PEREGRINE BOOKS

MEDIEVAL POLITICAL THOUGHT

Between the fifth and twelfth centuries, when vast stretches of Europe were still uninhabited, a society grew up which had to learn the very rudiments of how to manipulate the ordering of public life. It was during and just after this period that many of the basic political concepts of today were formed.

In this study Professor Ullmann traces the origins and development of political ideas in Western Europe – ideas as familiar as sovereignty, parliament, citizenship, the rule of law, and the state. He shows this development being forged out of the conflict between the descending and ascending theses of government, with their Roman and Germanic sources, and explains the dominance of ecclesiastical powers in medieval society.

From implicit belief in theocratic kingship to the beginnings of popular sovereignty, Professor Ullman's book provides an introduction to medieval concepts of government which is both scholarly and pertinent to the politics of today.

Walter Ullmann has been Professor of Medieval Ecclesiastical History at the University of Cambridge since 1966. Born in 1910, he studied at the Universities of Vienna and Innsbruck. He did research at Munich and Cambridge Universities, and has for many years specialized in the history of legal and political doctrines of the Middle Ages. After holding a lectureship at Leeds University he became, in 1949, a University Lecturer at Cambridge. From 1957 until 1965 he was the University Reader in Medieval Ecclesiastical Institutions at Cambridge. He is also a Fellow of Trinity College, Cambridge. In January 1965 he went to the United States to become Visiting Professor of Humanities at Johns Hopkins University. He was Birkbeck Lecturer at Cambridge for 1968 to 1969.

Walter Ullmann's publications include: *The Medieval Idea of Law* (1946), *The Origins of the Great Schism* (1948), *Medieval Papalism* (1949), *The Growth of Papal Government in the Middle Ages* (1955), *Principles of Government and Politics in the Middle Ages* (1961), *The Relevance of Medieval Ecclesiastical History* (1966), *The Individual and Society in the Middle Ages* (1967), *Papst und König* (1967), *The Carolingian Renaissance and the Idea of Kingship* (1969), and over fifty papers in learned British and foreign periodicals. He has also edited for the Henry Bradshaw Society the only existing account of the English Chapel Royal in the Middle Ages (1961) and is General Editor of 'Cambridge Studies in Medieval Life and Thought'.

Walter Ullmann, who holds several doctorates and is a Fellow of the British Academy, is married and has two sons.

WALTER ULLMANN

MEDIEVAL POLITICAL THOUGHT

PENGUIN BOOKS

Penguin Books Ltd, Harmondsworth, Middlesex, England
Penguin Books Inc., 7110 Ambassador Road, Baltimore, Maryland 21207, U.S.A.
Penguin Books Australia Ltd, Ringwood, Victoria, Australia
Penguin Books Canada Ltd, 41 Steelcase Road West, Markham, Ontario, Canada
Penguin Books (N.Z.) Ltd, 182–190 Wairau Road, Auckland 10, New Zealand

—

First published as *A History of Political Thought: The Middle Ages*
in Pelican Books 1965
Reprinted with revisions 1970
Reissued as *Medieval Political Thought* in Peregrine Books 1975
Copyright © Walter Ullmann, 1965

—

Made and printed in Great Britain by
Hazell Watson & Viney Ltd, Aylesbury, Bucks
Set in Monotype Times

This book is sold subject to the condition
that it shall not, by way of trade or otherwise,
be lent, re-sold, hired out, or otherwise circulated
without the publisher's prior consent in any form of
binding or cover other than that in which it is
published and without a similar condition
including this condition being imposed
on the subsequent purchaser

TABLE OF CONTENTS

CONTENTS

PREFACE

WITH the now generally noticeable increased interest in political ideas goes a heightened awareness of the need to understand how modern political concepts have become what they are. If the value of historical inquiries is to find out not so much what there was, but how and why things have become what they were and are, an inquiry into the historical development of political ideas stands in no need of justification. This is all the more true in regard to a history of political thought in the Middle Ages, of which the present age is, in more than one respect, the direct heir and descendant. The somewhat detached attitude towards the medieval period, which could be witnessed a generation ago, has given way to an accelerated and sometimes very keen interest, because it has become widely realized that an intelligent assessment of modern ideologies necessitates at least some knowledge of how these have come about. In this country in particular public institutions, such as the monarchy, parliament, the law, the courts of justice, rather clearly reveal their medieval ancestry, but also – and perhaps more important – they reveal the ideas which originally brought them into being and still sustain them today. The ideas concerning sovereignty, democracy, political authority, political obligation, the duty of obedience, lawful command, justice, are with us today in a manner in no wise different from that which they were in the Middle Ages.

Admittedly, in some respects the Middle Ages show features which do not strike familiar chords. But it is necessary to separate the form from the contents of a thing and to see the essence, the inner core. Stripped of its irrelevant paraphernalia, the medieval period in which, as far as the West is concerned, political ideas in the modern sense were born, is the period of Europe's apprenticeship, puberty, and adolescence. If ever the principle of historical continuity has relevance, it is within the precincts of the history of political ideas: it is these which have not only given the medieval period its complexion, but have also slowly and frequently painfully given birth to our ways of thinking on political matters and matters of public concern. Ideas could only, as a rule, be expressed through language – it was the word which clothed a rough idea and enveloped it with flesh, and thus made it a vehicle of further communication. A sensitive ear can hardly fail to notice the kinship between the medieval and modern connotation of a political idea. The fact that the Middle Ages were the ages of faith, in which Christianity played a decisive and determinative role, and that modern man is less influenced by religious considerations, is an all the stronger incentive for looking into the past, if only to find out why and how it was that our ancestors thought and acted in the way they did, and why and how it was that modern ideas and actions seem to be different. And the inquirer will then find that, although political ideas often enough took different forms, in their substance there is a remarkable genetic continuity. Some of the political ideas prevalent in the Middle Ages may not endear themselves to us, may even produce a sense of intellectual detachment, but this reaction, however understandable it may be, in fact reminds us how necessary it is to see what we were before we have become what we are.

It was these and similar considerations which have prompted me to attempt a brief outline of political ideas as they developed, progressed, matured, decayed, and changed in the medieval period which in time spans the age between the fifth and the fifteenth centuries. A good deal of work has recently been done on the history of political thought in the Middle Ages, work, that is, which greatly contributes to a better and more fruitful appreciation of the historical process itself no less than of the presuppositions which in actual fact created political ideas. I have therefore refrained from going into details which, however important in themselves, do not materially assist the understanding: the aim has been to present a genetic exposition of that political thought which imprinted itself on the Middle Ages and in consequence potently influenced and shaped the modern world. That in so doing I have concentrated more – and especially in the earlier period – on the official and semi-official governmental measures which allow us to see political ideas in practice, is therefore explicable. That there is consequently no chapter explicitly devoted to St Augustine is understandable, quite apart from the consideration that to give what might be called a simplifying sketch of his 'political' ideas is dangerous, because easily misleading; moreover, to understand his thought adequately, one has of necessity to be familiar with his own theological premises for which an outline of medieval political thought does not provide sufficient space. Individual Augustinian elements have of course been given due prominence. Very similar considerations apply to Ockham at the other end of the period – to appreciate his 'political' thought one has to familiarize oneself with his nominalism and his own theology; apart from this, the projected edition of his political works which is to have seven volumes, has not yet gone beyond the third volume, and work on him is still in full flux. What I have aimed at is to present within manageable proportions a brief outline of the main topics. I have tried to combine the topical with the chronological method, because my experience has been that this combination offers reasonably good prospects for the understanding of political ideas in their proper historical context. In the Middle Ages political thought was frequently enough embedded not in learned books or in pamphlets, but in media of communication which in themselves would have seemed at first sight to have little to do with political ideologies: the royal coronation orders are one such instance. It was therefore advisable to reconstruct the subject from a variety of sources of information. Since thought in the Middle Ages was considerably more integrated than our own, political ideas also manifested themselves in a number of ways which have since lost their function as forces which contribute to the integration of thought and life. Modern political thought is, historically seen, merely an offshoot of the many diverse agencies which in their sum-total constituted medieval political thought. For those readers who might wish to pursue the one or the other subject I have appended a short list of the primary source material and secondary literature.

18 September 1964   W.U.

PREFACE TO THE 1970 EDITION

In order not to increase costs unduly by resetting Chapter 3 which needs some revision in the light of recent work, I have added a brief Supplementary Note in Appendix B. A short additional bibliography for those readers who would like to inform themselves on one or the other topic by reference to more recent literature, will be found in Appendix A.

Cambridge
17 April 1970   w.u.

PREFACE TO THE PEREGRINE EDITION

The inclusion of this volume in the new series gives me an opportunity of adding to the Select Bibliography a number of items which have appeared or come to my knowledge since the last revision in 1970 and which interested readers might find useful (Appendix B). A revision of the text itself has not been shown to be necessary. The continued demand for this volume and the welcome response by students of political ideas has been most gratifying. May it continue to serve the purpose for which it was originally written, that is, to introduce the enquiring layman and student to the ever fascinating cluster of problems of how and why the Latin West has assumed its distinctive political and constitutional complexion.

Trinity College, Cambridge
August 1974   w.u.

INTRODUCTION

THE frequent assertion that the medieval period stretches well into modern times has special relevance to the impact of medieval political ideas upon the shaping of those political concepts which only in the modern period have come to full fruition. Indeed in no other field but that of ideas is a continuous development so conspicuous. But by the same token it would be unhistorical and in fact naïve to think that the political ideas of the later Middle Ages had no ancestry in the earlier medieval period. There are few branches of historical studies which are so useful in demonstrating the historical process itself as the study of the history of political ideas. In fact, it is the same kind of approach which we adopt when we come to assess the character of an adult person. In trying to explain the traits of his character, we do not begin by looking at the finished product, at the fully grown man. On the contrary we try to find out relevant details of his childhood and youth that shed light on those influences and agencies which had impressed themselves upon the adolescent and the maturing man. In other words, we attempt to explain what factors, circumstances, elements, and so on, were formative in moulding his character.

To understand how current institutions and political ideas have become what they are, a very similar genetic approach strongly suggests itself. For they did not emerge out of nothing and are firmly embedded in the historical process itself. And the medieval period offers a particularly good opportunity to see how political ideas and institutions have in actual fact come about. This period, a space of more than a thousand years, witnessed in Western Europe the emergence and growth of a society which had as yet no experience of political matters, no readymade or suitable pattern on which to model itself as far as matters of public government were concerned. When the impetus of the Germanic invasions had spent itself, and more or less orderly and peaceful conditions came about again, there arose the problem of how to preserve public order and peace, of how to regulate public life, of how to arrange matters which were of concern to all members of society. These may be classed as problems of a political order, and from the conceptual point of view could be put into the category of political ideas. This society, in many respects still primitive, had to find its own solutions.

Man has always asked where in the final resort original power in the public field was located. What is it that makes law binding? Why is law binding at all? Today, in the West, the answer is not difficult. But the present-day manner of thinking – and practice – are the result of fierce and bloody conflicts which were wholly conditioned by the ideological forces set up in the Middle Ages. For, historically speaking, there were two main theses of government and law in the medieval period. Both were operative, though at one time the one, at other times the other, was predominant.

The one conception of government and law, which was also chronologically the earlier one, may be termed the ascending theory. Its main feature is that original power is located in the people, or in the community itself. This was the thesis of government which Tacitus described when he portrayed the manner in which the Germanic tribes were governed. Since original power resided in the people, it was they who in their popular assemblies elected a war leader or a duke or a king, and the like. He had no power other than that which the electing assembly had given him. He was said to represent the community and remained therefore accountable to the popular assembly. Consequently, there existed a *right* of resistance to the ruler's commands as a leader. This right of resistance explains the ease with which a king was deposed and done away with, if in the view of the people he no longer represented their will. Although in course of time the practice developed to elect men into kingship only from certain families, the principle still remained the same. Metaphorically speaking power ascended from the broad base of a pyramid to its apex, the king or duke. The popular assembly controlled the ruler's government, and it was mainly as a court of law that the assembly worked effectively. This ascending theory of government may also be called the populist theory of government, because original power was anchored in the people.

Opposed to this theory was the descending thesis of government. Here original power was located in a supreme being which, because of the prevailing Christian ideas, came to be seen as divinity itself. St Augustine in the fifth century had said that God distributed the laws to mankind through the medium of kings. And in the thirteenth century St Thomas Aquinas expressed the same idea when he said that power descended from God. One can here also see a metaphorical pyramid but it was at its apex that the sum-total of power was located. Whatever power was found 'below', was derived from 'above', for, as St Paul said, 'There is no power but of God.' Here one can speak only of delegated power. It was God who had appointed a vicegerent on earth, and it was, in actual fact, this vicegerent who was held to have embodied original power. Within this thesis the people had no power other than that it had been given 'from above'. Every officer was appointed 'from above' – and not elected by a popular assembly. The supreme officer was responsible to God alone. This theory of government can also be called the theocratic theory, because eventually all power was located in God.

The history of political ideas in the Middle Ages is to a very large extent a history of the conflicts between these two theories of government. As a result of the overpowering influence of Christianity the Germanic peoples adopted the theory inherent in Christian doctrine – which was almost wholly of a Latin–Roman complexion – and the ascending theme was, so to speak, driven underground, not to emerge again as a theoretical proposition until the late thirteenth century. From then onwards the descending thesis of government receded more and more into the background, until only a few remnants are left today.

This adoption of the descending thesis of government makes understandable the very pronounced ecclesiastical and Latin complexion which political thought assumed in the earlier Middle Ages. For its bearers were predominantly, if not exclusively, clerics who were sufficiently educated to express themselves adequately. Until well into the eleventh century there was no such thing as an educated laity ; there was no general education for laymen, and whatever education there was, was in the hands of the clergy and almost wholly for the benefit of the clergy. The chanceries and offices of kings and emperors were staffed by clerics, not by laymen. This very strong ecclesiastical character of early political thought marked it off both from ancient – Greek and Roman – as well as modern political thinking. The following chapters show, however, how basic and decisive this early medieval political ideology was for the subsequent development, which cannot be understood without an appraisal of the preceding doctrines. What is called political thought in the Middle Ages was overwhelmingly shaped by the thesis centred on Christ. In some ways one could speak of an attempt to apply medieval Christian doctrine to problems of government, which is only another way of saying that medieval doctrines were in their earlier stages ecclesiastical. They may well appear somewhat strange and rather abstract to readers in the twentieth century, since the presuppositions of political thought seem so fundamentally different from those with which modern man is familiar. Nevertheless the distinction between modern and medieval thought is basically one of degree, and not one of kind. Precisely because of the comparatively uncomplicated and unsophisticated character of early medieval society, the historian can trace its fundamental concepts with greater confidence than those appearing in fully-developed societies where they may well have lost their pristine freshness.

From the late Middle Ages onwards political doctrines have been set forth by scholars, theoreticians, and philosophers. This was not the case during that period in which the foundations for the later emerging political theories were laid. From the fifth to the eleventh century very few individual writers can be detected who had made it their business to expound political theses. No books, tracts, or pamphlets were written on those topics which have at all times formed the contents of political thought. For it was the governments themselves, the popes, kings, and emperors, who by their governmental measures created, shaped, and applied political ideas. Whatever there was in political doctrine was contained in the actions which the governments themselves took, and these actions were as often as not responses to actual and concrete situations and challenges. In the earlier Middle Ages political thought has to be extracted from the official pronouncements of the respective governments as well as from the historical process itself. That is the reason why the earlier part of the history of political ideas is intrinsically bound up with the actual history of the time. The vehicle which served the governments to express their political views was, for ostensible reasons, the law. For the business of any government is to govern, and government can be executed – within civilized societies – only by means of the law. The close integration between ideas of government and the facts of government is a feature which stands in need of particular emphasis.

This brings us to another marked feature, namely the intimate connexion between what may be called political science and jurisprudence, that is, the science of the law. Whatever we are inclined to call 'political' was for the greater part of the Middle Ages expressed within the terms of the law. It was the law issued by the various governments which attempted to translate the aim of society into reality. This indeed is what characterizes any civilized society – whether pagan, Christian, Muslim, Jewish, communist, or capitalist. Hence the law as a vehicle of government pursues a definite aim – what the aim was depended then (as now) on views and doctrines which were there before the law was made – and this is why medieval law was conceived in terms of society's purpose, aim, or end. This so-called teleological conception of law was particularly important throughout the Middle Ages.

Medieval law was, one might well say, applied political doctrine, and in fact for large stretches of the medieval period the law was the only means which allows the historian to recognize pure political doctrine, because it was enshrined in, and applied by, the law. Fortunately, the legal records of the Middle Ages are plentiful, and from them the underlying political ideology can be ascertained. We may express this important principle also in another way. The law attempted the translation of the idea of justice into reality, but what corresponded to justice

15

depended on the view of the respective government on what it considered just. It was in the contents of justice that political ideas in the Middle Ages can be recognized, and it was the concept of justice which flavoured – and makes understandable – political ideology in the Middle Ages. The idea of justice found its embodiment in the law. From here one can readily understand the crucial importance of the problem of where original power was located, for on that question hinged the answer whether or not a government was entitled to issue the law.

In approaching the age in which our modern political ideas came to be born, we should bear in mind that in that period man was not yet familiar with ways of thinking which are familiar, and also indispensable, to us. We view human activities from certain angles and put them into more or less neatly confined departments. Thus we speak of religious, moral, political, economic norms, and we are inclined to say that this or that activity is religious, or political, or moral, and so on. The codes of these various norms are by no means identical, and it is often difficult to reconcile all the norms. But this atomization of the norms determining human actions is of rather recent date. For the larger part of the Middle Ages there was no such splitting up of human actions into different compartments. The Christian idea itself militated against any kind of departmentalization. That one and the same human activity could be viewed from a moral and a religious and a political angle was not a way of thinking with which medieval man had been acquainted. What counted then was the undifferentiated Christian: religion was not separated from politics, politics not separated from morals, and so on. What mattered was the Christianity of man, and not his social or moral conduct. His actions were not thought, at least in the public sphere, capable of being judged by any other norm than by the Christian. This wholeness point of view, or what may be termed for want of a better name this 'totalitarian' standpoint (though we hasten to add this has nothing to do with modern connotations of totalitarianism), is a feature which it is as well to keep in mind when one wishes to see how ideas and concepts which we call political have originally come about. The Christian who alone mattered was he, as St Paul had it, who had been baptized: by virtue of his baptism he was made 'a new creature' and had shed 'the man of nature', thereby partaking in the divine attributes themselves. The point here is that the faithful, that is, the Christian, was, in theory at least, distinguished from mere natural man. As a Christian he was incorporated in the Church.

Whilst the early and high Middle Ages did not distinguish between religious, political, moral (etc.) norms, but considered only the faithful, there was nevertheless a crucial distinction between the members of the Church, that is, the clergy and the laity. It would be quite erroneous to think and speak of the Church in the sense of clergy only. Since both constituted the Church, the problem of the relations between the two formed an essential topic in the Middle Ages. Clergy and laity were epitomized in priests and kings and focalized as priesthood *(sacerdotium)* and kingship *(regnum)*.

The concept with which the medieval period before the thirteenth century was not familiar was that of the State, understood as an independent, self-sufficient, autonomous body of citizens which lived, so to speak, on its own substance and on its own laws. This concept came about in the thirteenth century as a result of the influence of the Greek philosopher, Aristotle. Kingdoms and empires counted as parts of a larger unit, of the whole body of Christians, and did not count as individual, self-sufficient, autonomous, sovereign bodies. It is not therefore without interest to note that the very term 'political' did not enter the vocabulary of governments and writers before the thirteenth century. The absence of this term is not indeed difficult to explain. That it – rather hesitatingly – began to make its début then was intimately linked with the simultaneous emergence of the concept of the State. Before then neither the concept of the State nor that of the political was there. The term which was used was neither 'State', nor 'political', but 'government' *(gubernatio* or *gubernaculum* or *gubernator),* and this was linked with the Roman term of laying down the law – *jus dicere* (jurisdiction). In a roundabout way we return to the fundamental question: where was original power located, and, consequently, who had the right to lay down the law? However

17

often it is repeated that there was a conflict between Church and State in the Middle Ages, the assertion still does not make historical sense. What there was, was a conflict between the *sacerdotium* and the *regnum*, but this conflict was fought *within* one and the same body, within one and the same society of Christians, and not between two autonomous and independent bodies, a Church and a State. In the final resort 'political' thought dealt with the problem of the ultimate authority of the government to lay down the path to be followed by society, which was nothing less than the problem of sovereignty.

The prevailing theory of government in the Middle Ages, the descending thesis, should not, however, be seen in isolation, but should be viewed as an effluence of the dominating religious idea itself and an offshoot and practical application of the de-ductive method of reasoning. It was this deductive method which ensured the resilience of medieval thought and in par-ticular of the descending thesis of government. For from some generally acknowledged and unquestioned universal principles, such as the divine government of the world, specific principles and theories were deduced. From the most comprehensive prin-ciple the remotest ramifications were derived and the last ounce was squeezed out. Clearly this is a highly developed logical method by which the most insignificant item can be traced back to a comprehensive, all-embracing, general principle. What may have been merely implicit in a universal principle became by the deductive method explicit. In short, the history of the ideas relating to public government in the Middle Ages is part of the history of ideas as it unfolded itself in the European Middle Ages.

CHAPTER 1

THE FOUNDATIONS:
THE ROMAN AND BIBLICAL
BACKGROUND

I. THE ROMAN CHURCH IN THE ROMAN EMPIRE

As a result of recent research it is more and more recognized that it was in the late Roman period from the fourth to the fifth century that the foundations were laid for the basic conceptions and ideas relating to government. This period is also of particular significance in so far as none of the ideas were as yet contaminated by any Germanic elements: there was still no intellectual contact between, and therefore no cross-fertilization of, Roman and Germanic conceptions. This was perhaps the only period in the Middle Ages, in which this contact was absent. Hence governmental conceptions were purely Roman and this holds true of both agencies, the Church of Rome and the empire of Constantinople, which were the chief framers of governmental schemes relating to a Christian society.

The point which deserves emphasis is that, despite its approaching nadir, the Roman empire still disposed of a first-class administrative apparatus, which clearly manifested, in its essentials, the tenor of Roman government – that is, a highly geared-up constitutional and legal system which had evolved as a result of a long historical process and which still demonstrated all the characteristic features of what ancient Rome stood for. In actual power and concrete influence the Roman empire, now governed from two residences – Rome as well as Constantinople – was a shadow of its past, but institutionally and constitutionally it had lost extraordinarily little, despite recurrent economic crises, despite incessant military attacks from outside, and despite the diminution of the standing of Roman citizenship. Governmentally, the Roman empire was still, within the precincts of the contemporary world, the one entity which could legitimately be classed as civilized, because in it the law reigned supreme. And this Roman empire was still seen, at least by those within it, as a world-embracing one: this vocation the Roman empire, even in its last decades, had not lost. The decree of the emperors Valentinian II, Gratian, and Theodosius I in 380, by which the Christian religion was made the religion of the empire, was not only a step of universal historical significance, but also the instrument by which the papacy (the Church of Rome) became focalized as a governmental institution. From the point of view of the development of governmental ideas, it is hardly possible to exaggerate the importance of this imperial decree. True enough, there was now one religion only which enjoyed the sanction of the governmental machinery of the empire, and thereby a religious, if not also an ideological, force assisted the unity of the empire, but this step also entailed possibilities which were not, and perhaps could not be, foreseen by its authors. For the faith thus prescribed in the decree was that 'which the apostle Peter had given to the Romans' and therefore, as the decree furthermore stipulated, the subjects of the empire were to live according to 'apostolic discipline and evangelical doctrine'.

The Church of Rome was not established or even legitimized by this imperial decree: what the decree did was to credit the Roman Church with institutional functions, the very ones which in one way or another the papacy had already claimed. The papacy from now on began to act as a proper governmental institution, and it acted by means of the law. This legal complexion of the early (and medieval) papacy is a feature that has caused a good deal of misunderstanding, but from the papal and historical point of view it appears to be well-founded. In the first place, manipulation of the law was not the invention of the papacy itself, but suggested itself to any institution which had exclusively grown up on Roman soil and had received so much stimulus from its Roman surroundings. Moreover, the fact must be stressed that, long before the papacy had effectively emerged as a governmental institution, Christian dogma and doctrine had been clothed in the language of the law. At the cradle of Latin theology stood a jurist – Tertullian – who exercised enduring influence. Religious maxims and principles, in short Christian doctrine, came to be handed out in the form of legal maxims and principles. To the creators of Latin Christianity and Latin dogma the relations between God and man were legal relations, conceived in the framework of rights and duties and moulded into a Roman jurisprudential scheme. The result of this legal manipulation of doctrine was that the Latin world, in any case amenable to legalistic thinking, and later also the Germanic world, were given their faith, their religion, their dogma in the shape of the law.

In the second place, the law as an instrument of doctrine had a very conspicuous ancestry in the Bible. Though it has only fairly recently been recognized, the Bible, and above all the Old Testament, was strongly imbued with legal material, and, in consequence, quite a number of basic governmental principles in the Middle Ages had been modelled on the Bible. But for a work to exercise any influence it must be written in an idiom understandable to contemporaries. It is here that the Vulgate – the Latin translation of the Hebrew and Greek Bible – by St Jerome in the late fourth and early fifth centuries assumed crucial importance. The language used by Jerome was that of the cultured Roman classes of the fourth century and his translation contained terms and notions which rather closely corresponded to the language of the Roman jurists. What is important to stress is that, whilst the Latin terms of the Vulgate may have been linguistically correct, they nevertheless conveyed Roman-legal overtones and undertones not necessarily in consonance with the original Hebrew or Greek meaning of the term. In any case, the strongly legal complexion of the Bible was presented through the Vulgate in a thoroughly juristic garb (that of the Roman law) as far as matters concerning government were affected.

The influence of the Latinized (or Romanized) Bible upon the development of governmental ideas was crucial. Although down to the fifth century there was no elaboration of or doctrinal reasoning for the function of the Roman Church, practice and usage did attribute to it a seniority and a pre-eminence so far as questions of organization and doctrine were concerned. A claim to a practical exercise of supreme authority can be witnessed throughout the period prior to the fifth century. Pope Clement I's letter to the Corinthians (*c*. 92) was a testimony of the authoritative position which the Roman Church claimed, and throughout the subsequent period the position of the Roman Church as the senior or principal church received practical, though not uncontested, support. But there was no papal theory or doctrine or working out of the thesis that the Roman Church in a very special way occupied a position which put it on a level fundamentally different from that of other churches. To be sure, there were some isolated statements made by writers, such as Cyprian, who struck up chords which were later to become the backbone of papal ideas relative to government in a Christian society, but from the papal quarter itself no literary or documentary proof has come down from which one could gather any exposition of the papacy's own standing in Christendom.

The imperial decree of 380, already mentioned, made necessary the doctrinal exposition of governmental authority claimed and partly exercised by the Roman Church. The period between the pontificate of Damasus (died 384) and Leo I in the mid fifth century may well be spoken of as the period of gestation in regard to the ideas animating the papacy's function as a governmental institution. And these ideas culminated – entirely in consonance with the theocentric standpoint* – in the monarchic position of the pope. There was no basic difference between the concept of the monarchic function of the pope and that of the emperor. There was, however, a distinction, and that concerned, first, the reason for the monarchic position embodied in pope and emperor, and secondly, intimately connected with it, the view taken of the society over which the monarchy was to be exercised.

The concept of papal monarchy was derived by the papacy from the interpretation of the passage in St Matthew xvi, 18–19:

Thou art Peter and upon this rock I will build my church. . . . And I will give unto thee the keys of the kingdom of heaven : and whatsoever thou shalt bind on earth shall be bound in heaven : and whatsoever thou shalt loose on earth shall be loosed in heaven.

That St Peter had in actual fact died in Rome was taken as a

* That is the view that God was the centre and pivot of the universe.

matter of fact throughout the period. But the papacy had not, as far as the extant material allows one to judge, made this a pivotal point. Certainly one of the strangest features is that these crucial Matthean verses, which were destined to play a quite unparalleled importance in subsequent ages, had not before been adduced as the exclusive title-deed of the papacy's functions. No doubt, the decree of the three emperors hastened the process of clarification ; no doubt also that the growing practice of consulting the Roman Church demanded a doctrinal exposition ; furthermore, it cannot be doubted that the availability of the Bible in a contemporary idiom, comprehensible to everyone, was a factor which potently assisted the exposition, particularly in conjunction with the juristic milieu in which the Roman Church found itself working. For within the Roman environs any governmental idea was a juristic one.

The difficulty of a satisfactory doctrine did not, at that time, concern so much the person of St Peter as the succession to his functions. However much it may have been taken as a fact that Peter died a martyr's death in Rome, neither the gospels nor the Pauline letters nor any other available facts indicated anything about a successor to St Peter. And in any case the fact of someone's death in a particular locality had no necessary connexion with the legal thesis of a succession. But a spurious document made at the end of the second century, and written in Greek, seems to have supplied the wanting historical evidence. This document was translated at the very end of the fourth or possibly in the early years of the fifth century by Rufinus of Aquileja, who is well known for his rendering the famous *History* of Eusebius into Latin. And it was through this translation of the document which might well have been assigned to oblivion that the historic theme of a Petrine succession was launched on its triumphant career.

According to this document, which purported to be a somewhat lengthy letter written by Pope Clement I to St James (the brother of Christ) in Jerusalem, the pope informed his addressee of the last dispositions which St Peter had made when he felt his death approaching. The letter stated that in front of the Roman community St Peter had handed over to (Pope) Clement his own binding and loosing power, so that what henceforth would be bound by Clement and his successors on earth would also be bound in heaven. In other words, St Peter in a most visible and concrete manner appointed, by way of a testamentary disposition, a successor to his own position and, in the same document, also referred specifically to those who were to succeed Clement. The significance of this is that, in the garb of a historical event, witnessed by the Roman Christian assembly, a transfer of powers was executed. It is here not necessary to point out the excruciatingly difficult problems which the letter created: for, according to common knowledge, it was Linus who followed St Peter in Rome and of whom, indeed, St Paul spoke. What is, however, necessary to state is that this letter was quoted over and over again, throughout the medieval period, as the one historical and concrete fact supporting the doctrine of papal monarchy, based on the Matthean passage. The letter was incorporated in the earliest extant collection of papal laws, and was already in the mid fifth century cited by a council held in far-away Gaul.

However much this letter (the so-called *Epistola Clementis*) had clothed an abstract idea – that of a transfer of powers to an appointed successor – in a tangible and factual event, it was still necessary to expound its allegedly historical contents in a doctrinal manner. And within the Roman milieu that exposition could be undertaken only with the help of the Roman law. Juristic thought is the abstraction of factual events – and this truism is particularly relevant to the present topic. For both the Matthean passage and the apparently historical and visible transfer of powers by St Peter to Clement concerned facts capable of juristic elaboration. It is, considering the milieu of the Roman Church, no coincidence that the fifth century witnessed the emergence of a number of juristically relevant papal enactments and doctrines which in one way or another presented the juristic abstraction of biblical and historical facts.

Pope Leo I (440-61) summed up both the historical and doctrinal development of the preceding generation and, by virtue of his mastery of Roman law and its technique, presented an idea which, within the confines of the Roman Church, has stood the test of time. Leo's thesis culminated in the exposition of the monarchic function of the pope: he was the juristic successor to the powers and functions given by Christ to St Peter. This succession concerned the continuation of Petrine functions and powers: the pope, according to Leo, continued to exercise the same powers which Christ had originally given to St Peter. The pope simply inherited, according to Leo, the office which Christ had conferred on St Peter.

The papal thesis was that Christ had established in that one statement (St Matthew xvi, 18ff.) both a particular society as well as the government appropriate to it. Indeed, in all the history of societies and governments this is a unique feature, because, as far as it is known, there never was any deliberate foundation of a society with, in the same breath, the establishment of a particular form of government. There was a remarkable unanimity on this point amongst all, whether pro-papal or anti-papal, throughout the Middle Ages: where disagreement entered was the scope and extent of the monarchic government to be exercised by the pope. At any rate, Leo I fixed the theme of the pope as the 'unworthy heir of St Peter' *(indignus haeres beati Petri)*. It is a formula which, because it was so succinct, has not yet been properly appreciated. The formula contains, however, a whole programme and one that satisfied, within the predominantly religious climate, all the juristic aspirations of the time and beyond. In actual fact, the two crucial notions were the heirship of the pope and his unworthiness for this position. According to Leo, it was the personal merit of St Peter to have recognized Christ at Caesarea Philippi, and for this reason he received plenary powers from Christ to bind and to loose. This was St Peter's personal and peculiar merit and could not therefore be transmitted. And no one after Caesarea Philippi could legitimately claim any like merit or distinction.

It was quite otherwise in regard to the powers and the office which, in Leo's view, Christ gave to St Peter. Operating as he did with the Roman law of inheritance, he considered that these powers (of binding and loosing) were entirely objective and independent of the person to whom they were originally given. They were held to be capable of being transmitted. The transmission was effected by inheritance, for, according to Roman law, the heir continued, in law, the legal status of the deceased. The heir entered into the same (legal) assets and liabilities which the dead person possessed: the latter was continued in the heir. But the personal qualifications of the deceased could not, for understandable reasons, be transmitted, and it was this consideration which prompted Leo I to employ the succinct formula of the 'unworthy heir' of St Peter. The Petrine powers were transmitted and therefore continued in the pope through inheritance – the Petrine merits could not be transmitted.

Two crucial consequences followed. First, the powers of the pope were exactly the same as those of St Peter. There was no difference, in law, between them: the pope was St Peter who continued to function in the pope, however unworthy. The fundamental importance of this view lay in the neat separation between the office and the person holding the office. There were few doctrines which were so important as this distinction, for it maintained that the personal qualifications of the office-holder were of no concern. What was of concern was the office which he occupied. Whether the pope was a saintly individual or a malicious scoundrel or a nonentity was of no moment. The point was that he legitimately exercised his office and that his decrees and laws and orders, in other words, his governmental acts, issued from his official function as pope. They did not acquire binding character, because the pope happened to be saintly; vice versa, they did not lose one iota of their obligatory character because the pope who issued them happened to be a scoundrel. Few themes relative to government have had before them such a useful career as this distinction between office and person. Even when the papacy in the tenth and eleventh centuries sank to its depths, no opponent retorted that its governmental actions were invalid because they originated in reprehensible characters: as long as it could be established that a decree had emanated from the office, was official, and that the pope was validly elected, it had the stamp of legitimacy: it was binding.

Secondly, it was the Leonine thesis of papal, that is, Petrine monarchy, that no pope succeeded his immediate predecessor but succeeded St Peter directly and without intermediaries. That is to say, governmental powers were not transmitted through predecessors; there was no handing on of Petrine powers. Each pope was (and is) considered an immediate successor of St Peter in his function as monarch. This side of the papal position is technically called the *potestas jurisdictionis,* because it was with the laying down of the law, with declaring what was and what was not to be done, that the papal office concerned itself. It was different with the other side of the papal position, that is, the *potestas ordinis* function as bishop of Rome, which indeed was handed down in a temporal sequence from the apostles to the actual occupant of the see of Rome, but this 'power of orders' had nothing to do with government and concerned itself exclusively with sacramental matters, such as ordination, confirmation, consecration of churches, and the like. In this latter respect the pope was in no wise different from any other bishop. This side of the pope's power is of no further interest to us. But because solely the pope, as heir and continuator of Petrine powers, possessed what Leo I called the plenitude of power *(plenitudo potestatis)* and because this plenitude of power was solely concerned with *gubernatio* (government) and therefore the law, the pope occupied not only the *principatus* of the Church (another term borrowed from the Roman constitution), but was also in no need of any specific clerical order. Any layman, provided he was baptized, could (and can) become pope. The essential point was that the pope was validly elected: once validly elected, he was the heir of St Peter. Throughout the Middle Ages there were numerous popes who at the time of their election had not even been ordained as priests, let alone consecrated as bishops. In actual fact, before the mid eleventh century it was not even possible for a bishop to become pope, because as a bishop he was said to have been married to his diocese – hence the episcopal ring – and a marriage was then indissoluble: had he become pope, so it was held, he would have been married twice.

The position of the pope as *gubernator,* as a governor, was therefore according to the Leonine thesis exclusively juristic and conceived from an entirely objective standpoint. The juris-

27

tic interpretation of the office further entailed an important
theme with an equally important corollary. Leo's explanation
of the Matthean passage was that St Peter was set up as the
'builder' of the Church, as the one who, by his government, was
to act as the instrument of Christ. For Peter's powers were the
same as Christ's own powers, because he had been given the
'keys of the kingdom of heaven' by Christ so that it could be
maintained, as Leo did, that Christ's powers were the same as
Petrine powers, and these again were identifiable with papal
powers. The corollary was that in his function as *gubernator*
the pope formed, so to speak, an estate of his own, stood outside and above the Church, and was, in this capacity, no member of the Church. It is impossible to exaggerate the significance
of this. For the office which the pope occupied was descended
from Christ through Peter, and, as 'builder' of the Church, St
Peter (= pope) had to direct the path of this Christian Church.
The papal concept of monarchy differed in no wise from the
contemporary imperial one – or for that matter, later, from the
royal one – because the Church was not an autonomous body
that lived, so to speak, on its own laws and was independent of
any other agency. On the contrary, the Church was, in public
and governmental respects, entirely dependent on its 'builder'.
It was this thought which stood behind the statement, employed
invariably since the fifth century, that the Church was entrusted
or committed to the pope: the *ecclesia mihi commissa*.* The
significance of this was that the Church as the body of the faithful was considered devoid of indigenous powers: what it possessed, what functions its individual officers had, were seen as
'derived' from the pope. This 'derivational principle' was, even
before Leo I, alluded to in pictorial terms which portrayed St
Peter as the source of a river, from which other rivers flowed
or branched out.

Governmentally speaking, this idea of the Church being committed or entrusted to the pope meant that it came to be considered on the same level as a minor under age who, because of
his minority, needed a directing and guiding hand. But equally

* We shall see later that exactly the same can be observed in the kingdoms.

important was the other conclusion: since the Church, the body of the faithful, did not give any powers to the pope, it had no legitimate means of depriving him of his powers. That was one more important item within the complex structure of governmental ideas in the Middle Ages, not indeed confined to the ecclesiastical sphere. In expressing the thought in clear and unmistakable language, however, priority belonged to the papacy. Some thirty years before Leo I put forward his theory, another pope had already proclaimed the thesis that the pope's judgments and decisions were not subject to any further review or appeal: he was supreme as governor. Pope Zosimus in about 420 had in a genuine document declared this principle which by the end of the fifth century was raised to a constitutional principle of the first magnitude, though this time in a spurious document antedating the principle, namely that the pope could not be judged by anyone and hence could not be deposed. The current law of the Roman Church still has: *papa a nemine judicatur*. Here we have in fact a classic instance of a fundamental principle expressed in juristic language, and the principle was nothing less than that of sovereignty (=superiority or supremacy) of the pope himself by virtue of his office. In modern parlance the concept of sovereignty refers to a State, but in the Middle Ages this concept of sovereignty appeared, not as a territorial notion, but as a personal one. The essence of the concept of sovereignty was that the Ruler's function was not susceptible to any legitimate judgment, because he was superior. Those whom he governed were his inferiors, or again, in the language of the fifth-century Roman imperial constitution, they were *sub-diti,* sub-jects of the monarch. The pope – as also the later medieval king – was removed from all judgment by his subjects, because they themselves had nothing to do with his function and had not conferred any office upon him.

In the emergence of the concept of sovereignty the Bible, and notably the Old Testament, proved itself of particular importance, for the position of the Ruler, usually a king, was portrayed in language that engendered the idea itself. Here one read frequently enough of the Ruler set *over* the people, exercising his rule *over* the *subjects*, and the like. Within the framework of the concept of personal sovereignty no members of the Church had any claim to demand, as of right, any particular action or law or decree from the pope. The sum-total of all governmental power was in the pope (hence the concept of plenitude of power) and whatever power was possessed 'lower down' was the effect of the pope's having it explicitly conferred or having implicitly approved of it. In other words, since the members of the Church had no right to any office, they possessed it merely as a matter of grace, exercised by the 'superior', that is, sovereign pope, who could not be put before a tribunal composed of those upon whom the papal favour had shone. In this papal theory the pope formed an estate of his own, unaccountable to anyone on earth.

The concept of grace should on no account be confused with the theological sense the term also began to acquire. From the governmental standpoint it simply expressed the idea that the subject as such had no right to any governmental action, though he could always propose or suggest or supplicate for governmental measures. Once again, the papacy was the first in the field with this concept as a governmental idea, and again the idea was suggested in the Old Testament which used the term and the notion in precisely this sense. And the Pauline doctrine 'What I am, I am by the grace of God' also promoted the idea that the Christian had no right to anything. What he was, was the effluence of God's good will which showed itself as a divine favour, as a divine grace, as a divine good deed. The idea of a good deed, of a *beneficium,* captured the meaning of grace in its governmental sense exceedingly well, and we shall presently see that it was precisely this which formed the backbone of the papacy's stand against what it considered imperial encroachments. Whether expressed as a grace or as a good deed, the thought underlying this conception was that of a concession made by divinity. The principle of concession was essential to all theocratic forms of government.

This sketch of the papal doctrine in the mid fifth century may be supplemented by a brief consideration of a non-papal source of politological ideas. This source is, for inscrutable reasons, usually overlooked, although it exercised throughout the Middle

Ages a very great influence on both ecclesiastical and royal governments. Very little is known about the author of these highly influential tracts, written in the second half of the fifth century. He is usually referred to as Denys the Areopagite (or Pseudo-Denys) because he referred to himself as the Denys mentioned in the Acts of the Apostles (xvii, 33–4), the follower of St Paul. Most likely he was a Syrian who successfully managed to hide his real personality and to persuade everyone in the Middle Ages that he was in fact St Paul's pupil. It was Pseudo-Denys who supplied a semi-philosophic or semi-theological explanation of the origin of power in a Christian world, and it was he who actually invented the idea and coined the term of hierarchy *(hierarchia)*. Setting out from Hellenistic, Pauline, and neo-platonist premisses he maintained that there was but one supreme being which possessed the sum-total of all power and that was God, called by him the principle of unity. From this supreme being all power was derived and thus order in this world was guaranteed. For order, according to him, consisted of the differences in the grades and ranks of officers, arranged, however, so that each of them stood in direct dependence to his immediate superior officer. The differences in ranks and function and order were expressed by the term hierarchy. God had erected in the heavens different orders and they found their copy on earth. The ecclesiastical hierarchy was, for this author, simply a continuation of the celestial hierarchy.

This author worked out quite a detailed scheme concerning the hierarchical structure of ecclesiastical power. All power, he said, flowed downwards or descended from that one supreme being to the different grades, so that there was a kind of a pyramid in which the apex embodied the sum-total of power. In the proper distribution of power downwards by the hierarchs themselves the author found the guarantee for harmony and order. The Pauline view that there was no power but of God found in these works of Pseudo-Denys confirmation and some practical application. What he was furthermore insistent upon was the principle of obedience of the lower ranking officer to his superior officer. This idea of subordination – clearly foreshadowed in the Bible – received with Pseudo-Denys its pronouncedly descending or theocratic complexion. The importance of these tracts lay in that they gave a semi-philosophic or semi-theological basis to the already widely accepted descending point of view: they made explicit what was hitherto in any case implicit.

II. ROMAN IMPERIAL POLITICAL IDEAS

It is now time to consider the governmental doctrine of the imperial side in late Roman antiquity. However similar papal and imperial theories of government were, there was one essential difference. Papal governmental ideology was the product of biblical and religious abstract reasoning and argumentation, though clothed in the only available language, that of the Roman law and constitution. The imperial governmental ideology was the product of historical argumentation which was reinforced by arguments from the Bible. In some ways, therefore, the picture was the reverse. The one started from the Bible and presented its conclusions with the help of Roman law. The other continued a historic reality and buttressed the historical fact with an appeal to the Bible.

The development of the imperial doctrine in the late Roman and Christianized empire culminated in the function of the emperor as monarch in the literal meaning of the term, which meant in fact that he was both king and priest. His priestly functions were firmly based on the practice of pagan antiquity, they were not weakened, but as a result of the monotheistic Christian religion greatly stimulated. Christian monotheism powerfully contributed to the strengthening and elaboration of the idea that, just as there was one God in heaven, so there was only one monarch on earth. Recent research has shown beyond question that Christ Himself was viewed as emperor, and that this in turn underscored the monarchic position of the emperor himself. It was especially Eusebius in the fourth century who was chiefly responsible for this imperial ideology, linking monotheism with the concept of Roman emperorship: before Augustus, he declared, there was polytheism and therefore a multiplicity of rulers, but, since Christ's advent, which was contemporaneous with Augustus's rule, there was only one God and so there should be only one emperor who alone was in a position to guarantee peace, piety, and true religion. The motto characterizing imperial ideology became 'one God, one Empire, one Church', and one can with justification speak here of an 'imperial theology'.

In assessing the roots of this official imperial doctrine, one should not forget that it was an amalgam of the Christian ideal, Hellenistic conceptions, and above all oriental views, all however tending to stress the uniqueness of the emperor himself. It is of course no coincidence that the inflated imperial conception did not reach its full extent until well into the fourth century, after the transfer by Constantine of the capital to Constantinople. (This was an event which had far-reaching consequences on governmental doctrine as well as on the Byzantine empire.*) The combination of regal and sacerdotal power already mentioned was the hallmark of the emperor's singular position. It expressed his function as Christ's vicegerent on earth. Christ's fullness of power in heaven was held to have been embodied in his vicegerent on earth. The emperor's laws and decrees and commands were the laws, decrees, and commands of divinity made known through the emperor. Hence, just as during a divine service there was silence, so there was when imperial decrees and laws were read out or promulgated. St John Chrysostom at the turn of the fourth and fifth centuries went so far as to advise subjects that they should listen to Holy Scripture with the same awe and reverence as that with which they listened 'in sacred silence' to the reading out of imperial laws.

It was in his function as God's vicar on earth that the person of the emperor as well as his office was surrounded with a halo of sacredness and sanctity which underlined his singular status amongst mortals. He performed liturgical ceremonies in consequence in his function as a priest. For instance, on Palm Sunday he represented in the procession Christ Himself entering Jerusalem; on Maundy Thursday with his own hands he washed the feet of the twelve poor men; at Christmas and the

* See below, pp. 59ff.

subsequent twelve days he dined with twelve members of the Byzantine aristocracy. Of particular importance in this context was the emperor's function as promulgator of dogmatic decisions in the field of doctrine. Indeed, he was the 'living law', which meant that his will alone, and no other factor, had the force of law. 'The will of the prince' (not consent of the subjects), was the material ingredient of imperial laws. And since he was responsible to God for the empire, he had also to watch that his subjects possessed the appropriate faith – hence his legislation in doctrinal matters. Apart from that, taxation, organization, military command, decision of peace and war, and so forth, were exclusively within his competence. The descending theme of government found in the imperial Byzantine network its practical manifestation: every officer, of whatever low or high rank, stood in the same relation to the emperor as he himself stood to divinity. The emperor himself appointed officers, and they were and remained responsible to him alone, just as he remained responsible to divinity. He stood far above his subjects and was, constitutionally, not accountable to them. All public power was exercised in the emperor's own name.

This quasi-divine position of the emperor was most suitably emphasized by the appropriate ceremonial symbolism which is a highly important factor enabling later generations to reconstruct its underlying ideology. All actions of the emperor bore the stamp of divine actions. Thus ceremonial imperial feasts appeared as divine services; all processions were introduced and accompanied with a strictly regulated liturgical ceremonial, acclamations, hymns, and genuflexions; all the buildings which formed the imperial palace were sacred, because its centre, the hall of the throne, was the most sacred of any sacred building in Constantinople. It was in this hall that the imperial throne stood, the symbol manifesting the exalted position of imperial majesty. It was here that the emperor, after having received the acclamations of the subject people, turned towards heaven to forward the people's wishes and prayers to divinity itself, a characteristic symbolic gesture denoting the emperor's mediating role between Christ and the Christian people. These symbolic manifestations were to make clear that the emperor was the vicar of the Pantokrator – the omnipotent Ruler – and that he himself was the Autokrator on earth, the autonomous Ruler, unhampered by any human agency. The senate deliberating with the emperor was called the 'sacred consistory'* of the emperor or 'the Court of the Holy Senate'. Moreover, pictorial representations of Christ were adapted to the pictures of the emperor himself. Pagan imperial cult was simply continued in the Christian empire. Whilst the emperor himself had become Christian, his government carried on the pagan idea of the empire. And since it was divinity itself that spoke through the mouth of the emperor – as Justinian in the sixth century was to declare: 'The laws originate in our divine mouth' and the law was a 'divine precept' – he himself was not only 'divine', hence his appellation as 'divus Justinianus', and the like, but also had to appear in a divine manner: his 'divine right hand' used red ink for the imperial signature, and the subject receiving an imperial document bowed deeply and kissed the roll reverently.

This system of government, called perhaps inelegantly, Caesaropapism, culminated in what for all practical purposes was the exercise of power and authority by divinity through the emperor: indeed, he was Autokrator and Kosmokrator, ruling the 'world' identified with the Roman empire, as if he had been God Himself. Hence he was in every respect above the law, since there was no body, no authority, no tribunal that could sit in judgment on him. It was the same kind of personal sovereignty which we have met with the pope. Nevertheless the emperor's monarchic government was not considered to be a *carte blanche* for tyrannical government. On the contrary, because he alone knew what the divine plan demanded, he was the foremost guardian of the laws and could change them at will, if divine justice demanded any change. Hence it was that the imperial laws continued to be called 'sacred laws', because divinity in the person of the emperor spoke through them. Ecclesiastical organs, such as councils, had no standing, unless summoned and approved by the emperor. The decrees of the

*This designation was later applied to the College of Cardinals, the pope's senate.

35

councils became imperial laws, provided the emperor had sanctioned them. Ecclesiastical officers were imperial civil servants,
appointed and dismissed by the government. Conceptually, a
division between the Christian Roman empire and the Christian
Church was not possible for the imperial government: this entity was either the empire or the Church, but it could not be
both. No separation of emperor and God seemed possible,
because the former was the latter on earth. Hence also the
ancient pagan idea of the Roman emperor as the 'Lord of the
world' reappeared in the garb of the Christian universal idea
of rulership. It was not only his right, but also his duty to spread
Christianity and hold together the *ekumene*, the totality of all
cultured peoples, by means of the Christian faith. Perhaps the
best and most persuasive expression of the imperial idea relating to the ecclesiastical organism was the address of Constantine
the Great to the assembled bishops at Nicea, who were told
that they were the bishops for the internal matters, whilst he
was the bishop for the external, by which he meant that the
legal, organizational, administrative, and purely external arrangements and management of Christianity was his task, not
theirs. We shall meet exactly the same view later with the medieval king. The 'priestly' character of emperorship did not refer
to the sacramental, charismatic, and pneumatic qualifications
of the emperor, but simply to his function as governor, as law-
giver, in other words, to the external mechanics of his government. No emperor (and for that matter no medieval king)
claimed to be able to ordain or consecrate or do any of the
specifically sacramental acts which presupposed the possession
of a charisma.

Although the descending theory of government reached its
most pronounced manifestation in the imperial Byzantine
framework, there was, in the fifth and sixth centuries, little
literary activity which would have argued or discussed or
elaborated the idea in any scientific way. Nothing demonstrates
better the difference between the practice of the emperor's government and the theory put forward on behalf of the pope's
government than the manner in which the monarchic function
of either was said to be derived from divinity. Within the latter

it was the abstract exegesis of the Matthean verses which yielded the monarchy of the pope, within the former it was partly history, and partly the sensual (as opposed to the purely abstract) manner in which the emperor was shown to be appointed by divinity. The emergence of the idea of a coronation was perhaps the most easily comprehensible demonstration of the visible appointment of the emperor by God. The first pictorial representation of the divine appointment occurred in fact soon after Constantine the Great, when on a medaillon a hand was seen to reach down from the clouds to put a crown on the head of the emperor. From the mid fifth century the coronation of the (Byzantine) emperor by the patriarch of Constantinople became an important ceremony: it served to declare, but did not constitute, the divine derivation of powers and the appointment of the emperor himself by divinity.

Whilst the East was always more inclined to metaphysical and philosophical speculations, the West – and in the fifth century this meant for all practical purposes, Rome – was more earthbound and realistic and, above all, more inclined to the legalistic point of view. By the second half of the fifth century the imperial government at Constantinople found in the Roman papacy a severe obstacle to the uncheckered implementation of its governmental ideas, and as a result of Leo I's superb mastery of Roman law the papacy could in fact challenge the very bases of the imperial government by means of the most germane of all Roman institutions, government by law. The papacy was now in a position to turn the Roman inheritance, the Roman law, against the Roman emperor residing in Constantinople. Both the elaborate coronation ceremonial and the pointedly anti-papal legislation of the Council of Chalcedon (451) prompted the papal challenge. The twenty-eighth chapter of Chalcedon laid down that Constantinople – significantly enough called New Rome – had the same rank as Old Rome; the seventeenth chapter declared that the civil status of a city determined also its ecclesiastical status. Both decrees in fact were clearly designed to reduce the status of Old Rome to an insignificant place, entailing considerable diminution of the papacy's standing. The governmental actions of the emperor, which immediately followed, particularly his appointment and dismissal of high-ranking ecclesiastical officers, forced the pope to remonstrate. Moreover, in order to pacify the warring factions in the East, the emperor, Zeno, issued an edict in which the faith of his subjects was laid down. On the one hand, it was its legal doctrinal equipment which enabled the fifth-century papacy to take up the challenge, and on the other hand this challenge forced the papacy to declare itself on a number of vital points and principles.

III. GROWTH OF ROMAN-BIBLICAL IDEAS

That the papal and imperial standpoints were irreconcilable was not only the result of the factors already mentioned, but also followed from the fundamentally different view which pope and emperor took of the entity under their control. Each of them looked at it from a different standpoint. To the emperor it was the Roman empire, pure and simple, which had become Christian; to the pope this same body was the Church (comprising clergy and laity) which happened to be the Roman empire. Because this body was, for the emperor, the Roman empire, it was his duty in consonance with his monarchic function to govern it in every respect, be it in purely mundane matters or in spiritual affairs or in organizational respects: divinity had entrusted him with the government of the Roman empire; but since the Christian religion played a conspicuous role and was of paramount importance for the cohesion of the empire, he considered it one of his prime functions to intervene in religious disputes and in the organization of ecclesiastical bodies by giving them appropriate officers in the shape of patriarchs and archbishops, and so on.

But because this same entity was, for the papacy, the Church, and because the emperors themselves more and more stressed its Christian complexion, the popes in the second half of the fifth century began to ask – now that they were equipped with a doctrine based on Roman law – whether the emperor was entitled to govern monarchically simply because he was emperor. The problem, as the papacy saw it, was this. Who was to lay down faith and doctrine, who was to give the law for this Christian body corporate, who was to control the sacerdotal organism – emperor or pope? The question posed by the papacy assumed that Christianity not only seized the whole of man and determined his life in every aspect, but also demanded the whole, and not merely part, of man. For both governments the wholeness, the totality of man, counted, and not his religious, political, moral conduct. Hence, since the emperors themselves so strongly emphasized the Christian character of the empire, the popes began to ask certain crucial questions. Who was qualified to define the doctrine, purpose, and aim underlying this corporate union of all Christians, and to turn doctrine into the enforceable law – emperor or pope?

The papacy was always to be in a better position to give an answer to this sort of question. As already indicated, the popes held that doctrine must be enunciated by those who were qualified to pronounce upon it. The purely abstract principles of faith must be cast into intelligible language – who else but the pope was qualified to do this? Since the empire was Christian, it was all the more necessary that the Christian religion be given its precision and contents, for Christianity was then a living force that was of the most crucial importance for all social life and that permeated into every one of its departments – had the emperor the necessary qualification for pronouncing upon doctrine, had he the necessary knowledge which officers to appoint within the ecclesiastical organism? The translation of the abstract principles of faith and doctrine into concrete measures and terms, into law, is government. Since the emperor was a Christian, he was, according to the papacy, subjected to papal jurisdiction, subjected to the papal law. At the same time it should be stressed that the papacy – in the fifth century as well as in the succeeding ages – concerned itself with those fundamental principles which affected the basic structure of the corporate body, and not with issues which were merely peripheral or even irrelevant to it.*

* If one were to give an example taken from modern conditions the question of right-hand or left-hand driving would not, on the surface, be one that fundamentally affected the Christian character of society, and the

It was in the working out of the answers to these problems that the late-fifth-century papacy made a number of basic pronouncements, so basic in fact that they remained valid throughout the medieval period, and possibly beyond. To begin with: what was the function and standing of the emperor – or for that matter of any Christian king – within the corporate body of Christians? 'The emperor is within the Church, not above it' St Ambrose had already declared in the late fourth century, and this cue was readily taken up in the fifth century, when the father–son relationship between pope and (Christian) Ruler came to be metaphorically used. And for anyone acquainted with the position of the Roman father in the Roman family there could be no doubt what the implications of this theme were. Leo I had directed attention to the purpose of secular rulership when he said that the Christian Ruler's predominant duty was the protection of the Christian body corporate. This teleological argument could not but help to invoke the Pauline statement that 'The prince does not bear the sword without reason'. The reason for the prince's bearing the sword was that he had the duty to assist the realization of the divine plan on earth; he had received the sword in order to administer the mundane things through the application of Christian principles.

This view of the ruler's function, based as it was on Pauline views, denied autonomous character to any secular ruler. But this is not to say that, according to papal views, the emperor had not an important role to play in the execution of the divine plan. On the contrary, since there was no power but of God, God had created secular rulership, but it had a merely auxiliary function in the divine scheme of things: he was to eradicate evil by the sword – that was the reason why divinity had conferred on him actual power. His duty was to learn, not to teach, as Gelasius I (492-6) also insisted in his protests to the emperor, for the emperor was the son of the Church, not its master. And it was precisely in this context that Gelasius operated with the Matthean verses, declaring the pope's all-comprehensive power

papacy would have taken no interest in this question, unless it could be shown that the basic structure of society was touched by it.

of binding and loosing: everything could be bound and loosed. This theme of the unrestricted legal power to bind and to loose was given by Gelasius its basic character which, within the papal precincts, was to remain so throughout the Middle Ages. For it was, according to the same Gelasius, the duty of the emperor to subject his rulings to ecclesiastical officers, provided, as we should add, that these rulings affected the structure and well-being of the whole Christian corporate body. That emperor, Gelasius said, who recognized this state of affairs, who subordinated his (basic) rulings to the priests of Christ, could justly call himself a 'catholic emperor'.

What these Gelasian statements amounted to was the assertion of the pope's *superioritas*, his sovereignty, in matters fundamentally touching the Christian complexion of society, and consequently the emperor's inferiority, his subjection to papal rulings, in these matters. This sovereign status of the pope Gelasius also made clear in one of his best-known statements, in which he referred to the pope's *auctoritas* and to the emperor's (mere) *regia potestas*. Both terms were in fact taken from the Roman constitution in which the 'authority' of the Ruler was over and above mere 'power': the 'authority' of the Ruler consisted of his outstanding qualification and was the faculty of shaping things creatively and in a binding manner. The 'power' referred to the execution of what 'authority' had laid down. All this had of course nothing to do with any Church–State problem. Not only did this dichotomy not exist, not only did the whole output of Gelasius's work contain no hint at the awareness of this dichotomy, but the whole problem and conflict would never have arisen, had there been a dichotomy between a Church and a State. For the question was precisely who, pope or emperor, gave the final and authoritative decision in matters vitally affecting the fabric of one and the same body? There were not two bodies, one a Church, the other a State, but one only, which the emperor viewed as the Christian Roman empire, and the pope as the Roman Christian Church. Nevertheless, the Gelasian statements were the first clear enunciation of the concept of sovereignty within a Christian corporate body.

The papal concept of sovereignty was buttressed by the super-

imposition of a Christian argument. The pontifical 'authority'
in a Christian world was all the greater as it had to render an
account of the doings of the kings on the day of judgment. It
was the pontiffs who had then to say how the kings and emperors had discharged the trust which divinity had conferred
on them. For, as the same Gelasius furthermore declared, thereby giving considerable precision to the papal theme of government, the rulers had no right to their rulership. Rulership was a
special favour of divinity, was a good deed *(beneficium)* and
nobody could claim a right to a good deed or a favour. Rulership in a Christian world, Gelasius maintained, was a privilege,
which divinity had bestowed on the individual king. Rulership
was, in other words, a concession made by God. In a way, Gelasius turned the thesis so much propagated by his contemporary
emperors, of the derivation of their power from God, against
them: it was for the popes who in this Christian world were
the heirs and successors of St Peter, to pronounce on the day of
judgment how the emperors had dealt with the divine trust and
favour of their rulership.

In one of his tracts Gelasius considerably deepened these
ideas and once more struck up a theme that was to imprint its
stamp on medieval governmental thought. In this tract he rem-
onstrated against the imperial conflation of regal and sacerdotal
power, maintaining that only Christ had been both king and
priest and that it was since Christ that the offices of king and
priest had been distinguished. Neither should meddle in the
affairs of the other. What Gelasius wished to impress upon his
readers was the difference in the functions of the king and
priest. The latter should not be entangled in matters of this
world for which divinity itself had provided by the institution
of kingship. For the fruitful pursuit of the aims of Christian
society each should adhere to his own office. Carnal matters,
he declared, were the proper domain of the kings, who for their
own salvation needed the pontiffs because the latter alone were
qualified, by virtue of their vocation, to lay down the conditions
on which salvation could be achieved. What he did not propound in this important declaration was any sort of equipollent
dualism in a Christian society. What he did set forth, and this

is indeed important enough to make him one of the great thinkers on Christian government, was the principle of division of labour. Sovereignty (the *auctoritas*) concerning basic and vital matters, remained with the pope, but the execution of what the papal sovereign had laid down, the actual handling of the mundane (the Gelasian 'carnal') matters was the task of the king. This principle of division of labour rested – in the final resort – upon another Pauline thesis, that is, that to each part of an organic whole special functions were assigned. Consequently, each member of society should adhere to the scope of the office which was eventually of divine origin. But final authority, in a Christian society, was the pope's alone. Eventually the principle of division of labour was intimately linked with the concept of monarchy. That was also the reason why the same Gelasius operated so much with the highly geared-up concept of the *principatus* which was the usual term for Roman monarchy. And only through the vehicle of the law could this papal *principatus* become a reality in the public sphere. The power to bind and to loose could be exercised over the emperor himself, since, as Gelasius said in the same tract, 'the lower placed cannot absolve the higher placed'. Moreover, since 'the disciple was not above the master', the imperial government had no right to sit in judgment over the pope who, as he was insistent, was removed from all earthly control and jurisdiction.

Some general observations on the Gelasian themes are called for. The pronouncedly regal-sacerdotal scheme of the imperial government in Constantinople and the mature papal ideology presented a contrast which human ingenuity was unable to bridge. In actual fact the Gelasian remonstrations and consequent deepening of the papal idea occurred in the middle of the first serious schism between East and West which lasted some thirty years. The incessant Eastern stress on the historical justification of the emperor's functions was matched by the incessant papal protestations of the papacy's biblically founded role. As the history of the millennium of this conflict showed, no compromise was possible. This early quarrel had already all the ingredients of the later medieval conflicts between the secular and the spiritual powers: the one standing on the concrete facts of history, the other on the abstract doctrines of Christianity.

Perhaps more important is the influence of the Gelasian ideas on the science of government. Modern ears may not be attuned to the arguments and modes of reasoning employed by the fifth century, but in assessing the historical development of ideas one should try to abstract from the formal presentation the matter or substance itself. Although the themes were worked out by the papacy within a wholly christocentric intellectual framework, they nonetheless contained principles which concern all modern 'political' thought also – the concept of rulership, of the reason for the necessity of rulership, the law, the concept of office and its functions, division of labour, sovereignty, and so on, are all familiar topics to the student of modern political science. The only difference between this and its early progenitor is the form in which the answers are presented.

CHAPTER 2

THE WESTERN ORIENTATION

I. IMPERIAL CAESAROPAPISM

THE ending of the first schism between East and West in 519 was no more than a patched-up truce concluded by the employment of some ingenious face-saving formulae. The strong assertion of the papacy's primatial-jurisdictional functions in the preceding pontificates was only apt to provoke the imperial government at Constantinople all the more, and in Justinian (527–65) it found an amateur theologian as well as a convinced 'Roman Caesar' of quite extraordinary capabilities and energies. It is perhaps not insignificant that even before this Macedonian peasant became the 'Lord of the world', popular legend at Constantinople had it that, whilst it was undeniable that the Roman Church was founded by St Peter, his brother St Andrew had founded the patriarchate of Constantinople – the story was invented to show in characteristic Byzantine manner that both sees were founded by apostles who were, moreover, brothers. The implication was clear enough. Constantinople was to have at least the same position as Rome had, and any prerogatives which the Roman Church had were at least equalled by the sister foundation. When we recall for a moment the relevant decrees of the Council of Chalcedon* we will have no difficulty in appreciating the trend. It was also at the same time – the turn of the fifth and sixth centuries – that Rome witnessed the publication of a novelistic best-seller, the so-called *Legenda sancti Silvestri*, which dealt with the alleged conversion of Constantine and which was to serve as the model for one of the most influential papal forgeries in the Middle Ages.†

Justinian's preoccupation was the restitution of the ancient Roman empire in all its wondrous respects. The re-conquest of Italy and the accompanying military and governmental measures are of no concern to us. What is however of direct concern is that in his vocation as Roman emperor he was aware of

* See above, p. 37.   † See below, p. 59.

the need to recover the Roman law and to codify the whole available law in conveniently accessible volumes. This was one of his first governmental actions, though there had been attempts at codification in the fifth century resulting in the *Code* of Theodosius. But Justinian desired to make available the whole of Roman law, both private and public, and for this reason he appointed a commission in 527 which with startling rapidity produced in about six years what came to be known as the *Corpus Juris Civilis* consisting of three parts which, to this day, forms the basis of our knowledge and study of Roman law. General jurisprudential principles and the private laws were contained in the *Digest* of fifty books, divided into titles which consist of a number of individual 'laws' relevant to the subject-matter of the titles. Here the statements and views of the classical Roman jurisconsults were conveniently assembled. Most of them are known to us only through the *Digest*. The statements were in reality excerpts from the then still extant writings of the jurists; the commission was however empowered to make the necessary adjustments, and these are known as interpolations to the original dicta. The whole *Digest* was given by Justinian the force of law, so that all the private statements of the jurists were raised to legal enactments. What was hitherto dispersed in numerous writings, judgments, repositories, etc., became now a handy and allegedly harmonious work of law. The laws of the Roman emperors, the so-called imperial constitutions, largely dealing with public law, were contained in the *Code* which consisted of twelve books, again subdivided into titles and laws, the latter chronologically ordered down to Justinian's time. Any imperial constitution that was not in the *Code,* was deprived of legal force. The third part of the codification was a short text-book, the so-called *Institutes* of Roman law, which was to serve as a handbook for the law students at Beirut. The laws of Justinian himself after the promulgation of the *Code* were collected as so-called *Novellae (novae leges:* new laws), and from the twelfth century on were added as the fourth part to the *Corpus Juris Civilis*.

The significance of Justinian's codification can hardly be exaggerated. It lies perhaps less in the purely legal contents than in the ideology and the Roman culture which it conveyed. The *Corpus* was studied throughout the Middle Ages to a greater or lesser extent, sometimes merely in excerpts or summaries, but was always regarded as the sum-total of Roman juristic wisdom. It superseded all other similar works, as far as the *Code* was concerned, and in the *Digest* created something completely new. Here were available for the first time in medieval Europe books which contained all Rome had ever stood for – the law. To say that this codification became one of the most formative agencies of Europe would be no overstatement. The general principles relating to justice, to the concept of law, the division of law, its enforcement, and so on, became central to the medieval conception of law; whilst the *Code* (and the *Novellae*) set forth an unadulterated monarchic form of government in the guise of the law. And the *Code* of Justinian was later, when it came to be the subject of scientific treatment in the medieval Universities, one of the main sources of the doctrines relating to government. Its language, structure, composition, in short the indispensable requirements of formulating legal enactments – quite apart from the subject-matter – served as models for all subsequent generations. It was all so conveniently available.

It was in his legal output that Justinian expressed himself on the question of sovereignty within the empire. To him there could be no doubt that he as Roman Caesar was the supreme, sovereign Ruler who directed and ruled the empire in accordance with Christian principles emanating from the fount of all Christianity, the divine majesty of the emperor himself. In fact, the very first title of his *Code* bore the heading 'On the Trinity and the Catholic Faith', in which the subjects were instructed in the faith by the law. No less important was his legislation concerning the functions and structure of the priesthood itself: of course, as the monarch he was bound to see that the clerical officers of the empire consisted of suitable persons. This principle of suitability (which will engage us later), though identical with that upheld by the papacy, nevertheless differed greatly in the practical application. He who was considered suitable by the papacy, was not necessarily suitable in the eyes of the emperor. This decree of Justinian (*Nov.* 6) was in fact a rather gentle, though quite effective, reversal of the Gelasian thesis, to which attention has already been drawn. That in this scheme of things there was no room for a jurisdictional primacy of the pope is evident. What Justinian – and subsequent emperors – conceded was an honorary rank to the pope, a concession that is understandable if one takes into account the revered position of Rome itself and the predilection of Justinian for the Roman character of the empire. After all, it was Rome that gave the empire its complexion, and therefore the bishop of that city, the pope, had to be given some honorary precedence over other patriarchs. Consequently, his government legislated on the orthodoxy of faith as well as against heresies; there was legislation that only orthodox Christians could serve in the army, from which clerics were debarred, heretics were not allowed to propagate their faith and their books had to be burned; the clergy were forbidden to attend theatres, circuses, or race meetings; they were not allowed private oratories; their liturgical duties and their duty of residence were regulated by imperial laws; and so on. The participants of the Council of Constantinople in 536 entirely supported the imperial scheme when they declared that 'nothing must be done in the Church against the command and will of the emperor'. What the government of Justinian showed was the pure monarchic principle at work, in which all power flowed from the divinely instituted and inspired majesty of the emperor, whose interventions in purely theological disputes become understandable. The basic features of this descending theme of government were partly Hellenistic, partly Roman, partly Christian, and there can be no doubt about the consistency and inner resilience of this amalgam. A governmental ideology was faithfully reflected in the law and constitution.

Clearly, this ideology and law were diametrically opposed to the fundamental ideas which the papacy held should prevail in a Christian society. And the history of the sixth century incontrovertibly proved that the imperial scheme was concretely applied, with the consequence that the papacy was faced with one of its most difficult dilemmas. As Romans and popes they were, of course, subjects of the emperor, and in this capacity they had no right to remonstrate against the regal-sacerdotal monarchy of the emperor. Their dilemma was this. If they acquiesced in the imperial scheme, they became unfaithful to their own vocation, to their office, to their function as successors of St Peter upon whom Christ had put the duty of 'building', that is, governing the Church. If, however, they attempted to live up to their vocation, they were bound to protest against the untrammelled exercise of monarchic authority, but protestations against the divine majesty of the emperor were fraught with severe dangers amounting to the crime of *lèse majesté* in the person of the emperor. From the constitutional standpoint the drastic measures taken by the imperial government against those who denied the imperial right to legislate comprehensively were perfectly understandable and justified. For the papacy – and for that matter for the imperial government – no compromise was possible: either the pope was sovereign or the emperor.

It is against this background that the importance of Gregory I's pontificate (590–603) must be set. Before becoming pope, he was an ambassador of the Roman Church to the imperial court. He had therefore personal experience and knowledge of how strongly entrenched the regal-sacerdotal scheme was in Constantinople, and the only sensible conclusion he reached was that it would be dangerous and foolhardy for the Roman Church to persist in its protestations and remonstrations against the emperor's government. Dangerous, because of the severe constitutional consequences, and foolhardy, because of the lack of any prospect of changing the imperial scheme of government. This is not to say that Gregory acquiesced in it – far from it: it was a situation which was regrettable but which it was not in his power to change. But, and in this lay Gregory's juristic acumen and far-sightedness, none of the disadvantages would exist if the popes were to press their own governmental theory in regions in which the emperor's government and jurisdiction were ineffective. Hence Gregory's turning to the West by sending missions to Gaul and England. Indeed, in these regions he could – and did – strike up all the resonant chords of the papal

view of government; above all he was able to stress the primatial function of the papacy, unimpeded by any problems concerning its constitutional position. The realism of Gregory was
the necessary prerequisite for making the papal government a
reality in the Middle Ages. Indeed, with every justification was
he called 'Father of Europe'. Western, that is Latin, Europe
was the result of this step; not only did the West as a cultural
factor come into being, but it became also strongly impreg-
nated with Roman, that is Latin, features. It was from the
farthest corner of Europe into which he had sent missionaries,
that Northern and Central Europe were to be christianized by
English and Scottish missionaries.

Gregory I did not contribute any startlingly new tenets to
papal theory, though by his superb command of language he
impressed ideas (even by then well-worn) upon the receptive,
fallow Western soil. The Roman Church, according to him,
was the epitome of the whole 'Body of Christ which is the
universal Church', and this body was made up of the nations
and kingdoms recognizing the motherhood of the Roman
Church and the fatherhood of the pope. Particular praise was
bestowed upon the Franks in Gaul, because they showed true
orthodoxy. What is highly significant is that there was a strong
contrast in the manner of his dealing with Western kings and
the emperor in Constantinople. Whilst the former were addressed as his 'dearest sons', the latter was the 'Lord emperor' – the
reason for this difference being that he did not wish to provoke
the wrath of the emperor. Nor did he ever employ the danger-
ously pregnant concept of *principatus* towards the East, though
towards the West the term was frequently used by him. Moreover, in his communications to Western kings he stressed that
the earthly power was at the service of the celestial power
which should be the model for the former – a clear reminder of
the influence of Pseudo-Denys.* It was the language of governing authority which made Gregory lay down the sanctions for
disregarding papal decrees and measures: excommunication,
that is exclusion from the corporate union of Christians, was a
penal measure which, he said, could be employed against

* See above, p. 31.

kings as well as clerics. The clergy was to be the organ which transmitted papal decrees, because in this way they acted as 'cultivators' of the Church of God. The sovereign function of the pope was buttressed by the reference to the spurious statement of Constantine to the bishops assembled in the Council of Nicea – which Gregory had from Rufinus' translation of Eusebius – that 'You are gods, constituted by the true God: it is not right that we sit in judgment over gods.' Nor was Gregory less emphatic on the differentiation of hierarchical ranks and orders within the universal Church, because its smooth working was conditioned by inequality of functions. This was a principle that was to gain great importance in the high Middle Ages. Above all, Gregory I called the corporate union of Christians the 'Society of the Christian commonwealth' (*societas reipublicae christianae*), which was to be directed by the successor of St Peter acting through suitable lower officers.

One of the reasons for the great influence of Gregory the Great upon Western Europe was that virtually all his writings were preserved and, most important, that his official correspondence contained in his Registers and kept in the Archives were transmitted to later papal generations. The intimate contact which the papacy from now on maintained with the West resulted in the amalgamation of purely Germanic with purely Roman and Christian elements, a process made easier by the fairly favourable conditions which existed once the dust of the invasions had settled down. In Northern Italy, amongst the Lombards as well as in Spain and France, peaceful and orderly conditions prevailed which considerably facilitated the spread of papal governmental ideology. The gulf between East and West became thereby ever wider. A new civilization grew up, virile, assertive, and forward-looking, a civilization which was Roman-Latin as well as Germanic, and which had as yet little appreciation of the highly geared-up and mature culture of the East. Whilst Latin became the *lingua franca* of of the West, Greek remained the official and ordinary language of the East. Through the numerous avenues which were opened up by Gregory's far-flung missions, Roman spirit, above all the Roman law, could gain a firm foothold in Western regions. Because of the lack of literacy amongst the broad masses, the spread of ideas came to be greatly helped by the adoption of Roman liturgy. Liturgy in many respects took the place of literary exposition. It was a means by which often profound ideas could be presented by ritual gestures, actions, and so on, each of which was to convey an easily understandable symbolic meaning. That liturgy was overwhelmingly Roman-directed and inspired; it later stimulated and promoted reflective thinking about the ideas which were expressed by the liturgical symbols.

But one of the vital organs that so greatly contributed to the acceptance of the theocratic-descending thesis of government was the Latinized Bible. For some inscrutable reason this hardly ever receives mention. It is indisputable that the Vulgate played a most important role in the softening up of the fertile and yet untilled soil of Western Europe, cultivating it for the reception of purely Roman ideas. One has merely to state that the Bible was the one book with which every literate person was thoroughly familiar, in order to grasp its potent influence. And the dissemination of the Latin Bible took place in pre-cisely those regions of Western Europe which were particularly susceptible to Roman influence. This is specially true of the chancery personnel of the rulers, who, without having ab-sorbed learned treatises on governmental ideology, nevertheless applied a very definite system of government in their chancery products. For here in the Bible there were found – as we have already stated – a number of topics which had direct relevance to public government. In fact, the Latin Bible was one of the major factors which assisted the Romanizing-Latinizing pro-cess. What needs stressing is that the Bible in its Latin shape was held to have contained not only the truth itself, but that Truth in Latin. The divine word was written and spoken in Latin. It really does not need much historical imagination to visualize how potently the constant occupation with a model so strongly soaked with theocratic as well as Roman-Latin elements shaped the thought of the very men who did the governing. One can go further and say that the Latin Bible not only was the most important factor which directed the West to Rome, but also to a degree not yet fully realized facilitated the spread and influence of the ideas enshrined in Roman law.

These observations also furnish an explanation of the different complexion between West and East. In the East Roman-Latin elements were absent; the West interpreted the Bible essentially as a legal document. Moreover, the fewer obstacles, physical, geographical or otherwise, the Latin Bible experienced in Western Europe, the stronger its influence was. This appears to be at least part of the explanation of why there was no trace of a theocratic-descending form of government in the Scandinavian countries and Northern Europe until very much later than in the Southern and Western parts. Nor do we find the influence of Roman law in Northern Europe to any extent comparable to that in the West and South. The Latin Bible became known in Northern Europe far later than anywhere else. It was this factor which at least partly explains the different complexions in these parts of Europe. Moreover, the legal records upon which our knowledge of matters relating to government is based rather faithfully reflect the divergence of Roman-Latin influence. The thickest and densest production of legal records can be found in the very same regions which were subjected to the combined influence of the Latin Bible and the Roman law, and the less noticeable this influence was, the fewer the legal products were, with the consequence that, for instance, in Scandinavia legal records did not begin before the high Middle Ages. It is therefore significant that in the Scandinavian countries the ascending theory of government enjoyed a longevity which stood in contrast to the prevailing theocratic-descending thesis observable throughout Southern and Western Europe.

II. THE KING BY THE GRACE OF GOD

There was perhaps no more telling text in the Bible than that in the gospel of St John when Christ addressed Pilate in these words:

You would have no *power* at all against me, if it had not been *given* to you from *above*.

This text in its literal meaning – power given from above – linked with the already mentioned Pauline statements 'There is no power but of God' and 'What I am, I am by the grace of God', presents the nucleus of medieval royal theocratic government. Although this kind of government was developed without any – so far – observable concrete papal influence, in essence the papal and royal-theocratic standpoints were identical, both agreeing that within a properly conceived christo-centric framework there was no room for a thesis upholding a right to power, a right to rulership, a right to an office. It will be recalled that Gelasius I spoke of a divinely conferred 'good deed' (*beneficium*) upon the emperor, and now within the royal theocratic form of government we find exactly the same point of view, arrived at without any intervention by the papacy.

As a matter of fact, the visible result of the change from the earlier ascending theory of government to its descending counterpart can be found, as far as records can show, amongst the Lombards in Northern Italy. The Lombard kings began from the late sixth century on to call themselves 'King by the grace of God' – the 'Rex *Dei gratia*' – and there is additional proof that the Anglo-Saxon kings in the seventh century had become familiar with the thesis of the king deriving his power from God and that kingship was conceived as a gift of God. From the eighth century onwards this designation became standard with all kings of Western and Southern Europe. The meaning of this appellation seems clear enough. The king, who had hitherto been elected by the people or by its representative body, made it abundantly plain by this designation that his kingship rested upon the good will, the favour, the 'grace' bestowed on him by God. The essential point is that thereby the close links which he had had with the people were severed, because the people conferred no power on him, could not therefore take it away by legal means, and was merely committed to him.

Several important consequences arose out of this location of original power in God. The title unmistakably conveyed the thesis that the king had no right to his governorship. No one has a right to claim a good deed, to demand a favour from anyone. This was simply the transference of the Pauline idea to public government. And just as the king himself had no right to his rulership, in the same way the people were not entitled to demand from the king, as a matter of right, any governmental action. This theocratic form of government was also demonstrated by the king conceding to his subjects, as a matter of royal grace, offices and rights which they otherwise would not have had. The underlying idea was that all power came from God through the king who then distributed parts of it to his subjects. This was the essence of the all-important principle of concession, according to which the subjects received offices, functions, rights, etc., as a matter of royal concession, as an effluence of royal favour. When therefore the Queen today declares that she has 'graciously' approved of this or that appointment, she uses language which not only clearly conveys the idea of royal grace, but which has also a very distinguished pedigree reaching back to the seventh century.

The principle of concession emerged as an operational instrument in one of the oldest historical records which inform us of the basic conceptions relating to the king's government. The so-called Marculf Formulae were a chancery handbook used by the Frankish kings in the seventh century and contained many of the ideas which have just attracted our attention, especially those relative to the king's grace, as well as to the complementary principle of concession. They were a Germanic product which exhibited the influence, at least in governmental matters, of the Christian theme and therefore of the Latin Bible. This handbook also showed quite clearly how the Frankish chancery conceived of the sovereignty, that is, the superiority, of the king. What mattered was the 'will of the prince', precisely because he was the recipient of divine favours. To all intents and purposes the king was God's vicegerent on earth. The people itself was merely the recipient of royal favours: it was subjected to the will of the king, hence they were subjects in the literal meaning of the term; the king could also withdraw his royal grace from the subject, in which case the subject fell into the king's disgrace, and was unable to expect any further favours. It is important to keep these ideas in the forefront of our minds because, as we shall later see, the royal coronation orders, and especially the unction, powerfully buttressed them in a liturgical garb. It stands to reason that on these presuppositions the old-established right of resistance could no longer be upheld. The subject had no right to resist the king's command, however much he might have considered it unjust or unlawful, because the king acted as God's vicegerent: and once again St Paul was at hand to support this lack of rightful resistance.*

The people itself, so far from having autonomous or indigenous powers, was in fact and in theory entrusted or committed by God to the king's government. Because of its inability to order its own affairs, doctrine was not only to put the people of a kingdom on the juristic level of a minor under age, but royal practice and doctrine, as exemplified in the thousands of charters and dozens of formulary collections used by the chanceries, very significantly treated of the people as being in the *Munt* of the king. That is to say, the *Munt* (Latin *mundium* or *mundeburdium*; Anglo-Saxon: *mund-bora*) expressed the idea of protection in a telling way. It was the same kind of protection which a father affords a child, in no wise different from the protection which a guardian gives to his ward, or in Anglo-Saxon England the husband gave his wife.† The protector was supposed to know best when the interests of his entrusted ward demanded action. The protector, however, acted in the interests of his trust. And according to medieval conceptions, the guardian had, through possessing the *Munt*, jurisdiction over his ward. This was exactly the idea underlying the king's guardianship or what the Anglo-Saxons called *mund-bora*; protection by the king entailed jurisdiction over the protected subject (*protectio trahit subjectionem*). Nevertheless, the interests of the ward (or of the people) did not always coincide with his wishes. The ward, or the people, may well express wishes, aspirations, desires, and

*Romans xiii, 2.   † Cf. also the German *Vor/mund*.

the like, but the guardian, or the king, is not bound by them. As Charlemagne's adviser said, merely repeating what a fifth-century pope (Celestine I) had already said: 'The people are not to be followed, but are to be taught.' Royal-theocratic government culminated in the idea of giving protection to the people, because it – like a ward – was entrusted to the king's care. Once again the concept of sovereignty appeared: the king stood outside and above the people. This was clearly and concretely brought into clear relief by the symbolism that attached itself to the throne when the king was seated high above the people surrounding him.*

The concept of protection (*Munt*) also explained why already in the early laws of the seventh and eighth centuries Lombard and Visigothic kings employed a terminology which unmistakably reflected ideas animating royal governments. For the vehicle by which protection was practically and effectively given was that provided by the law. Through his law the king furthered the well-being and the peace of the kingdom entrusted to him and also laid the foundations for orderly development. The law was given to the subjects or the people, not made by them. It is therefore understandable why law from the eighth century onwards became overwhelmingly royal law, and why this ousted the hitherto prevailing folk-law, the mainly customary law made by the folk (the people). Similarly, until the ascending thesis gave way to its counter-part, there also prevailed in the kingdom the peace guaranteed by the people itself – the so-called *Volksfriede* – which, on the application of the descending form of government gave way to peace guaranteed by the king (so-called *Königsfriede*). For the supreme duty which divinity was said to have laid up-on the king was the preservation of peace. In giving protection and in preserving peace, mainly through the law, the king acted entirely on his own insight, knowledge, and understanding; he was alone responsible to God for keeping the peace in his king-

* This superiority (sovereignty) has always been expressed in linguistic terms, such as 'Your royal *High*ness'. The untranslatable German '*Obrig*keit' or the '*Hoheits*gebiet' and so on, no less than the very concept of Majesty, meaning the greater or higher, express exactly the same ideology.

dom. The conception of monarchy thereby gained considerably in practical importance. In the eighth century the king effectively emancipated himself from the fetters which had bound his ancestors to the people: he visibly detached himself from the people. It was a veritable reversal of things.

The people committed to the king's government included in the seventh and eighth centuries the clergy, particularly the episcopacy. The Frankish kingdom in the eighth century furnished good examples of the monarchic government by the king. It was he who convoked ecclesiastical synods, presided over them, and sanctioned the decrees of the councils. Equally important these councils were composed as much by the clergy as by the (aristocratic) laity. Although there is no shred of evidence that the Frankish Rulers were in any way familiar with the Byzantine regal-sacerdotal schemes of things, it is nonetheless interesting to see that the actual development in the West tended towards the same kind of government which was observable in the East. But there was, in the West, no theorizing, no high-falutin speculation, but only practice.

III. FUSION OF ROMAN AND FRANKISH IDEAS

Development down to the mid eighth century had not shown any close relationship between the Franks and the papacy. The journey of Pope Stephen II in 753–4 to the Frankish kingdom was to be of decisive influence, not only for the history of Europe, but also for the development of governmental ideas. Indeed, shortly before this journey was undertaken, the Frankish leader, Pippin, had established closer contact with the papacy, with results he himself could hardly have foreseen. In order to have some sort of backing for his *coup d'état* against the king, Childeric III, Pippin asked the pope, Zacharias, whether he who had actual power should be called king or he who, though called king, wielded no power at all. The pope's answer was favourable to Pippin, adding for good measure that he, by apostolic authority, ordered Pippin to be king. Although its revelation of papal ideology was to prove extremely profitable to a later papal generation, the answer had, however, little bearing on the immediately following events. The purpose of Stephen's journey was to use the genuine Frankish veneration for St Peter and his office, in order to emancipate the institution of the papacy from the framework of the imperial constitution and thereby to escape the consequences of the regal-sacerdotal rulings of the imperial government. The pretext for invoking Pippin's help was the alleged threat of the Lombards to Rome. The handle with which the aim was to be achieved was the spurious Donation of Constantine.

The stages by which the papacy extricated itself from the imperial framework are not relevant here and it will suffice to say that the result was the establishment of the so-called papal state, an entity that was carved out of the body of the empire and was governed by the pope alone. This remained in existence until 1870 and is now reduced to the Vatican City. Pippin and his son, Charlemagne, gave promises of security for this entity which was, to use modern terminology, recognized in public law, though not by Byzantium. Stephen II's actions and letters were a faithful reflection of papal governmental ideology.

The document itself deserves some attention. The Donation of Constantine, though primarily aimed at Constantinople, had, nevertheless, by virtue of the general principles it embodied, applicability also to the West. The forgery was, as is now generally agreed, made in the bosom of the Roman Church, that is, in the papal chancery at the latest in the early fifties of the eighth century, and certainly before the visit of the pope to the Franks. It is impossible to exaggerate the influence which this fabrication had upon medieval Europe generally and on the papacy specifically. The contents of this forgery relied on the already mentioned *Legenda sancti Silvestri*, of the late fifth century, written in the very period which witnessed the first serious clash between papal and imperial conceptions of government. The chief point made by the government in Constantinople was that Constantinople, New Rome, was the capital of the empire, to which all other cities, including Old

Rome, were subordinated. This was, as will be recalled, based on the decrees of Chalcedon.* If it was so, the question arose, How did Constantinople actually become the capital of the empire, thereby degrading Rome? It was undeniable that Constantine had built the new city transferring the government from Rome to his own city, Constantinople. What the author of the *Legenda* tried to hint at, and what the author of the Donation explicitly brought out, was that the transfer of the imperial government from Rome to Constantinople took place with the agreement and acquiescence of the pope, Silvester. A historical fact was interpreted in purely ideological terms.

The *Legenda* informed its readers that Constantine had conferred on the Roman Church the privilege of its being the head of the whole clergy in the Roman world. It also contained a long description of Constantine's alleged conversion to Christianity, and in sometimes unsavoury detail the author depicted how Constantine as a sign of his utter contrition for all his evil deeds, prostrated himself before the pope, divesting himself of his imperial emblems, including the imperial crown; his contrition made him weep bitterly and he wetted his purple mantle that lay on the ground. This was meant to be a realistic portrayal presented in sentimental and romantic language which should not, however, disguise the thought behind it. For nobody had ever doubted that Constantine was emperor after the transfer to Constantinople, and when the *Legenda* described in some considerable detail how he had divested himself of his imperial insignia, especially the crown, in front of the pope, the question clearly suggested itself: Who re-invested him with his imperial insignia, and who put the crown back on his head? The *Legenda* left the question unanswered, and it was the fabricator of the Donation of Constantine who provided the answer.

According to the Donation, Constantine wishing 'to give the Roman Church imperial power and dignity of glory, vigour, and honour', handed to the pope all his imperial insignia and symbols, lance, sceptre, orb, imperial standards, purple

* See above, p. 37.

mantle, imperial pallium, purple tunic, and so forth.* They all became the pope's property. Moreover, as a sign of his humility Constantine performed the office of a '*strator*', that is, he led the papal horse for a short distance. Furthermore, the pope was given the imperial palace as his residence as well as the whole city of Rome, all provinces of Italy and the occident. Lastly, Constantine wished to put the imperial crown on the pope's head, but – most significantly – the pope refused to wear the imperial diadem. Constantine nevertheless decreed that the pope might use the imperial insignia. In this document the pope was called the vicar of Christ, a designation unknown at the time. Amongst the constitutional rights conferred on the pope were his right to appoint consuls and patricians.

This 'grant' of Constantine left nothing to be desired in its comprehensiveness and totality. The pope thereby became a veritable copy of the Eastern king and priest: he became a papal emperor. Although this idea became of crucial importance in later medieval Europe, at the time it had little bearing. What was of prime importance to the forger was to explain how and why Constantinople had become the capital. Although the pope refused to wear the crown, it was, according to the Donation, his property. The forger's intention was to convey the idea that, since nobody had ever doubted that Constantine did wear a crown after moving to Constantinople, he wore it with the pope's agreement and acquiescence. If the pope had so wished, he could have worn it: the crown was his, but he left its use to the emperor. The further implication was that as a result of the pope's refusal to wear the imperial crown – the highest symbol of rulership – it migrated to Constantinople which was thereby raised to the status of the capital, because the imperial government and symbol of rulership were there. The immediately emerging thesis was that the crown was on Constantine's and his successors' heads on sufferance by the pope, who, if he so wished, could also re-transfer it to Rome. The crown was to be at the disposal of the pope. The true state

*'In imitation of our own power' Constantine also laid down that the papal horses should be white horses and that the pope's non-liturgical dress should be white.

of affairs, according to the forgery, was the very opposite of what Byzantium asserted.

The governmental doctrine revealed in this document concerned the function, the purpose, and the aim of rulership within a Roman-Christian world. To show this was in the last resort the real intention of the forger. In order to demonstrate his papal doctrine of government he had to have recourse to the facts of history, but he utilized them in such a way that they became tools of the papal-Christian idea of rulership. It is perhaps difficult nowadays to put one's mind back to the mid eighth century, when, first, the papacy had had practical experience of the actual working of the Byzantine regal-sacerdotal scheme which deprived the popes of any worthwhile deployment of its primatial rights, and, secondly, ideas were most suitably expressed in allegorical and concrete terms. For one must not forget that the emperors in Constantinople had made a particular point about their Christianity – but it was, from the papal point of view, a Christianity that violated the most vital of all vital themes, namely the function of the papacy as the divinely instituted governing organ of all Christians. It was only a few years earlier that the emperor had legislated on, and prohibited, the veneration of images, declaring his right to do so, because he was both king and priest. It was precisely this with which the papacy could not agree, asserting that the governance of all Christians belonged by right to it. The popes asserted their superiority (sovereignty) in the Christian world, a sovereignty which was symbolized by the crown. This was why the forger made Constantine hand over the imperial crown to the pope. But although the Eastern emperors had so much stressed their Roman character of rulership – throughout the millennium of Byzantine existence – the popes argued that a Roman emperor should follow the Roman Church. If he did not, he ceased to be a Roman emperor and became a Greek emperor or a Greek king. This was precisely what the emperor at Constantinople was told soon afterwards. The wearing of the imperial crown at Constantinople was a favour granted by the pope – and a favour could be withdrawn. Like any other favour, nobody had a right to it. All this was simply the Pauline and

Gelasian theory of rulership clothed in eighth-century symbolism.

This, in brief, was the handle which enabled Stephen II to approach the Franks with some confidence. Incidentally the earliest 'copy' of the forgery extant is one of eighth-century provenance and is still preserved in the Bibliothèque Nationale at Paris whence it came from the monastery of St Denis where Stephen II stayed for some time on the occasion of his memorable visit. More important is that a number of his actions and statements were faithful reflections of this document. The whole territorial settlement can reasonably be explained only by recourse to the gifts of Constantine. The territories claimed by the pope were the property of St Peter, because donated to him by Constantine, and the faithless Lombards, he told Pippin, had stolen them. It is at this point that the function of Pippin as a Christian king and his indubitably genuine veneration for St Peter came into play. As Christian king he had the duty of protecting those who could not adequately protect themselves, a category which included churches, monasteries, etc. And here the essential point driven home by the pope was the old papal thesis of the Roman Church being the mother of all other churches, including those in the Frankish kingdom. If, as the pope vividly presented the situation to Pippin, the Lombards were not forced to restore the territory that belonged to St Peter and were to be allowed to continue with their depredations, the Church of St Peter and hence the mother of Pippin's own churches would go under. The extension of royal protective duties from the Frankish domains to the Roman Church was the gist of the pope's request to the king: precisely because of the Christian idea of kingship embraced by Pippin, these requests were bound to fall on fertile soil.

In order, however, to make sure that they were implemented, the pope applied another governmental idea of the papacy, and one that was explicitly contained in the Donation of Constantine, the appointment of Pippin as patrician of the Romans. In this concept was foreshadowed the later papal doctrine of the secular Ruler as an auxiliary organ of the papacy. The significance of this appointment lay in that a papally imposed duty of protection was added to the kingship of Pippin. Hitherto Pippin's kingship contained the kind of autonomous protection which was called *Munt*,* but his being made a patrician changed the substance of protection: he was to become active when instructed by the pope to act. The one kind of protection was autonomous; that of the patrician was comparable to that of an officer whose *raison d'être* was protection.† This latter was called in the sources *ad-vocatus*, that is, his help was called upon. In the appointment of Pippin as patrician the pope supplied a vital principle of government, and the title-deed he found in the forged Donation. This appointment was, from the papal side, the first breach into the royal monarch's fortifications. That Pippin himself, not being quite clear about the implications of the title, never used it, is beside the point; his son Charlemagne used it from the day of his succession – a measure of the advance which insistent papal policy had made in the meantime. Nevertheless, Pippin acted in the manner of a protector by conquering the Lombards and handing over the conquered territory to St Peter, that is, he 'restored' it (the future papal state) to the 'rightful' owner.

On the occasion of the pope's meeting with Pippin in 754 he also anointed him. This is not the place to review the history of anointing prior to this unction. But by this time it had become customary amongst the Visigoths in Spain, the Franks, and the Anglo-Saxons, and the idea took its origin from the Old Testament. The essence of it was that thereby an intimate link between king and God was established. It was the visible act of conferring divine grace on the king.‡ It should be noted

* See above, p. 56.

† A somewhat rough comparison between the two kinds of protection may be seen in the position of a guardian of a child or an insane person, and of the police. The former may well be approached by his ward for his services, but he decides what is in the best interests of his ward and may therefore have to refuse his ward's wishes, if he considers them unreasonable or against his best interests. The police on the other hand act when we call upon them against criminals, etc.; they have no right to interfere in our affairs in our interests, and they are called upon to help, because this is their *raison d'être*.

‡ See also below, pp. 71, 86

that the unction was as yet unknown in Rome. It reveals a somewhat well-prepared plan that the pope performed it, and he did not fail to stress that he acted as a mediator between God and the king. God Himself through him, the successor of Peter, had anointed Pippin for a definite purpose, namely of making him a special protector of the Roman Church.* In a number of communications to Pippin the pope repeated this. Here the papacy employed its much favoured teleological argument. The king, the pope said, had been distinguished by this act of anointing, and he became thereby consecrated to service to the papacy. Ideologically, therefore, upon the kingship of Pippin were imposed his duties as an officer, as a patrician of the Romans, and these duties were solemnized by the anointing. In his numerous communications the pope made the function of Pippin quite clear when he declared that through unction he had become the strong arm of the Roman Church that would see that justice was done to St Peter. This, indeed, was also the theme of the urgent and insistent letter which St Peter 'himself' wrote to Pippin. In the papal act of unction Pippin was, according to the numerous papal communications, instituted king. Undisputed facts once again had to yield to a programme.

Although Pippin acted as requested by the pope, there is no means of telling how far he himself accepted the implications of the theoretical papal standpoint. What however was of evident value was that the papacy's memory was always kept alive in its own ideological storehouse, that is, in its Archives and Registers. And what was of equal value was the dynamic initiative pursued by the papacy in its attempt to translate the blue-print of its programme into reality. No less important at that time was the intellectual superiority and experience of the papacy, and precisely in matters of government. One has but to mention the strong and overwhelmingly legal Roman milieu in which the papacy had grown and developed, to understand the expertise and skill with which it tried to master

* The fact that St Boniface had already anointed Pippin in 752 was not once mentioned in the whole papal transaction: it was as if it had never taken place.

situations. Nor should the essential difference between East and West be left out of account in an assessment of this papal ideological initiative. The genuine veneration which the Western peoples had for St Peter and his successor was a feature completely absent in Byzantium. Rome counted, as far as Byzantium was concerned, as the birth-place of the empire, and for this reason received its share of attention. For the West, Rome was the place where St Peter was said to have died, where his successor lived, where the epitome of the whole Christian Church, founded by two apostles, was situated, and for these reasons it was a place of special reverence. What was a historical fact for Byzantium, the New Rome, was an ecclesiastical or religious matter for Old Rome and the West. If to these factors one adds the Roman-inspired Latin Bible and the thoroughgoing legalistic interpretation of the Bible, one will readily understand why governmental thought in the West was so overwhelmingly ecclesiastical in its complexion. But because it was so strongly ecclesiastical, governmental thought could hardly fail to be shaped and influenced by the Roman Church, the papacy.

IV. THE CONCEPT OF EUROPE

As a result of these influences there was at the end of the eighth century a further application of its own governmental principles by the papacy. This was conditioned by the auspicious dealings between the papacy and the Franks in the mid eighth century, and appeared as the final act by which the papacy hoped to detach itself completely and irretrievably from the Byzantine framework. From the papal point of view the coronation of Pippin's son, Charlemagne, on Christmas Day 800 carried the idea of the patriciate to its logical conclusion. For, as we have seen, as a patrician Pippin was created an officer: an office was superimposed upon his kingship by the pope. By crowning Charlemagne the pope transformed the office of the patrician into the dignity of Roman emperorship. The title-deed to dispose of the imperial crown was plainly derived from the Donation of Constantine, in which the pope

THE CONCEPT OF EUROPE

allowed the Byzantine emperor to wear the crown which,
strictly speaking, was the pope's. What Pope Leo III did was to
're-transfer' the imperial crown from Byzantium to Rome –
with which action he completed the policy so auspiciously
begun by his predecessor, Stephen II. The coronation was to
be the final and solemn act by which Rome was to become
once again the centre of the Roman empire. For there could
not be two Roman emperors, each being the 'Lord of the
world'. As far as the papacy was concerned, the Eastern
emperor had for the reasons already stated, forfeited the right
to call himself an emperor of the Romans and had sunk to the
level of a mere Greek king or emperor. According to the
papacy an emperor of the Romans could only be he who was
a Roman, that is, who adhered to the Roman Church. Differently expressed: government in a Christian world must be
Roman directed and inspired; this meant acknowledgement
of the primatial position of the Roman Church, the papacy
itself – the very point strenuously denied by Byzantium.

The immediate reasons prompting the papacy to act were
the manifestations of a true regal-sacerdotal scheme in
Charlemagne's own government. In contrast to Byzantium
the kind of kingship which he exercised was not based upon
any grand speculation or theology, but on the consideration
that he as the recipient of divine grace (as he made abundantly
clear in his intitulation as 'King by the grace of God'), was
charged by divinity to guide and lead the kingdom entrusted
to him by God. It is one of the most interesting features
in the development of European governmental thought that
two governments as different in their genesis as the Byzantine
and the Frankish governments arrived at an identical form
of rulership. And there were indeed ominous signs that the
papacy might well be confronted by the same forces which
it had hoped to have banished. For on the occasion of Pope
Leo III's visit to Charlemagne in Ratisbon (799), he became
acquainted with the latter's plan to erect a 'second Rome' at
his residence at Aachen where there was the 'sacred palace' for
Charlemagne and a building called the Lateran to house the

pontiff. Little imagination was needed to see in the architect's plan a vivid reminder of the Byzantine set-up where the patriarch of Constantinople was the emperor's domestic chaplain. Nothing is more persuasive and dangerous than the embodiment of ideas in visible shape and concrete masonry. An additional spur for the pope to take the initiative was provided by the vacancy in Constantinople, because a woman, Irene, occupied the throne there.

All that does not mean that Charlemagne was in every respect taken unawares. He was in Rome in December 800, because his help was invoked against some Roman opponents of the pope. There were discussions about his becoming emperor and there can hardly be any doubt that he agreed to become emperor. Where, however, the difference between him and the pope lay, was in the kind of emperorship. To be an emperor pure and simple was only a question of title: after all, the Anglo-Saxon kings liked to call themselves emperors and there were others too. An emperor was simply he who gave orders, in no material respect different from a king. One might well say that an emperor was a streamlined king. But what the stage-managed conferment of a crown* by Leo III on Christmas Day produced was not just the creation of an emperor, but of the 'Emperor of the Romans'. That was a technical designation which meant, in agreement with the ancient Roman emperorship, one thing only: supreme governorship of the world. But this was not what had been discussed between Leo and Charlemagne. Leo's action had the effect of making the Frank an 'Emperor of the Romans', as the acclamations by the assembly made clear, and it was the name given to the newly crowned emperor, as the reports had it. To this kind of emperorship Charlemagne objected. For universal governorship, that is Roman emperorship, he had not intended nor had agreed to accept. His governmental intention was to be in the West what the Byzantine was in the East. What he wanted to see was a parity of position, a kind of coexistence with the

* What sort of crown did he place on Charlemagne's head? Where did he get it from? There were no imperial crowns lying around in Rome. Research has not yet unravelled this question.

East. But if he accepted the function intended for him by the pope, the emperor in the East would have ceased to exist as an 'Emperor of the Romans', and he alone would have had that role which he never intended to play. The papal plan was defeated, because Charlemagne refused the role allocated to him by the pope. But this was only a temporary check on the advance of papal governmental principles, as subsequent history was to show.

The governmental idea animating Charlemagne was that of being the 'Rector of Europe', and it was here that the concept of Europe became operational. Europe was for him Latin Christendom, which he indeed had done so much to strengthen. Reaching from the Pyrenees to the Elbe, this entity – the 'Kingdom of Europe' – was governed by him as the divinely appointed monarch. In this scheme of things the pope's duty was to pray for the monarch's success. Charlemagne was simply a Frankish monarch who had no understanding of the whole involved and (to him) abstruse Roman emperorship ideology. He was a realist who governed his kingdom in an autonomous way, in which the Christian element in its Roman complexion played a vital role. Europe and Church were identical in his scheme: they constituted the corporate union of all Latin Christians. It was of this that Alcuin, his main adviser in these matters, spoke declaring it to be the practical manifestation of St Augustine's City of God. Hence he appeared as the vicegerent of God on earth, as the vicar of Christ whose decisions were those of God – all in keeping with the theocratic-descending standpoint. His government of Europe was in many respects a classic demonstration of the theocratic monarch at work: legislating on all sorts of liturgical, religious, sacramental, monastic matters; appointing bishops and clerics; convoking ecclesiastical councils which were merely consultative organs, because their decrees had to have his approval to become law; and so on. In practice there was very little difference between this government and the one in Byzantium, with one exception, and that was that he accepted the ingredients of the Christian faith from Rome, because he

acknowledged that the exposition of the faith was the undisputed task of the pope. But deciding which items of this
Roman-expounded faith were to become law and therefore
part of the government itself was his, the king's task. This
important difference was to prove itself of crucial concern
to later royal (and imperial) generations. In Charlemagne's
reign this thin end of the wedge could not possibly be perceived in its complexity, for the acknowledgement of the
teaching primacy of the Roman Church was necessary for the
papal deployment of its jurisdictional primacy, that is, the right
to demand action by means of the law. This was a difficulty
which Byzantium escaped by not acknowledging any teaching
primacy of the Roman Church, and a difficulty which post-
medieval monarchs also avoided by breaking with the Church
of Rome altogether.

The creation of the Frankish king as an Emperor of the
Romans had far-reaching repercussions on a wider front,
however, not so much in his own time, as in the following
centuries. The Byzantines, from their standpoint, could never
understand how there could be an emperor who was not also
an Emperor of the Romans. However much Charlemagne tried
to persuade them that he was merely an emperor who governed
Latin Christendom, they were never really convinced of his
explanations. More important, through the accentuation of
the Western 'Empire' as a wholly Latin-Christian body, the
gulf between East and West considerably widened. The implications of the concept of Europe – and this is what Byzantium
clearly perceived – was that the 'Greeks', that is, the Eastern
empire, did not belong to Europe. From the point of view of
the history of civilization the period around the turn of the
eighth and ninth centuries was of fundamental importance:
Europe was portrayed as the embodiment of Roman-Latin
culture, and this was conceived almost wholly in religious
terms; the empire ruled from Constantinople was considered
alien to Europe. What had begun in the fifth century as a
matter of purely ecclesiastical disputes, leading to the first
schism, became now hardened and intensified on the territorial

plane of a Europe and the outside world. The Continent was divided between its Latin and its Greek component parts, in which only the former was Europe. Principles of government were to be henceforth moulded in the West by the – at the time – irresistible Roman influence, whilst the East continued to be Greek and receded from Europe's vision. This Roman influence could be seen in a somewhat concrete form in the decades subsequent to Charlemagne's reign. His successors went precisely the way which he had refused to go; they accepted what he did not accept, the papal view of the Western emperor as the sole and legitimate Emperor of the Romans. The crucial question then arose: Which of the two, the Eastern or the Western, was the real Emperor of the Romans? It was a question which was not finally answered until the conquest of Constantinople by the 'crusaders' in 1204.

Already the Frankish kings, including the Merovingians, had powerfully, though quite unwittingly, assisted the process by which the Roman-inspired governmental thought was to achieve its later resounding victory, and thereby help the clerical section of the Church to its dominating role. This is the significance of their practice of royal unction, modelled on the Old Testament, the mastery of which was the strength of the Frankish royal advisers. They considered that in the Old Testament the prophet by virtue of his knowledge of the divine will appointed a king of the Jews by pouring holy oil on him. They further considered that the divine grace was visibly bestowed upon the recipient of the oil. In agreement with the Old Testament they spoke of the king as 'The Lord's anointed' (the *Christus Domini*), and it was indeed in keeping with the Old Testament that Charlemagne was spoken of as a new David, as a king who had, so to speak, risen from the Old Testament. The king's claim to be 'King by the grace of God' was therefore powerfully buttressed by the liturgical ceremonial of the unction. The outward distinction of the King was paralleled by the internal effects which unction was believed to have produced: the king's whole being was transformed by the influx of divine grace and a powerful link was thereby established between him and God. Hence, 'The king's heart is in the hand of the Lord', which, transferred to public government, entailed a very special protection for the king: 'Do not touch mine anointed', one read in the Bible (Psalm cv, 15), and the inaccessibility of the king to his subjects received its biblical sanction. It was something approaching the crime of sacrilege for the subjects to lay hands on the king. The unction was a perfect means to bring the essence of theocratic kingship into relief. Throne and unction were visible means to show how much the king stood outside and above the community which divinity had entrusted to him.

Hindered by external factors, the East was unable to undo what had been done on Christmas Day 800, though the aim of Byzantium to reconquer Italy remained a strong element in its policy down to the second half of the twelfth century, and in the West it might well have appeared to the papacy in the first decade of the ninth century that it had exchanged the one king-priest for another. The effective resistance of Charlemagne put a temporary check on papal advance. But dynamic initiative was the hallmark of papal policy in its attempt to bring its own ideas of government to fruition. And this is precisely what the ninth-century papacy successfully accomplished, preparing the way for later development. What the fifth century is for the papacy, the ninth century is for Europe.

A further achievement of Charlemagne's government was to realize the need for an adequate education of the clergy. The so-called Carolingian Renaissance was powerfully supported by Charlemagne himself, and the educational measures stimulated by the government provided distinctly beneficial effects. Yet the education benefited exclusively the clergy, and above all the episcopacy, and no attempt was made, nor even envisaged, at a corresponding education of the laity. This is important in our context, because the educated clergy was to become the bearer of the intellectual movements which were to give the ninth century its complexion. Partly as a result of the critical spirit awakened by a higher standard of education, and partly as a result of the ground which the Renaissance covered – the resuscitated Latin and patristic works – there was an additional accentuation and impregnation of the still fallow Western soil with Roman-Latin elements. The following generation which had directly benefited from the educational efforts of Charlemagne was to propound themes and theses and theories concerning public government in a Christian society which were in stark contrast to the systems of government that could be witnessed in practice. The great forgeries concocted in the middle of the century no less than the liturgical arrangements concerning the king's coronation, to mention but two topics, were the work of those who succeeded the early Renaissance generation, itself so largely engendered by Charlemagne, the 'King by the grace of God'. And it was through the later confluence of the papal and Frankish episcopal efforts that the pronouncedly ecclesiastical character of medieval government thought was to come about. It is time we turn to a survey of the development in the ninth century.

CHAPTER 3

THE POST-CAROLINGIAN DEVELOPMENT

I. CLERICALIZATION OF POLITICAL THOUGHT

PERHAPS at no previous time had the papacy displayed greater initiative than in the ninth century. We recall that Pope Leo III's intention in crowning Charlemagne still remained unfulfilled, since the Frank showed himself impervious to the Roman-papal set of ideas. Apart from this, the coronation itself lacked all liturgical and ecclesiastical character; although performed in a church (the basilica of St Peter's), no anointing of the king-emperor took place, and no prayers were said, nor was there any other item that would have raised the action onto a specifically liturgical plane. It was nothing but a stage-managed action within the confines of a church. None saw the deficiencies better than Leo III's immediate successor. In order to drive home the papal theme of creating the 'Emperor of the Romans', Stephen IV (816–17) once again travelled to the Frankish kingdom, where Charlemagne's son, Louis I, had succeeded, already made a co-emperor by his father in imitation of Byzantine practice. The meeting between Stephen IV and Louis I at Rheims in 816 was memorable for two reasons: (1) the pope now produced the crown supposedly worn by Constantine, with which he actually crowned Louis I. Nothing could be more suggestive and more persuasive than the production of Constantine's crown – its absence in 800 was no doubt felt to be a defect which had now to be remedied; (2) the pope anointed Louis I on the same occasion, so that anointing and crowning were now combined in one liturgical act. Both were to form the essential elements of any subsequent coronation. Whilst the anointing was of Frankish (or possibly Anglo-Saxon or Visigothic) origin, the idea of coronation was Byzantine.

The coronation of 816 presented basic concepts relating to public government in the shape of readily understandable symbols. The symbolism of unction was now understood to mean that because Christ's grace flowed into the king, he thereby became the 'Type of Christ' or the 'Figure of Christ'. In actual fact, there was no essential difference between the anointing of a bishop and of a king, except that the royal (and imperial) unction did not confer what was called an indelible character, that there was no laying on of hands, and that the king (or emperor) did not receive the 'cure of souls'. The liturgically correct place of unction in both instances was the vertex of the head to symbolize headship. We shall see later how imperial unctions came to be administered, not on the head, but on the back between the shoulders.

Whilst in 816 it was the pope who travelled to France in order to complete what was left unfinished in 800, seven years later it was no longer necessary for him to undertake a journey, for when Louis I's son, Lothar I, was in Italy, he was invited to come to Rome at Easter to be crowned Emperor of the Romans. He, too, had been made a co-emperor by his father. Once again the initiative lay in papal hands. The coronation was performed at the main altar of St Peter's, which was henceforward to be the proper place for imperial coronations. A further detail of some significance was added. During this coronation the emperor received a sword from the hands of the pope. Again there was a precedent in the eighth century, when in 758 Paul I, who had succeeded Stephen II the year before, had sent a sword to Pippin. The sword was at all times understood as the symbol of physical strength, and the conferment of the sword by the pope was to symbolize not only that the emperor had received his 'strength' from the pope, but also that there was a duty for him to protect the pope. It is not therefore surprising that this symbol was to obtain deep ideological significance. The emperor was later said to receive his actual power from the pope. Thereby practical meaning was attached to St Paul's 'The prince does not bear the sword without cause', and in this context it meant that the 'cause of his bearing the sword' was 'to execute wrath upon him who does evil'. What was evil and what should therefore be eradicated was to be left to those who in a Christian society were qualified to pronounce upon it. Thereby the auxiliary function of the emperor was clearly demonstrated – in 823 there was little hope for a practical application of this idea, but papal governmental ideas were sometimes far ahead of their practical employment. The sword ceremony clearly brought out the idea of the emperor as an assistant of the pope in the eradication of evil. Later, from the eleventh century onwards, the sword was taken from the altar of St Peter – the same place on which lay the pallium for the pope – the idea clearly being that the sword (just as the pallium) came from St Peter himself. In the ninth century the concrete meaning attached to the sword was, as a contemporary (Agobard of Lyons) tells us, 'the subjugation of barbarous nations so that they may embrace the faith and widen the frontiers of the kingdom of the faithful'.*

Whilst in 823 it was the pope who invited the king, it was in 850 the father who requested the pope to crown his son (Louis II) Emperor of the Romans. And this coronation and unction was the sole constitutive act setting up Louis II as emperor, as he had not been made co-emperor by his father. And quite in agreement with the Donation of Constantine, the emperor (before his coronation) led the horse on which the pope sat the length of an arrow-shot. Although each of the three coronations added a significant detail to the coronation, the coronation seventy-five years after Charlemagne's shows the papal initiative still more convincingly. No invitation had to be issued, no request had to be submitted, because the pope, John VIII, called upon Charles the Bald: he was, as the pope made clear, called, elected and confirmed by him himself, and made emperor of the Romans 'through the privilege of the apostolic see'. Celestial inspiration, John VIII claimed, dictated his choice, or, as he said on another occasion, the emperor 'was postulated and desired by us and called by God'. Here we are presented with a quite remarkable translation of abstract governmental thought into reality, and also, which is at least as important, the acceptance of the papal governmental theme by the successors of Charlemagne. There can be few parallels in history which could be compared with this single-minded, pur-

*Agobard made the text of the ancient fifth-century Good-Friday prayer specifically refer to the secular Ruler's sword.

poseful, and dynamic initiative of the ninth-century papacy. It demonstrated how advantageous it was for a governmental institution to have a blue-print or a programme, provided that the bearers of the programme pursued it ruthlessly and that it was tuned into the ethos of the time. When we remember the masterly fashion in which the papacy always justified each of its steps by reference to the divine order, divine law, and tradition, and also the strength of the contemporary christocentric outlook, the advance becomes more easily understandable.

What Charlemagne had so strenuously rejected as a matter of principle, namely any kind of *Roman* emperorship, became gradually in the course of the ninth century the policy of his successors. They thereby adopted the very reasoning and standpoint of the papacy, according to which true *Roman* emperorship could be had only from the pope, thus degrading the Eastern emperor to a mere Greek ruler: the universality of rulership and dominion rested with the true emperor of the Romans, crowned by the pope. There are numerous testimonies which bear out the wholesale adoption of the papal thesis by Charlemagne's successors. Of these numerous examples only one can be given here. The communication of Louis II, in 871, to the Byzantine emperor was a classic presentation of the ideology underlying papal as well as Western imperial ideas. It denied that the Byzantine could legitimately be a Roman emperor, because he was not created as such by the pope; the pope could not have made him emperor of the Romans, because he was no Roman, for only he was a Roman who acknowledged the primatial function of the pope. The Byzantine was no more than a Greek prince. Moreover, the Greeks, as was well known, held the wrong doctrine altogether: true doctrine – orthodoxy in contrast to heterodoxy* – could only be found in the West, the communication claimed, and the papacy as the guardian of orthodoxy must be entitled to confer the highest available rulership, so as to have an efficient protector and defender. And Louis II had no qualms in saying to his Eastern rival that he had received the authority to rule from the apostolic see. The significance of this communication is

* The communication itself used the term cacodoxy (wrong doctrine).

obvious. Papal ideology had been translated into reality within a very short period. In the mid eighth century the pope appeared as the supplicant – little more than a century later he had transformed with his ideology the complexion of Europe, which was now ruled by the creature of the pope, that is to say, the Emperor of the Romans.

The translation of pure governmental ideology into practice was accompanied by numerous literary assertions directly bearing upon doctrines of government. For instance, to Anastasius, the learned librarian (c. 860), the pope was the vicar of God distributing power on earth, because he was the doorkeeper of heaven. The comprehensiveness of the Petrine binding and loosing powers was here stated in unambiguous clarity: what the pope shut, nobody could open again. In other words, supreme jurisdictional power, or sovereignty, lay with the pope in a Christian society. However much some of these statements were directly modelled on, if not culled from, the Bible, the significant fact remains that biblical statements had become directly applicable to the pope. This has rightly been called the monopolization of the Bible by the papacy,* and was clearly observable in Nicholas I (858–67), who declared that the popes were set up as princes over the whole earth, a statement which applied Psalm xlv, 17–18. Whatever, Nicholas I further declared, was found in the Church, was in its fullness in the Roman Church which was the epitome of all ecclesiastical power. Because there was no one on earth, he maintained, repeating old doctrine, who could judge the pope, all Christians were his subjects who received from the pope whatever power they had. Supreme jurisdictional power rested solely with the pope whose decrees were binding upon every Christian. The corporate union of all Christians, presided over by the pope and committed to his government, was what Nicholas called 'the society of all the faithful', directed by the laws given to it by him, because he alone was the heir of St Peter. The same Nicholas I also held that at the imperial coronation the emperor was 'conceded' his right to rule, because he was given the right to use the sword. And at once the teleology of functions appeared.

* E. Kantorowicz.

The reason why he had received the sword was 'for the sake of exaltation and peace of his mother, this holy and apostolic church'. By now the pope determined the reason for the Ruler's bearing the sword. What sort of Roman emperor was the Byzantine who knew not even Latin, but only Greek, Nicholas asked the emperor at Constantinople in a communication.

The 'society of all the faithful', as the corporate body of both laity and clergy, was for Nicholas I a union held together solely by faith in Christ. If, he said, this bond of faith was in any way permitted to be broken, the whole society would collapse. On the basis of such considerations he gave detailed instructions to princes regarding their duties. The extermination of heresy was one of them. Kings were subjects of the pope: they could not be allowed to sit in judgment over those who were their masters, because the pupil was not set over the master, as the Bible had it (Matthew vi, 24; Luke xvi, 13). The principle he wished to express was that of clerical immunity from secular or royal judgment, because this principle followed from the functionalist approach of the papacy. In the 'society of all the faithful' precedence must be given to ecclesiastical laws over the laws given by princes; subsidiary character might be attributed to secular laws, if there was no specific ecclesiastical enactment and if they did not contradict any canonical principle. Royal laws, in short, must fit in with the purpose for which this society existed and must be in agreement with the faith expounded by the Roman Church. For the function of all laws, as Nicholas I said, was to produce 'orderliness' in society. If the king were to issue laws outside his scope of jurisdiction or even against the purpose of Christian society, he was to be disobeyed – but this was no genuine right of resistance, because disobedience must be sanctioned by those who were qualified to pronounce upon it. This tallied, as we shall presently see, perfectly with the tenor of the royal coronation orders. In fact, according to Nicholas, a king who had proved himself a tyrant was on the same level as a heretic, and this was for him – as for many of his successors – the case if he disregarded the laws and decrees of the papacy – a sure sign of revolt on the part of the king. For Nicholas the pope was sovereign, because his decrees were final, given as they were 'on the authority of Almighty God'.

The ideas of Nicholas I became accentuated by his successor, Adrian II (867–72). He dealt specifically with the petrinity of the pope by declaring that, since Peter was instituted by Christ, the decrees of his successors had the same force as if they had been issued by Christ Himself. Since justice was the basis of the law, Adrian II held that papal decrees embodied the idea of justice to a pronounced degree, a point which we meet later in its full maturity in Gregory VII. The comprehensiveness of papal jurisdictional power was evidently derived from the Petrine commission, as was repeatedly made plain by the pope: 'whatever' in the commission meant 'whatever'. He felt himself entitled to order barons to take up arms and to make active military preparations under pain of excommunication. It was legitimate for the pope, Adrian further declared, to decree the exclusion of any Christian, including a king, from the society of the faithful, for the stability of a kingdom rested upon the king's doing his duty as a Christian king.

Even this brief sketch of the views of two ninth-century popes will have shown the stimulus which the actual application of papal governmental ideology had provided. Their language was that of the governor (*gubernator*) who issued commands, which were claimed to embody justice. It was evident to the papacy that the contents of justice could be substantiated only by those who were qualified, or as an eighth-century pope (Gregory II) had said, by those who had 'the sense and mind of Christ'. Over and above all stood the principle of division of labour, according to which each functionary, be he king, emperor, or bishop, had to confine himself to the scope of those functions with which he was entrusted. Adrian II, or for that matter, Gregory I, were insistent that 'everyone should be content within the terms of his office', a view that may also reflect the static nature of society.

II. THE GREAT FORGERIES

The intellectual movement in the ninth century was exclusively the work of the Frankish higher clergy. To a large extent the papacy found in the Frankish episcopate a very strong ally. Although the Carolingian Renaissance had made possible the advances in liturgy, theology, philosophy, it was the higher clergy which took an active interest in matters concerned with the government of a Christian society. The frequency of Frankish Councils after the death of Charlemagne testified to the awareness of the episcopacy as the leading factor in Christian society. These numerous episcopal synods from 816 onwards expressed theories and doctrines which considerably buttressed the papal doctrines and at the same time began to corrode and undermine the royal theocratic form of government. The participants were exclusively episcopal; the lay element had no means of making its standpoint clear, even if there had been an educated laity (which was not the case). Moreover, the royal advisers were exclusively clerical. The incrustation of governmental thought with ecclesiastical elements is therefore readily explicable.

The views expressed in these councils in one way or another dealt with what the decrees called the 'right ordering of Christian society'. And the numerous decrees were insistent on the thesis that in a Christian society it was the priests alone who were qualified to pronounce upon the bond that brought society into being, to pronounce on the faith. Hence, in applying this fundamental tenet, there were decrees dealing with prohibition against Sunday work, with the proper private and public conduct on feast days, with matrimonial matters (though it is interesting to see that the Council of Rome in 826, presided over by the pope, still adhered to the old doctrine that the wife's fornication was a valid ground for divorcing her and for the husband to marry again), whilst other decrees, such as those issued at Paris (829), laid down the function of the king as that of a 'minister', that is, of one who had to rule with equity and justice – though the contents of justice were defined not by himself, but by the specially qualified clergy. It was in keeping with the trend of legislation that the point of view of Isidore of Seville of the early seventh century was invoked, according to which the function of the king was auxiliary, because he had to strengthen the word of the priests by the sword. In this was seen the main contents of the ministerial function of the king. The synodists also invoked the (spurious) statement of Constantine to the bishops at Nicea: 'God has given you power to judge, rightly therefore are we judged by you, but you cannot be judged by man.' Upon this followed the assertion of clerical immunity from royal control, since the king was merely a minister of God.

The progress of hierocratic thought can furthermore be measured by the effects which the clerically decreed sentences, such as excommunication, had in the public sphere. An individual excommunicated lost, as the Council of Pavia (850) laid down, the right to military service or to any public office; he was excluded from all courtly offices and dignities. If, furthermore, an individual proved recalcitrant and disobedient to episcopal orders, he was to be outlawed by the king and excommunication followed. In fact, the royal government markedly favoured this hierocratic trend, and royal legislation in many respects was complementary to the conciliar decrees. Even if the offence was one only in the eyes of ecclesiastical law, such as usury or the wilful refusal to pay tithes, the king nevertheless was entitled to proceed to outlawry and to confiscation of property. The important advance made was that clerical legislation formed the basis of the king's own measures of government, though there was no reciprocity, since royal decrees were said to display no effects in the clerical field. The effect of this kind of governmental thought as a precedent was very strong; and the ecclesiastical memory was powerfully assisted by the availability of written records. These views contributed a great deal to the shaping and moulding of the contemporary intellectual outlook no less than to the ascendancy of the hierocratic form of government.

A Germanic inspiration of which this is particularly true was the so-called proprietary church system, according to which the owner of the land was entitled to build a church on it, and this church became his property, with the consequence that he had the right to appoint the cleric to serve the church. In course of time this system was to engulf all the great episcopal and archi-episcopal churches. The system had quite understandably grown up in a purely agrarian society. It had its great advantages, as the landlord had in the clerk someone who knew the rudiments of reading and writing, whom he could also engage for all sorts of domestic duties, including some education of his children. But it became clear in time that, properly viewed, the system would lead to exactly the same state of affairs which prevailed in Byzantium, though the paths determining this development were basically different. Through this system the Western kings and emperors were in fact often enough enabled to provide for their own faithful and loyal household clerics the richest bishoprics, abbacies, and other prebends. The lay lord kept a rather firm control over his appointments. By the eleventh century there had developed a whole cluster of ceremonial which was largely derived from the feudal sphere and which culminated in the so-called investiture of the cleric with his office and benefice by the lay lord.

The system attracted severe criticism at the hands of some radical writers, as Bishop Wala's memorandum for the Diet of Aachen in 828–9 showed, or as Jonas of Orleans or Agobard of Lyons a few years later demonstrated. To them a church was a thing consecrated to God, and could not therefore be made the subject of any kind of legal transaction: it should be altogether removed from the control of the lay lords who should become patrons or protectors, but should not be able to dispose of the church or of its incumbent. This was precisely the step taken later, in the twelfth century, when the ownership of a church by a layman gave way to a mere patronage or advowson, exercised by the lay lord. But in the ninth century these views were, once again, merely programmatic declarations.

The stimulating character of the many-sided activities of the Frankish clergy can perhaps best be seen in the quite respectable output of forgeries perpetrated in the late forties and early fifties, partly at or near Rheims and partly in or near Mainz. The aim of these forgers – and considering the extent of their fabrications, there must have been whole ateliers of workers – was to buttress the hierocratic thesis by surrounding it with the halo of antiquity. As with most medieval forgeries, they did not in many cases invent anything out of the blue, but clothed an already virtually accepted thesis in the garb of an ancient decree. The substance or doctrine of a hierocratic principle was not always invented: what was invented was the 'official' decree or law which was to prove the doctrine, and these were most conveniently 'collected' within one handy volume. The great popularity of these forgeries was not least due to their being accessible in an easily available 'reference book'. There were three products of which only one is of direct interest to us, and this is *Pseudo-Isidore*, which purported to be modelled on the genuine Isidore of Seville and contained the literal 'transcription' of the papal and synodal documents from post-apostolic times onwards. The second large product was the collection of *Benedictus Levita* – the name is as much pseudo as is the work – working near or in Mainz, pursuing the same aim as *Pseudo-Isidore* by 'collecting' royal and imperial decrees. He 'cited' no less than 1721 decrees and laws altogether, of which no more than about 400 were genuine. The third product was simply a collection of chapter-headings, allegedly sent by the pope to Bishop Angilram in about 785.

Pseudo-Isidore was of crucial importance in the development of governmental ideas. Most of the basic ideas can be found here: all was so conveniently assembled within two stiff covers; numerous copies were made down to the fourteenth century. Its influence on the papacy in particular cannot be exaggerated. Nicholas I made the first use of it, and in all subsequent times the papacy found in the collection a veritably inexhaustible reservoir for its theses. The full extent of the forgery was not established until a century ago. All the papal decrees down to Silvester I in the fourth century were invented, and it is significant that the papal 'decree' which opened the work was the letter which Pope Clement I had written to St James in Jerusalem: * the contents of this letter, in any case extraordinary, were however not adequate enough for the forgers who could not resist the temptation to add more (another ten closely printed pages in the modern edition), in which their

* See above, p. 23.

imaginative faculties about the Petrine powers of binding and loosing were given full rein. The all-comprehensiveness of papal jurisdiction received special emphasis in the numerous and lengthy 'decrees', no less than the strict hierarchical ordering of society and the concomitant lowering of the royal (or imperial) status. To the forgers, the immunity of the clerics from secular control was of particular importance, and so was the thesis that all so-called major causes (*causae maiores*) were to be tried by the pope, a thesis which was later of great moment in establishing papal control over bishops and metropolitans. Another recurrent theme that again had a great future was that no council was empowered to issue binding decrees, unless summoned or approved by the pope.* *Pseudo-Isidore* brought the monarchic theme as far as the papacy was concerned into the clearest possible relief. Considering the weakly developed historical sense at the time, one can hardly be surprised that the anachronistic nonsense that now stares the reader in the face was not perceived at all. It was precisely the form in which this 'ancient' material was presented, that is, the legal shape of papal decrees, that gave these forgeries the stamp of authority which made it also so difficult for subsequent generations to see the true nature of the work. Next to the Bible, *Pseudo-Isidore* was the most useful handbook which the papacy ever handled. Rome and Rheims merged into one broad stream. That so many of *Pseudo-Isidore*'s pithy statements went into later collections of canon law is not surprising, and thereby with every collection a new lease of life was given the 'old' law which was only bound to increase its authority. The forgers harnessed their indubitably superior intellectual equipment to the furtherance of a governmental scheme that was to set its imprint upon the Middle Ages – and beyond.

III. POLITICAL IDEAS IN ROYAL CORONATIONS

A faithful reflection of the strongly clerical complexion of the ninth-century ideas can be found in the structure, liturgy,

* The Donation of Constantine was understandably given a prominent place.

THE POST-CAROLINGIAN DEVELOPMENT

symbolism, and prayer-texts employed in the royal coronation orders. Before the ninth century there was nothing comparable in Western Europe and they give considerable insight into the texture of medieval kingship. The coronation orders were the results of the ninth-century clerical, or perhaps better, episcopal efforts. And yet it was the kings themselves who, by bolstering up the theocratic form of government, made it possible for the episcopacy to shape the very ceremony which created the theocratic king. Both king and bishops worked together: the coronation service was always one of the most guarded prerogatives of the episcopacy. Since every gesture, every symbol, every prayer-text had a very concise and precise meaning, the coronation services sometimes reveal more than lengthy learned treatises. The most important texts originated in the ninth century and many have survived to this day, particularly in England where they are still used at the coronation.

Although the coronation orders have not attracted the attention of historians of governmental thought, it is clear that even a cursory glance at them will show that they manifested rather clear-cut doctrines, of which only one or two can here be given prominence. Since the kings themselves were so anxious to underscore their theocratic government, calling themselves 'King *by the grace* of God', the liturgical development of the ritual of unction suggested itself. And this development culminated in the bishops visibly conferring the grace by pouring the holy oil on the head of the king. The accompanying text made the mediating function of the metropolitan bishop plain: anointing was at the time held to be a sacrament, and the bishops were the only officers who could validly administer the sacrament. The crucial role of the bishops in this central liturgical act of the unction needs no commentary. It was that act alone which made the king. The earliest prayer-text was originally contained in the so-called Benedictional of Freising of the first half of the ninth century. This text also made clear the teleology of the unction. Its purpose was 'to constitute' the recipient 'king *over* the people whom the Lord God *gave* you for the *sake* of ruling and *governing* them'. The unction was not only to distinguish the king from all other mortals, but was also to show the legitimacy of his rulership, sanctioned as it was by divinity. Thereby the king became 'the Lord's anointed'. It was not until the twelfth century that the unction was devalued from a sacrament to a mere sacramental – only after it had become obvious what unparalleled advantages the character of the unction as a sacrament had for the king. The divine favour conferred by the officiating bishops, however, could be withdrawn, as ninth-century doctrine held: it did not constitute an indelible character, the essential difference between royal and episcopal anointings.

Through unction the king was set up ('constituted', as the text had it) over the people. The meaning was clear. The people had nothing to do with the conferment of this divine favour of his divine grace, for they were, as many other texts showed, committed to the king. The king stood outside and above the people. What had previously been asserted in abstract terms was here made visually concrete in the framework of the coronation. Further, the texts underlined the inferior position of the people by designating it as being subjected to the king's government: *populus tibi subjectus* or *populus subditus*. We meet here the concept that was basic to the theocratic governmental system, namely that of the sub/ject, the *Unter/tan*, who as an inferior had no rights against the superior king. Numerous other texts could be cited to show that the subordination of the people to the king was a central feature. Of course, they could ask for favours, they could suggest remedies, make proposals, and the like, but a right to their fulfilment they had not. This was the abstract theory which was concretely presented in the coronation service. The king's government was exercised *over* the people; he was no member of the people, and this was expressed in the throne which by virtue of the elevated position was to show the 'higher' seat of the king, as well as in the emerging idea of committing treason against the king, appropriately enough called 'high' treason. The designation of the king as 'Majesty' (*majestas*), though of late Roman origin, was to bring out his 'superior' position. He was indeed 'major' than anyone else in his kingdom.

What a royal coronation made so unambiguously clear was

the *superioritas* of the king (his sovereignty), because he was 'supreme' in the kingdom, as a number of other texts expressly declared. In this both royal and episcopal aims were identical: that royal sovereignty, the king's 'supremacy', had reference exclusively to the laity which, in the coronation texts, was called the '*plebs*'. The structure of the coronation services was carefully designed to exclude any possibility of the king's having any sovereign rights over the clergy, and quite especially the episcopacy. In this emphasis of the sovereign position of the king *vis-à-vis* the 'people' the aim of the king to detach himself from the people was clearly endorsed.

In this context, episcopacy and royalty spoke the same language. In fact and in theory the king became through the liturgical coronation service a *persona ecclesiastica*; he was, as it were, adopted by the officiating bishops and was built into the clerical structure.* The vital significance of this was that a thick line of division was drawn between the laity and the clergy, a line which abstract doctrine had asserted often enough, but which was now made manifest in the public act of coronation. The king found himself, so to speak, drawn into the clerical camp. The more the king emphasized his theocratic function, the stronger the link between the episcopacy and him became. However much the king was told to rule and govern, no ingenuity of interpretation could lead to the view that he also exercised government over the clergy.

Indeed, as the coronation texts also proved, the king had the duty to lay down the law, but this law was not to be in conflict with divine law, of which the episcopacy held itself the proper expositor. The great Hincmar, archbishop of Rheims, told his king in 860: 'You have not created me archbishop of Rheims, but I, together with my colleagues, have elected you to the government of the kingdom, on condition that you observe the laws.' Although there was always some election of a king, in the coronation service itself there was no allusion, let alone reference, to any preceding election. On the contrary, the texts made it abundantly clear that 'we (i.e. the bishops) have elected' the king. It was as if there had

* Cf. also below about the pope making the emperor a cleric, p. 109.

not been any foregoing election. The statement of Hincmar faithfully mirrors the tenor of the coronation texts.* In again unmistakable terms the coronation texts referred to the respective functions of king and bishop: whilst the latter had cure of souls, the former was 'an athlete of Christ' *(athleta Christi)* and a 'husbandman of God' *(cultor Dei)*. Here indeed we meet a practical application of the old Isidorian view that the king's duty consisted in drawing the sword when the word of the priests proved insufficient. The king was to be the 'terror' of evil-doers by playing his role as an athlete.

Whilst the sharp cleavage drawn between the people, as the subjects of the king, and the clergy, notably the episcopacy, was of considerable advantage to the king in the earlier period, there can be little doubt that in the high Middle Ages, when the king was locked in battle with the ecclesiastics, he might well have desired a restitution of the link which his theocracy had snapped. For this cleavage also contributed a good deal to the estrangement of the king from the people and of the people from the king. Above all, any attempt to control the king was defeated by the theocratic argument that the people had not been given any power and that, on the contrary, they were, like minors, entrusted to his government. That, in the final resort, is the explanation of why, within a theocratic government, the tyrannical king presented a problem that was insoluble. In assessing the significance of the coronation service one should not forget that the day of coronation was the one day in any medieval king's reign which really counted. Before his coronation he was a mere 'duke' or 'prince': hence the practice of dating the king's regnal years from the day of his coronation, and not from the day of his accession. Virtually all the relevant features of governmental doctrine presented themselves in the coronation orders in an impressive and impressionable form: the principle of concession, the principle of subjection, with its complement of obedience of the subjects, the principle of law-giving (as opposed to law-making), and above all the notion of sovereignty of the king. Perhaps no other medieval element has done so much to perpetuate

* See also about the meaning of election, below, p. 135.

the 'minority' of the people as the medieval coronation orders, which in their fundamental structure were of ninth-century origin. They fitted perfectly the strongly ecclesiastical complexion of this century, and by their constant application throughout the medieval period they became powerful conservators of theocratic kingship, and by the same token were barriers to the emancipation of the people from royal tutelage.

It is interesting to note the combined influence of *Pseudo-Isidore* and of the ideas underlying the coronation orders, as they were reflected in a number of councils. For instance, the decrees of the Council of Hohenaltheim in the year 916 combined quite skilfully some of the basic pseudo-isidorian tenets with those contained in the coronation of the king. The synodists emphasized the strict hierarchical ordering of society and in so doing they stretched out their protecting hand over the king, in order to safeguard his position against the dukes. Rebels against the king's government (the factual matter is of no interest to us) were stigmatized as God's enemies, because they revolted against 'the Lord's anointed'. Moreover, specially qualified as they held themselves to be, they took their stand on the supremacy of the divine law and therefore judged a number of lay princes who had allegedly risen against the king. They declared that anyone encompassing the death of the king, or threatening his life, or in any way entering into a conspiracy against the king, was to be outlawed and damned for ever.

Although these declarations had some immediate contemporary effect, these programmatic statements were not generally put into practice. What one witnesses in the tenth century is quite remarkable tension between reality and ideology. It was indisputable that the episcopacy was dependent on the king to a far greater degree than they would have wished, but they lacked the means, the coordination, and the indispensable authoritative backing which their own programme in fact postulated, that is, a centrally directed policy. The proprietary church system was the most effective obstacle to clerical power asserting itself fully: but the danger was there for the king. However much in practice he kept control of the higher clergy, there was no gainsaying the effect which the quite respectably developed ideology exercised. On the king's side there was nobody who had the necessary intellectual equipment to construct some royal lay thesis. Apart from this, had not the king delivered himself into the hands of the clerical party by his own insistence on the theocratic kind of government? Over and above this consideration there is the reflection that the higher clergy at least were intellectually far superior and far more experienced than the isolated layman who might have aspired at constructing a governmental thesis. The ecclesiastics had a programme which the king lacked. The overpowering force of the Christian idea itself was responsible for the very institution of theocratic kingship which in its turn opened up the gates to the intervention of the learned episcopacy. The king had indeed shed the bonds which had tied his ancestors to the people, but all the stronger were to become the ties which bound him to those who mediated the divine grace and actually made him 'the Lord's anointed'. And when once the fully matured papal ideology was brought into play, the ancient Gelasian thesis of the pope's rendering an account on the day of judgment of how the kings had discharged their divine trust was to receive its concrete and precise application. The development of governmental thought in the Middle Ages was largely conditioned by the predominance of the priestly element: they had the equipment, the literature, the sources at their disposal. What other section of the population could have had similar advantages?

IV. THE POLITICAL IDEOLOGY OF THE WESTERN EMPIRE

The actual historical situation in the tenth century was not conducive to the development of thought. Europe was still suffering from the aftermath of the invasions, both by the Vikings and by the Magyars (Hungarians). The Frankish empire had collapsed and disintegrated into a number of more or less viable parts; the economic situation was, partly also as a result of bad harvests, at a very low ebb; the instability observable in Western Europe was apt to bring to the fore particularist forces, at the time entirely devoid of any constructive programme and thought. That these circumstances precluded any intellectual development seems evident enough. In Germany the firm government of Henry I (919-36) contributed to the creation of order, and it is not without significance that this king was the only one of all Western kings who explicitly refused to be anointed. There can be little doubt that at the time of his accession the former Saxon duke had come to realize what latently grave disadvantages the unction performed by the chief ecclesiastics might have for him.* A further clear symptom of his governmental ideas was that his own chancery – at all times the training-ground for the higher ecclesiastics and the reservoir from which the king appointed candidates to episcopal sees – consisted, for five years, of one scribe. Nor had his court a royal chapel. This king's government was to reverse the trend which was noticeable before, namely the clericalization of kingship. But at the time this could have been no more than an aim – and this same king's government in fact showed that it was impossible to carry on without the active assistance of at least the higher clergy. He himself was forced in time to reverse his own governmental principles.

The case of Henry I is worth mentioning because it persuasively shows that without the participation of the ecclesiastical hierarchy no tenth-century king could govern in an orderly manner for any length of time. The reign of his son, Otto I (936-73), was to be the great turning-point. The papacy found itself in a situation which was not unlike that of 200 years earlier. Otto had shown himself the saviour of Europe from the Magyar menace and after years of effort had established peace in Germany and by conquest had become king of Italy in 951. The pope, John XII, appealed to Otto to help to drive out the resurgent and threatening Lombard armies. But what gave special flavour to his appeal were the menacing designs of Byzantium: the South of Italy, Apulia, and Calabria, etc.,

* The contemporary chronicler, Widukind, explained the king's refusal by – royal modesty.

were Byzantine territories, administered by Byzantine imperial officers, and it was in the fifties of the tenth century that renewed attempts were made to advance northwards. At however low an ebb the papacy was at the time, it clearly perceived the danger to which it was exposed by the imperial armies. The bait which John XII held out to Otto I was the imperial crown – that is, his recognition as the one Roman emperor who could not, understandably, tolerate any reconquest by Byzantium. The latter on its side, had not given up – nor was it ever to do so – the claim to be the legitimate embodiment of the Roman empire; its claim to re-possess Rome was also understandable.

The re-birth of the Roman empire in the West on Candlemasday 962, when Otto was solemnly crowned, was the prelude to the intimate connexion between the papacy and Germany in the subsequent centuries – a feature which is of no interest to us – and to the elaboration of a number of important governmental ideas. As far as governmental aspects were concerned, what is of immediate interest is that the Roman Church became approximated to a German proprietary church. Accordingly, the elected pope had to take an oath to the imperial legates who thereby were placed in a position of judging the suitability of the papal candidate for his office. This was the monarchic principle at work, because the monarch alone was entitled to say whether or no a candidate for an office was suitable. That had also been the reason for the wide extension in Germany of the proprietary church system, which had by now come to embrace all important episcopal and metropolitan sees. The newly created emperor had all the more grounds for applying this principle to the papacy, as his coronator, John XII, had indeed given ample proof of his unsuitability. The arrangement was embodied in the famous document called the *Ottonianum* of 6 December 963. It formed the constitutional basis for the strict monarchic control of the popes by the Germans down to 1059. In this period there were twenty-five popes, of whom no less than twelve were directly appointed by the emperors and five dismissed.

The idea of Roman emperorship in the West was the

intellectual offspring of the papacy, a fact basic to an understanding of medieval Western Roman emperorship. The creation of the Roman emperor was for the papacy the handle with
which it could and did successfully emancipate itself from the
East.* Throughout the subsequent period this original aim was
ever present. The Western emperors, since from the time of
Otto I they held themselves to be the true successors of the
Roman Caesars, attributed to their emperorship the (ancient)
Roman idea of universalism – we recall the emperor was designated 'the Lord of the World' – with the consequence that, in
sharp contrast to Charlemagne, their conception of Roman emperorship in no wise differed from that of the popes. This indeed
was what could already be observed in the ninth century,† but
from now on the idea gained practical importance. The Byzantine emperor was demoted to a mere Greek king, whose claim
to Roman emperorship, so the Western emperors said, was
born out of Greek arrogance and conceit. But the presupposition for the Western assertion was that the pope had crowned
them – without the pope there never could come about, nor did
come about, a Roman emperor in the West. The pope played
in the making of the Western emperor a constitutive role, in
stark contrast to the Byzantine arrangements, where the patriarch's role in the coronation was merely declaratory. In other
words, the presupposition in the West was that the papal ideology of Roman emperorship was accepted, and herewith the
basis of the papal ideology of Roman emperorship, the Donation of Constantine,‡ was also implicitly accepted. Furthermore, the Eastern emperor as true and indisputable successor
of the Roman Caesars (if historical criteria alone and not papal
ideological criteria are to count), was always autonomous and
a correctly understood Autokrator – the very feature which the
Western emperor lacked: he was made (and later also unmade)
by the pope who, as ever, employed the teleological argument
that the emperor was created for a special purpose, that of de-

* See above, pp. 64ff.   † See above, pp. 74ff.
‡ It should be mentioned that John XII, on the occasion of Otto I's
coronation, had a special ornamental copy of the forgery made for Otto's
benefit. See also below, pp. 98.

fending the epitome of all Christendom, the Roman Church: he was to be the strong arm of the papacy which considered itself as a governmental institution on a universal scale. This governmental idea was to find its metaphorical reflection in the well-known sun–moon allegory (according to which the moon received its light from the sun, whereby the sun was to represent the pope, the moon the emperor).

However weak the papacy was in actual authority in the century succeeding Otto I, every one of his successors was anxious for the imperial coronation. That this continued practice was only apt to strengthen the papal ideology itself goes without saying. It was precisely on this basis that, later, in the twelfth century, the papacy could put forward the ancient Gelasian idea of the emperor's rulership as a divine good deed, as a *divinum beneficium,* in the garb of an 'apostolic favour'. The concession principle was thus transferred to the most eminent of all secular Rulers. It was in his function as mediator between God and man that the pope transmitted this 'divine good deed' to the emperor. The German argument that attempted to challenge this basic papal principle was that the German king, who called himself not king of the Germans, but 'King of the Romans', by virtue of his exercise of royal power over Italy, had a right to emperorship and the pope a duty to confer it. When put to the test, this assertion was shown to be without any basis in history or ideology. In the making of the Emperor of the Romans the papacy had always found the occasion to drive home some of its most cherished ideas concerning the government of a Christian society: the concept of an Emperor of the Romans served the pope as an instrument of creating an assistant on a universal scale, an *advocatus,* the strong arm to execute his programme. For this reason the emperor was also called 'the special son of the Roman Church'.

The attractiveness of the concept of Roman emperorship for the German king is indeed not difficult to explain. Of course it is true that his coronation as a Roman emperor by the pope added hardly any tangible rights to his kingship. But the title conferred was not a mere dignity or higher standing or what

might be called prestige – medieval kings were not as sentimental or romantic as all that – but a title-deed to rulership
on a universal scale, which meant in practice that the Eastern
emperor became not merely a rival, but an adversary. The
papal antagonism to Byzantium was thus necessarily transferred to the Western emperor. In fact, in the opposition to
Byzantium there was no difference between the papacy and
its creation, the emperor in the West. That opposition had
one aim: either to reduce Byzantium to a complete dependence on the West or to annihilate it. The period from the tenth
to the thirteenth centuries shows that a number of means
were employed by the Western emperors to translate the
Western imperial ideology into practice. Marriages between
sons of the emperors to Byzantine princesses were one such
means; active military measures, for instance under Frederick
I in the twelfth century, were others. There was the peripheral
reduction of Byzantine influence by missionary enterprises to
the East, including Russia (the so-called German colonization
programme) from the eleventh century to the thirteenth century. Financial extortions of quite astronomical dimensions also
served to reduce the power of the 'East' (late twelfth century).
Last, but certainly not least, was the acquisition of Sicily by
the Germans in the twelfth century, which provided a first-class
springboard on the one sea that mattered, the Mediterranean.
The aggressive policy towards Byzantium pursued by Frederick I's son, Henry VI, the first occupant of Sicily, bears witness
to the deadly danger which now faced Byzantium: it found
itself encircled. Finally the crusading idea was one more means
of subjugating Byzantium, for, as the creator of the crusading
movement, Gregory VII, plainly said in 1074 (twenty years
after the formal schism between East and West), a union
between the two churches, the Church of Rome and Constantinople, was the aim of his (abortive) crusade. And when in
1204 Constantinople did fall to the 'crusaders', Innocent III
could indeed exclaim that the Church of Constantinople had
now returned to her mother, the Roman Church. What
mattered to the papacy from the fifth to the early thirteenth
century was the lack of recognition of its primatial role by

Byzantium; nay, the very denial of that role by the imperial government in Constantinople entailed, as we have seen,* most serious consequences for the papacy, which saw in the creation of the Western emperor the only effective means of making its primatial-jurisdictional role in government real. And what mattered to the Western emperors was the corresponding lack of recognition by Byzantium of their role as (sole) Roman Caesars. Byzantium was the key to the understanding of the development of papal 'political' ideas no less than of that of Western imperial 'political' ideas. Pure ideology determined the path of historical events, and that ideology stemmed from the notion of the Emperor of the Romans as the one 'Lord of the world'.

But since the Western emperor was no more than a personified concept created for special purposes by the pope, he lacked all the external apparel that was to show him outwardly as the supreme ruler. Hence it was from the late tenth century onwards that one witnessed the adoption of typical Byzantine emblems, rites, symbols, customs, nomenclatures, offices, and so on, which could be observed 'over there'. That therefore the very laws of the Roman emperors – that is, the law books of Justinian – were to become the laws of the Western emperors, is evident. The significant beginnings of this appropriation of the law books were already to be found in Otto III's reign, at the very end of the tenth century, and it would not be many decades before the full opulence of Justinian's *Code* was to be perceived in all its magnitude. The Western imperial laws were incorporated into the body of the *Code*. There were also accelerated manifestations of monarchic government measures within the Roman *orbis*, within the Roman-Christian world. For a time in the eleventh century the Western emperor combined the papal intitulation (*servus servorum Dei*) with that of the 'Emperor of the Romans' so as to leave no doubt about his true regal-sacerdotal, that is, monarchic standing. The governmental ideas enshrined in the title showed themselves practically in the appointment (and dismissal) of popes as well as in numerous other ways. Having become acquainted with the real

* See above, p. 49.

nature of the Donation of Constantine, Otto III,* translating the monarchic idea into practice, brushed this 'figment of imagination' aside in 1001, and gave, on his own authority, a number of territories to St Peter through his successor, the pope (Silvester II). The significance of this revoked Donation of Constantine was that the pope came to be the beneficiary of the living emperor himself who 'out of his munificence' bestowed gifts on the pope, 'the chief metropolitan within the Roman world', as Otto called him. Rome, not Constantinople, was in this document called the 'royal city' (*urbs regia*) and hence Rome was, as he also testified, 'the head of the world'. The sting was directed as much against Byzantium as against the papacy, that now had sunk, paradoxically enough by virtue of the operation of the papally created Roman empire ideology, to a position not essentially different from that of the patriarchate situated in Constantinople.

Precisely because the emperors were Christian monarchs, they earnestly directed their governmental attention to much-needed reforms of ecclesiastical institutions which by virtue of the proprietary church system were in any case under their control. The first half of the eleventh century was the age of reform, carried out by the imperial government. Purification of the sacerdotal organism by the emperors themselves had in fact become a governmental measure. Hence the, literally speaking, hundreds of clerical appointments by way of investiture which signified the conferment of both the clerical office and the benefice by the king or emperor. His monarchic function could hardly be demonstrated in a better way. It is purely hypothetical to ask what would have happened to the Roman papacy if the Germans had not become the prisoners of the

* Otto III became acquainted with the spurious character of the Donation through the deacon John who, on the occasion of Otto's grandfather's coronation in Rome, had to make the ornamental copy of the Donation. He quarrelled with the pope, John XII, who, before 964, had his fingers chopped off, hence his nickname 'John the deacon without the fingers'. He fled to Otto's court and revealed the secret. That was, to my knowledge, the first, and last, time in the Middle Ages that the character of the Donation as a forgery was stated. The document referred to in the text above was kept in the papal Archives and was not, of course, known outside until last century

Roman empire ideology. The same hypothetical question might well have been asked about the intervention in the eighth century of Pippin and Charlemagne, who were not Roman emperors, but intervened by reason of their concern for the violation of rights inflicted on the successor of St Peter.

No clerical regeneration or reform would have been complete if the 'head' of the priests, the popes themselves, were not also reformed. Hence the Emperor Henry III (1039–56), in his capacity as supreme Ruler translating the very idea of monarchic government in a Christian society, took drastic steps by removing popes and appointing his own nominees. And these were indeed of a calibre very different from those whom they replaced. Men were now in charge of the Roman papacy who called to Rome a number of learned ecclesiastics from across the Alps, France and Germany. These were the men who in one way or another had expressed grave doubts about the correctness of the assumptions underlying the governmental ideology of their contemporary secular Rulers. These men were zealots of the hierocratic cause; they were put into responsible positions in the Roman Church; they relentlessly pursued their programme; they were greatly helped by the fortuitous circumstance of Henry III's premature death which supplied them with the opportunity to reverse the state of things within barely twenty years. It was these men who were to bring the papal-hierocratic system of government to full maturity.

CHAPTER 4

THE HIEROCRATIC DOCTRINE IN ITS MATURITY

I. MAIN CHARACTERISTICS

IT may be helpful to state here the essence of the hierocratic ideology, according to which the pope as successor of St Peter* was entitled and bound to lead the community of the faithful, the Church. The means for the pope to do so were the laws issued by him in his supreme jurisdictional function, which claimed universal validity, and concerned themselves with everything that affected the vital interests and structural fabric of the Christian community. Obviously, from this hierocratic point of view, the judge of what was in the interests of that community, what facts, circumstances, actions, or situations touched its vital concerns, was the pope. He was the 'judge ordinary' and claimed to possess the specific knowledge of when legislation was required. The function of the pope was that of a true monarch, governing the community that was entrusted to him. A further essential feature of this theory was the hierarchical gradation of offices, which ensured what was called order and smooth working of the whole community. This order was said to be maintained if everyone remained within his functions which were assigned to him. Bishops had their special functions, and so had kings. If either king or bishop intervened in, or rather interfered with, the other's functions, order would suffer and disorder would follow. The limitation of functional action was the hallmark of the hierocratic thesis, or, in other words, the principle of division of labour was a vital structural element of the thesis. Supreme directive control, the supreme authority (sovereignty), remained with the pope, who, standing as he did outside and above the community of the faithful, issued his directions as a 'steersman', as a *gubernator*.

* See above, pp. 25f.

While considering the theory, the allegorical manner of expressing the relationship between priesthood and laity deserves consideration. The metaphor constantly used was that of the soul and body. The *anima–corpus* allegory was adduced a hundredfold to show the inferiority of the laity and the superiority of the clergy, to show that, just as the soul ruled the body, in the same manner the clergy ruled the laity, with the consequence that, as for instance Cardinal Humbert in the mid eleventh century stated, the kings were the strong arms of the clergy, for the clergy were the eyes of the whole Church who knew what was to be done. In interpreting this antithesis one should not be misled by pure allegory. What the metaphorical use of soul and body attempted to express was that, because faith in Christ was the cementing bond of the whole Church and the exposition of the faith the business of the clergy, the law itself as the external regulator of society was to be based upon the faith. Faith and law stood to each other in the relation of cause and effect. The 'soul' in this allegory was no more and no less than the pure idea of right and law, the uncontaminated Christian idea of the right way of living. What legal or legislative action faith required could be discerned only by those who had the eyes to see, the clergy. Differently expressed, since every law was to embody the idea of justice, and since justice was an essential ingredient of the Christian faith, the 'soul' in this allegory meant the Christian idea of justice. There can be little doubt that this thesis was the medieval idea of the 'rule of law', manifested the idea of the supremacy of the law. For the body of the faithful could, so it was said, be held together only by the law based on (Christian) justice, which on the one hand externalized the faith and on the other hand reflected the teleological thesis, for the law was considered the appropriate vehicle by which the body of the faithful was enabled to achieve its end. In short, the law was the soul which ruled the body corporate of the Christians. The legalism of the Middle Ages and quite especially of the hierocratic form of government, found its ready explanation. It was said often enough that only through the law could a public body live, develop, and reach its end.* Within the hierocratic thesis the king was subjected to sacerdotal rulings, the basic idea being that the king was not qualified enough to lay down the law in those matters which touched the essential fabric of Christian society. Fundamentally, this thesis of soul and body expressed simply the idea of governing a body public and corporate by means of the law.

As a consequence, the hierocratic ideology which emerged in its full maturity from the pontificate of Gregory VII onwards (1073–85) also laid particular stress upon the law. In fact, this pope went so far as to state dogmatically that it was 'legal discipline' that had led kings onto the path of salvation. After all, they were distinguished by divinity to be the trustees of their kingdoms and had therefore all the more grounds for showing themselves 'lovers of justice' (*amatores justitiae*), and justice, as an ingredient of the Christian faith, could be expounded only by the Roman Church, which was consequently called the 'seat of justice'. The king's duty was obedience to papal commands: he was a subject of the pope, to whom all Christians in any case were subjects. The teleological argumentation received its precision, notably by reference to the accumulated body of knowledge and learning as well as to the interpretation of the coronation orders: the purpose of God granting power to the king in the public sphere was to repress evil. If there had been no evil, there would have been no need for the power of the physical sword. Hence the pope claimed to exercise a 'universal government' (*regimen universale*) by means of the law which made no distinction between matters or persons. The Petrine powers were comprehensive, exempting no one and nothing from the pope's jurisdiction. With exemplary unambiguity for instance Gregory VII declared:

* It should not be too difficult to understand on this basis also the meaning of the Ruler as 'the living law' (*lex animata*). This whole cluster of ideas could of course only exist within the descending theory of government, in which the 'will of the prince' formed the material ingredient of the law. It was this will that, so to speak, breathed life into, or animated, the body corporate. This thesis was actually of Hellenistic origin, where the Ruler was known to be the *nomos empsychos*, of which the expression *lex animata* was a literal translation.

If the holy see has the right to judge spiritual things, why then not secular things as well?

On another occasion he stated:

For if the see of St Peter decides and judges celestial things, how much more does it decide and judge the earthly and secular.

From the papal standpoint it was true to say that the pope bore a very heavy burden, not only of spiritual tasks, but also of secular business, for he considered himself responsible for the direction of the body of the faithful under his control and in his charge. Obviously, the governmental power of the popes referred specifically to kings, because they disposed of the means of executing papal orders and decrees. Moreover, the king, for the reason already stated, was an 'ecclesiastical person', whose office concerned itself with the repression of evil. Both the kingdom and the king's soul were, as the popes repeatedly declared, in their power. But the developed hierocratic programme did make the qualification that the pope considered papal jurisdiction to come into play only when the basic and vital interests of the body of the faithful called for his intervention. None expressed this principle better than Innocent III (1198–1216) in his usual concise language. He stated that feudal matters as such were of no concern to the pope's jurisdiction, which came into full operation however when sin was involved. *Ratione peccati* (by reason of sin) was the technical expression to denote the overriding papal jurisdiction. Evidently, the judge of when sin was involved was the pope himself.

The process of monopolizing the Bible* had meanwhile made great strides. The popes applied to themselves the passage in Jeremiah i, 10): 'I have set thee over the nations and kingdoms ...', because this was, according to Innocent III, a 'prerogative' (the term occurs here for the first time) of the pope: this was nothing but the explicit expression of the monarchic principle. The same Innocent III declared that he was less than God but more than man, a statement that brings into clearest possible relief the very essence of the papal thesis, namely the superior status of the pope, his sovereignty, stand-

* See above, p. 78.

ing outside and above the community of the faithful. And it was precisely by virtue of his 'superior' status that the papal Ruler gave the law. The development in the twelfth century leading to the concept of the pope as the vicar of Christ only underlined this point of view. The papal vicariate of Christ in itself changed nothing in the papal function. It attributed no more powers to him than he already had. What the concept of the vicariate of Christ focused attention on were the vicarious powers which Peter was said to have been given by Christ: it was these which, by way of succession, came to be wielded by the pope. The concept considerably clarified the function of the pope, with the consequence that a number of biblical passages which referred to Christ were now directly applied to the pope, so, for instance, the Matthean passage: 'All power is given unto me ...' The vicariate of Christ in the pope demonstrated the pope as the point of intersection between heaven and earth. Hence it was that Innocent III said that what he had decreed was decreed by Christ Himself. And Innocent IV (1245–54) stated that the pope figured as Christ's 'corporal presence'. It was quite in keeping with this theory that the government of the pope was considered to be a true *monarchatus*, because, as the canon lawyers taught, in his hands the 'keys of the kingdom of heaven' had changed into the 'keys of the law'. This monarchic theory was succinctly expressed by Gregory IX (1227–41) thus:

When Christ ascended into heaven, He left one vicar on earth, and hence it was necessary that all who wished to be Christians were to be subjected to the government of the vicar.

By virtue of the thesis that God was the creator of everything on earth, the claim was raised by Innocent IV that every human creature (and not merely Christians) were subjects of the pope (who in the doctrine of the canon lawyers was *de jure*, but not *de facto*, the universal monarch). Indeed, the pope possessed – or at least claimed to possess – supreme overlordship over both bodies and souls of all men, as the same Gregory IX asserted. And before him a similar theory was expressed by Innocent III who held that the princes of the world had power over the body only, whilst the priests had power on earth as well as in heaven and over the souls also.

Because the pope functioned as the monarch of the body of the faithful, he claimed that his laws had reference to anyone and anything. Wherever the line of distinction between spiritual and temporal matters might have been drawn, for papal governmental ideology the distinction had no operational value. Since the end of the body of the faithful governed by the pope lay in the other world, anything that might be called temporal was subjected to that spiritual end. St Paul had often enough declared the superiority of the spiritual over and above the mundane, the visible, the corporeal, or the secular. And by the process of monopolization the papacy made these Pauline views its own. Some statements of Gregory VII have already been quoted, but there were dozens of similar views expressed by other popes in the twelfth and thirteenth centuries. There was also the actual government of the popes who intervened in what might well have appeared, to the less sophisticated contemporaries, purely temporal matters. In the final resort the papal standpoint was based on the view that Christianity seized the whole of man and the whole of his activities without splitting them up into different compartments, which view led to the 'totalitarian' system of government. If, indeed – and as we shall see, it was the royal opposition which argued in this way – the temporal was to be exempt from papal jurisdiction, this would not only have contradicted the all-embracing character of the Petrine powers of binding and loosing, but also the very essence of Christianity, at least as the papacy saw it. Neither things temporal nor the temporal Ruler could have had an autonomous, independent, autogenous standing in the papal scheme of government. Each was a means to an end. The pope, as monarchic sovereign, stood indeed outside and above the body of the faithful,* a body that was one – 'we are one body

* It should be made clear, perhaps, that this thesis – that the pope did not belong to the Church and that he stood outside and above it – had reference only to his capacity as a governor. In what doctrine called the pope's private capacity, that is, as a Christian, he was of course a member of the Church, and, therefore, had his own confessor.

in Christ' according to St Paul – and which suffered no division. In brief, unity of the body demanded unity of government, which manifested itself in the monarchy of the pope as the 'overseer' (*speculator*) over all matters of basic concern to the well-being of the body.

The correctly understood monarchic point of view also made understandable the unaccountability of the pope for his actions and decrees. The maxim 'The pope cannot be judged by anyone' was, as we have said, the medieval manner of expressing his sovereignty.* He was the final arbiter and judge on appeal; to appeal from his court to a council drew the charge of suspected heresy. His plenitude of power was, however, thoroughly juristically conceived. His powers had nothing to do with any divine omnipotence. The anti-papal charge, 'if the pope is the vicar of Christ, why does he not work miracles?' – mainly raised by the French in the early fourteenth century – was really beside the point. No pope had at any time asserted that the Petrine powers were anything but juristic powers which did not suppose any 'divine' or divinely omnipotent powers. In the papal monarchy one found the classic expression of the descending thesis of government. The material ingredient that gave the papal law the character of an enforceable rule was the pope's will: it was the application of the ancient principle of the 'will of the prince' (*voluntas principis*) as the element that imparted enforceability to the law. Given as it was to the subjects, they had the duty of obedience. And Gregory VII laid down that only he who accepted unquestioningly the decrees of the pope could call himself a catholic.

The distinction, so clearly elaborated by Leo I,† between the person of the pope and the office of the pope, was perhaps the most useful governmental doctrine that any institution had ever possessed, for thereby considerations concerning the person, character, or bearing of the individual pope were relegated to the background. What stood in the foreground was the office, and the law or decree that flowed from the office. The

* See above, p. 29, and, for the same principle which obtained with kings, see below, p. 132.
† See above, p. 26.

106

validity of a decree or law was not in the least dependent upon the personality of the pope: any charge levelled at the pope's personal bearing, could be (and was) dismissed as irrelevant. The sovereign status of the pope showed itself, finally, in the full freedom of the pope to change the law which any of his predecessors might have issued. No pope could bind his successor (just as no parliament can today bind its successor), and that seems to be the test of monarchic sovereignty of the pope. The idea underlying it was that no pope followed a predecessor in his function as pope, but succeeded Peter directly without any intermediaries. In the pope, Peter's powers continued (temporal succession was, of course, necessary for the pope's episcopal status). This immediate continuation of Peter's status and office in the pope was in the last resort the explanation why each medieval pope so studiously avoided saying that any of his predecessors had committed an error. For that admission would have been tantamount to saying that St Peter himself had erred, he who was credited with Christ's vicarious powers.

The application of any monarchic form of government necessitates a firm control of subordinate officers. For the papal monarchy this meant the control of the episcopacy. Without its control neither the king nor the pope could hope to exercise governmental powers effectively, hence the ferocious conflict between the papacy and the kings, predominantly the German king, during the Investiture Contest, the main phases of which occurred in Gregory VII's pontificate. The governmental, that is jurisdictional, subordination of the bishops to the pope proceeded only in stages. It began with the episcopal oath which the bishops had to take to the pope, and the payment of regular visits to the pope, and ended with the quite significant designation of the bishops as 'Bishop by the grace of God and that of the apostolic see' *(episcopus Dei et apostolicae sedis gratia)*. The implementation of a worthwhile control presupposed the elaboration of the constitutional relationship that existed – or was held to exist – between the pope and the bishops. Again, the working out took a long time, though it visibly began in Gregory VII's pontificate and was, to a large extent, foreshadowed in the pseudo-isidorian forgeries. It culminated in the assertion that the bishop received his power to govern the diocese from the pope, a thesis which left the sacramental standing of the bishop intact. Hence a deposition or suspension of a bishop by the pope referred to the former's governing powers which were withdrawn or suspended: he still remained bishop, though he was unable to exercise government in his diocese. This thesis was strenuously opposed by the episcopacy, because the bishops stressed the identity of their sacramental function with that of the pope, relying furthermore on the interpretation of Matthew xviii, 18 (as opposed to the papal reliance on Matthew xvi, 18),* and consequently were extremely reluctant to acknowledge the papal standpoint. The episcopalist thesis was not destroyed, but only driven underground from the twelfth century onwards, and it began to emerge in a different guise as conciliarism in the late fourteenth century. The papal standpoint was that governmental powers of the bishop were derived from the pope who possessed the plenitude of power, in which the bishops merely partook.

Similarly, the logical pursuit of the papal governmental programme also necessitated the claim to exercise control over the temporal Rulers. This control was basically different in the case of the emperor of the Romans and the other kings. The German king – papal ideology was firm on this – had no right to the imperial crown, which was an 'apostolic favour'.† By the late twelfth century the theory of the so-called 'Translation of the Empire' was evolved, according to which the pope had transferred the imperial crown from the 'Greeks' to the Germans: this was simply an attempt to interpret the Donation of Constantine in the light of history. The papal doctrine concerning the empire was classically expressed by Innocent III, who maintained that, because no one had a right to a favour, the German king could have no claim to emperorship. The king had to be approved by the pope as well as confirmed and crowned, for, if there were a right to emperorship, Innocent argued, he would not only have no choice, but would in fact be forced to crown a heretic, a tyrant, an imbecile, and the

* See above, p. 22.   † See above, p. 95.

like. Before the pope put the crown on him, he was no emperor of the Romans, but merely a candidate. What papal doctrine was always insistent upon was to examine the suitability of the king for emperorship, because he was to be the strong arm of the papacy.

Moreover, from the ninth century onwards, the papacy had taken great pains to distil its governmental ideas into the imperial coronation orders. The official (and last medieval) imperial coronation order was made by Innocent III, who in precise and unsurpassable manner managed to incorporate papal doctrine into the liturgical symbolism of the coronation. Once again, purely abstract thought was presented in physical and easily understandable gestures and actions. Each symbol – ring, sword, sceptre, orb, crown – was conferred with an accompanying prayer-text which left no doubt as to the meaning. The imperial unction was, in fact, liturgically on a lower level than the royal unction, because not chrism, but an inferior kind of oil was used, which was applied not to the head (as in the case of the king), but between the shoulderblades and on the right arm (with which he was to wield the sword). Another significant feature was the oath of the emperor-elect to the pope, promising fidelity, protection, and defence. It was no less significant that the emperor-elect was made a cleric by the pope: he was given the right to wear tunic, dalmatic, and mitre. In general, the imperial coronation order, made by Innocent III, combined Byzantine and Western royal features.

But what was most significant was the absence of any enthronement of an emperor: there was no throne. Perhaps in no other way did the medieval papacy manage so clearly to convey its views on the function of the emperor as in this: the emperor was an (exalted) officer, and no officer ever sat on a throne. The coronation rite also made clear that the power of the emperor as an officer or assistant of the pope on a universal scale came from God – no pope ever deviated from this Pauline principle – but it was the pope who acted as the mediary between God and the king to be made emperor. Autonomous powers the emperor had not. If he had had them, there would have been no need, so Innocent III was adamant in his repeated declarations, to supplicate for the papal favour. Nevertheless, the same Innocent was equally insistent that he did not wish to interfere in the elections of the German king as king – not, however, without also declaring that the German princes had received the right to elect their king from the pope. It was mainly in regard to imperial matters that Innocent III often repeated that he had both regal and sacerdotal powers in the fashion of Melchisedek, the Old Testament king and priest. And hence in the creation of the emperor this combined power of the pope showed itself most fully. The *factor proprius* of the emperor, the organ that brought him into being, was the pope, as Gregory IX stated.

Innocent III's thesis owed a good deal to St Bernard of Clairvaux who, a generation before, had introduced the hierocratically orientated Two-Sword theory into the discussion, a theory that was alleged to have had its origin in Luke xxii, 38, and which had been used in a different sense already by Charlemagne's adviser, Alcuin, as well as by Henry IV.* But, according to the doctrine of St Bernard the pope possessed both swords, that is, the spiritual and the temporal (material), the one signifying the pope's priestly coercive power, the other the regal coercive power. During the coronation the pope gave the latter to the emperor, who was then said to wield the sword at the bidding of the pope (*ad nutum.*) This Two-Sword theory was to signify that the actual physical power the emperor possessed was derived from the pope, or rather from God through the mediating organ of the pope. The ancient Isidorian doctrine† was given its allegorical clothing. Gregory IX explicitly stated that the Lord had given the pope both swords, one of which the pope retained and wielded, the other he gave away. Or, as his successor Innocent IV stressed, the power of the material sword belonged potentially to the pope, but actually to the emperor. This Two-Sword allegory had reference to the emperor only. What therefore at the end of the thirteenth century Boniface VIII asserted in his *Unam sanctam* could barely be squared with the actual development, for he applied the allegory also to the

* See below, p. 137.   † Above, pp. 81f.

kings who had never been crowned, nor had ever expressed an intention to be crowned, as emperors: a characteristic extension of a suggestive allegory. What, however, is significant is that the relevant decrees of the popes, especially Innocent III and IV and Gregory IX, were appropriately enough incorporated in the official canon law books under the title 'Of majority and obedience', which seems very important in view of the (medieval) meaning of 'majority', that is, sovereignty and the corresponding obedience on the part of the subjects.

Although the papal thesis concerning the empire logically led to the fourteenth-century view of the pope as temporary administrator and vicar of the empire during a vacancy, the papacy never established – doctrinally at any rate – such close control over 'mere' kings. For, unlike the emperor, kings were rarely crowned by the pope; he never in theory at least claimed to intervene in royal elections; few of the arguments developed in regard to the emperor could be applied to the kings. Nevertheless, Innocent III stated that 'by reason of sin' he could intervene in purely royal matters as well as 'upon examination of certain causes' *(certis causis inspectis).* This Innocentian standpoint brought out clearly the underlying idea of papal governmental principles, that is, to act when the well-being of the whole Christian commonwealth in his view demanded his intervention, because the pope was the 'Overseer'. The idea of *utilitas publica,* that is, the concern for the public weal and its well-being, was an ever present conception of papal ideology and was in fact raised to the level of a governmental principle by Innocent III, according to whom private interests had to yield to the demands of the public interest. That, in the overwhelming majority of cases, there was no friction between the kings and the popes should not lead to the assumption that, in papal theory, the papacy had no jurisdiction over kings, for in borderline cases and disputes (and they usually were the crucial ones) it was the pope who asserted the claim to overriding jurisdiction. In other words, the principle of division of labour was to be fully applicable in the relations between papacy and kings.

The royal view itself – the 'King by the grace of God' –

111

played into the hands of the papal doctrine. For on the old Gelasian view the popes had to render an account of how the kings discharged their trust. If therefore the kings, in the papal view, misused their trust, the popes considered themselves bound to take action and either to remove the king altogether or to inflict ecclesiastical censures upon him. The principle of suitability or of usefulness became especially operative. Gregory VII was very insistent on the operation of this principle, and this was one of the reasons why the German King Henry IV was first suspended from his kingship (in 1076) and four years later finally deposed. The deposition of kings was decreed when the pope had reached the conclusion that the king in question was unsuitable for his office, as again Gregory VII made clear. But just as the removal of a king was claimed to be the pope's right and duty, so was at times the making of a king his right and duty. Innocent III, for instance, declared in setting up the king of Bulgaria, Joannitza, that thereby he 'wished to ensure the spiritual and temporal well-being of the Bulgarian kingdom'. In any case, the king was an 'ecclesiastical person', which facilitated the emergence of papal doctrine and assisted its application. But whilst deposition of a king was the final sanction the pope could employ, the excommunication of a king was based on different criteria. He could be excommunicated, not so much because he was useless as because he showed himself a disobedient son of the Roman Church. The effects of excommunication were, however, equally stringent, for doctrine had developed the view (which later became also the law) that the excommunicate person was infected with a contagious disease and that therefore nobody was permitted to have any intercourse or contact with him. Consequently, if only his immediate family circle could be in touch with him, government was extremely difficult for a king. Deposition affected the king's title-deed to rule; excommunication entailed his exclusion from the Christian community.

By virtue of his sovereign function within the Christian society, the pope furthermore claimed the right – of which the papacy made significant use – to declare treaties between kings null and void; to annul secular laws, such as Magna Carta or, later in the thirteenth century, the German lawbook, The Mirror of the Saxons; to decree ecclesiastical censures against those who exacted unjust tolls or fees on the highways and rivers; to order the king to despatch armed troops in support of another king or against pagans and heretics; to sanction territories obtained by military conquest as legitimate possessions; to compel belligerent parties to stop hostilities and to enter into peace negotiations; to force by interdict or excommunication the population of a kingdom not to obey a king; and so on. The papal plenitude of power enabled the pope, as Gregory VII professed on the occasion of deposing King Henry IV, to take away kingdoms, empires, principalities, and in fact the possessions of all men (*possessiones omnium hominum*), as the case merited. This view was partly based on the thesis that private ownership of goods was an issue of divine grace: because the owner had shown himself unworthy of this divine good deed, the pope considered himself entitled to take away property.

Partly by reason of the demands of public interest, partly by reason of safeguarding the bond that cemented the universal Christian society, partly by reason of the papacy's duty to protect the faith from corrosion, the doctrine was advanced in the early thirteenth century (it became law by the middle of the century) that special tribunals should be set up which were to deal with aberrations from faith. The inquisitorial machinery as laid down by Gregory IX and Innocent IV was the mechanism which was to bring to book those who had shown themselves disobedient rebels to the papal law. The mechanics of this machinery does not belong to the development of governmental thought. What does belong to it is (1) the concept of heresy as a crime construed (by Innocent III) as high treason against the divine majesty, committed through aberration from the faith as laid down by the papacy, and as such had the appropriate, fearful sanctions attached, including confiscation of property of the descendants, even if yet unborn; (2) the duty of the secular Ruler to exterminate heretics from his domains. If he were remiss, he himself was to be

113

declared a heretic, his subjects were to be released from their obligation by the pope, and his kingdom was to be occupied by an orthodox catholic prince. This was actually the ruling of the Fourth Lateran Council (1215), which remained the basic decree for the rest of the Middle Ages, and to some extent also beyond.

The governmental ideology underlying these measures, however unfamiliar to modern readers, was nevertheless one that embodied a great many concepts, maxims, and topics which at a later age were to be evaluated as 'political'. From the historical angle one should not forget that these concepts – such as sovereignty, the law, the subject, obedience, and so on – were worked out exclusively within an ecclesiological framework, and it was only later, from the late thirteenth century onwards, that ecclesiology and politology became two distinct branches of thought. Then indeed all of these concepts were to become the working tools of the new science of politology. It was one of the anachronistic feats of the papacy that it solemnly proclaimed in pithy and concise form its own governmental doctrine, at a time when the peak of practical application of papal governmental thought had long been passed.

The decree *Unam sanctam* by Boniface VIII, issued in 1302, was an able and succinct summary of the papal doctrine, culled as it was from a variety of sources which were nevertheless skilfully stitched together. He made great use of the Bible in its papal interpretation, of Cyprian, Pseudo-Denys, St Bernard, Hugh of St Victor, Thomas Aquinas, and so on, and though not a single point was new, the significance of *Unam sanctam* was that it presented a summary of papal governmental thought at this late hour. Boniface set out from the ancient idea of the Church as an indivisible body and that no salvation was possible outside it (this was originally Cyprian's thesis and was a century earlier stressed by Innocent III). The principle of oneness manifested itself in that there was one Lord, one faith, one baptism (this was of Augustinian origin). The papal monarchic government was based, according to Boniface, upon this principle: the Church needed one head. A body with two heads was a monster, and that head was Christ Himself and on earth Christ's vicar (this had been put forward by the English canonist Alan in the early thirteenth century). Whatever Greeks and others had asserted, all Christians belonged of necessity to the 'sheep of Christ', and hence were subjected to the pope (this was the thesis of Thomas Aquinas, expounded in his booklet *Against the Errors of the Greeks*). But – by virtue of the principle of division of labour – the two swords possessed by the pope were not wielded by him, but one only, whilst the other was to be used by the kings (and not merely emperors) 'at the bidding and sufferance of the pope' (an extension of Bernard's thesis.)* In his exposition of the hierarchical gradation he relied on Pseudo-Denys and went on to declare that the inferior must be ruled by the superior or the 'supreme power', the latter denoting the sovereign, to whom everybody was subjected. This had with singular clarity been expressed a generation before by the eminent canon lawyer, Cardinal Henry of Susa (Hostiensis), who maintained that, since the pope was concerned with the law, the king's duty was to enforce the papal law: for the smooth working of Christian society it was necessary, the Cardinal said, that the law issued by a 'majority' of the pope was to be followed and obeyed by the royal power. For, as Boniface himself said, on the model of Hugh of St Victor (who assumed the authority of the Holy Scriptures: *nam testante scriptura*) the spiritual power had to institute royal power (clearly a reference to the coronation proceedings) which remained at all times subjected to the pope (this was derived from Gregory VII). Anyone therefore resisting the papal law, resisted the divine power itself – an application of St Paul (Romans xiii, 4). He concluded that in order to achieve salvation it was necessary for every human creature to be subjected to the Roman pontiff.†

*John of Salisbury's theory was not unlike Boniface's. Writing in the mid twelfth century he said that the sword as the symbol of coercive power was wielded by the prince, because the priesthood was forbidden to shed blood and had therefore conferred the sword on the prince, who however remained subjected to the priesthood. The prince for John was in a sense an 'executioner'.

† It should be noted that the phrase 'every human creature' was, in the re-issue of *Unam sanctam* by the 5th Lateran Council in the early sixteenth century, expunged and 'every Christian' substituted.

II. EMERGENCE OF POLITICAL LITERATURE

Any exposition of papal governmental thought, however brief, must at least make some reference to the many writings which supported the papal thesis and from which the papacy itself drew a good deal of its ammunition. The Investiture Contest during the pontificate of Gregory VII gave rise to a new literary species, the so-called publicistic tracts. In order to assess their importance one must bear in mind two points. First, that in its fundamentals the Investiture Contest was concerned with far more than the question of investitures of bishops and ecclesiastics by the lay lord or the king. The full magnitude of the conflict can perhaps be gauged when one realizes that the traditional order of things was to be replaced by an order derived from purely speculative and abstract ways of thinking. The section of the Church that was primarily affected was the laity. The bitterness of the conflict becomes more readily understandable if it is set against the latent tension between clerics and laity. After all, there were numerous testimonies of ancient origin which declared that 'the laity had an ingrained hatred against the clergy', testimonies easily available in the current collections of the canon law. With unmistakable clarity the Investiture Contest and especially the abrupt declarations of Gregory VII had shown that the lay people were to be subjects of the clergy and that no layman was to raise accusations against the clergy. The issues thrown up in the Investiture Contest touched the very fundamentals of all social and public life, because attempts were made to set aside the customary and also traditional modes of living. It is indeed difficult in the twentieth century to grasp or even to imagine the intellectual, quite apart from the social, upheaval that was caused by Gregory's application of – historically speaking – ancient and traditional kinds of ecclesiastical and especially papal ideas. This application did appear as a revolution. And since the issues were of so fundamental a nature, they stimulated a great literary activity on both papal and anti-papal sides. The significance of this literature was that for the first time in European history there were laymen – they were Italians – who took up the pen and began to write. Peter Crassus of Ravenna, writing in the eighties of the eleventh century, was one such example. The deeper issues of the conflict jolted, so to speak the laymen into activity. They came from the University of Ravenna, and it was to be less than thirty years hence that other laymen were to create another University, Bologna, destined to become the citadel of all legal studies throughout the Middle Ages.

Secondly, this literary output consisted of what might nowadays be called pamphleteering, with this difference, however, that the books and tracts, etc. were scholarly products which examined with great thoroughness and with appropriate references the claims of the two contestants. A scientific scrutiny was made for the first time of the very concepts upon which the hierocratic system rested: the source of authority, its essence, its scope, and limitations; the concept of law, of right, of the authority to issue the law and its scope. Of particular importance were teleological discussions of these products, no less than some specific topics, such as the obligatory nature of the oath – especially since Gregory had released bishops and princes from their oath to the king – and the right of the pope to decree the non-observance of the oaths, or the sacral nature of kingship, and so on. It was also in this literature that history itself was harnessed in order to justify or to refute a particular point of view. The aim of this literary activity was to create and shape public opinion – one more unique achievement of the time. Of course, the public addressed was still a tiny minority but one that counted. On the whole, the intellectual and scholarly level of these numerous tracts, of which only part is edited and published, was very high. Naturally, the lay side was only sparsely represented, and, despite some ecclesiastical misgivings on some specific points, the clerical side supported with greater or lesser conviction the papal side. That the episcopalist theme* drove a number of bishops and clerics into the anti-papal camp seems understandable.

The intellectual fermentation of the Investiture Contest gave rise to an upsurge of many branches of intellectual activities.

* See above, p. 108.

The rise of the Universities was closely linked with the issues of the conflict, and this applied with particular force to Bologna, which was in its initial stages a University of laymen for laymen, primarily concerned with the study of Roman law. It was not until the forties of the twelfth century that the ecclesiastical law, the canon law, was also scientifically treated at Bologna, not by laymen, but by clerics. The reason for the predominantly legal turn of studies is clear. From its infancy, governmental thought in the Middle Ages had always been conceived within the framework of jurisprudence, within the law. And it was especially in the constant reiteration of the papal doctrine that the popes enunciated the law applicable to public life in a Christian society. Hence the reaction to this legalism took a legal form. It was the already mentioned Peter Crassus who brought Roman law into the discussion, because this appeared to be the most appropriate instrument with which the legal argument of papal governmental thought could be attacked. What is important is that the study of Roman law became the concern of the layman, because this seemed the only basis on which the legal encrustations of this thought could be assailed. Admittedly, for this purpose the base was not very strong, since the orientation of Justinian's *Code* especially was also theocratic, but it was at least the work of a lay ruler and a work that contained secular Roman wisdom. The enormous lead which the ecclesiastical side had won in the preceding ages was too great to be made good by a lay scholarship only now in its beginnings. The hierocratic system could look back to a long period of evolution; it had matured and was also applied. The lay side may have had in its favour history and facts, but by and large it used the same language, the same Bible, the same patristic writers, the same allegories and concepts, which their opponents used in so masterly a fashion. Above all, the detachment from the people by adopting the theocratic theory of kingship was achieved at a very high price. What the lay side needed was a set of ideas that had nothing to do with the christocentric set of premisses, and this desideratum could not be had by setting against the hierocratic theme another theocratically conceived body of the law, such as the Roman law to a very large extent appeared to be. No doubt, the civilians, that is, the Roman lawyers in the medieval universities, produced excellent juristic works which also contained a good deal of what later proved useful for political thought, but in the twelfth and thirteenth centuries they were unable to dislodge the hierocratic system of government from its secure habitation: they lacked the means to do so.

On the other hand, the canonists, that is, the canon lawyers teaching and studying at Bologna, achieved great influence: they were, so to speak, the technicians of the hierocratic system. For government presupposed knowledge of the law and of the general jurisprudential principles, and the canonistic school at Bologna was to furnish properly trained personnel for the papacy. From the time of the publication of Gratian's *Decretum* (*c*. 1140) the papacy could always rely on first-class jurists whose juristic skill and expertise greatly contributed to the making of canon law itself. From now on, the overwhelming majority of popes were jurists who had either been professors of law at Bologna (or some other University) or had in some other ways distinguished themselves in law. The following two centuries were the centuries of the great lawyer-popes. Their legal output, the so-called decretal letters, distilled abstract papal doctrine into the pithy language of the law, the law of the papal monarch. The thousands of decretal letters were collected, first unofficially, and, from Innocent III onwards, officially, in law books which were not, in system and structure, dissimilar to Justinian's law books. The study of Roman law was always a presupposition for a fruitful pursuit of the study of canon law, but there was, nevertheless, a great difference between these two bodies of law. What distinguished the canon law from the Roman law was that the former contained living law, law based upon contemporary ideas and focusing attention on contemporary needs of society: if the need arose, any papal law could be done away with by a stroke of the papal pen, the result of the pope's sovereign status. On the other hand, the Roman law had that great disadvantage that it was, already at the time of its codification, 'historical', and that many important medieval legal issues were unknown to Roman law which, for instance, knew nothing about feudalism. The Roman law had to be made a living law by accommodating it to contemporary exigencies. Whilst the graduates in Roman law staffed royal and imperial chanceries, the graduates in canon law entered the higher ecclesiastical civil service, sometimes reaching the peak of the profession. It was the canon lawyers who supplied the juristic equipment and reservoir to the papacy.

The great issues of the Investiture Contest not only furnished a legal stimulus, but also fructified other branches of intellectual activities. It is not usually recognized that the so-called twelfth-century Renaissance was in fact conditioned by the great upheaval of the Investiture Contest. Whilst legal studies were predominantly concerned with the practical distillation of abstract thought into law, such as questions of right, of proper authority, etc., and hence in one way or another dealt with justice underlying the law, the philosophical and theological examination of the same fundamental issues proceeded apace, though, as yet, in the twelfth century outside the University lecture rooms. There was a community of interests and subject-matters, but all branches of learning were plagued by the numerous contradictions which their systems exhibited. One must bear in mind that the corpus of knowledge in all mental disciplines could look back to an accumulation of material over something approaching a millennium, but that body of knowledge, for evident reasons, contained vastly different and contradictory opinions and statements, a feature from which law suffered as much as philosophy and theology. Once again, it was a practical question which set afoot the method of inquiry known as the dialectical one. Pope Urban II's advice (in 1088), in reply to the query of a bishop as to what ought to be done with contradictory statements, was the step which brought in its train this method. A distinction ought to be drawn, he advised, between statements of an immutable character and statements and texts which were prompted by the exigencies of time, place, and the persons involved, and which could be called changeable. The basic thesis was that the unity of the human mind, being a divine creation, could not contradict itself in fundamental matters. Contradictions were merely apparent, not real. It was the mental operation of drawing a distinction, according to time, place, and person, which initiated the scholastic or dialectical method, without which no scholarship in the Middle Ages would have come about. The fructifying effects of this mode of inquiry were observable in the law – witness Gratian who entitled his work a *Concordia discordantium canonum,* thereby indicating his intention of reconciling the discordant, i.e. contradictory, canons. The effects were similarly observable in theology and philosophy. Abelard's contemporary *Sic et Non* was the philosophic counterpart to Gratian. What is usually called the twelfth-century Humanism was the result of the forces awakened towards the end of the eleventh century through the application of governmental thought.

John of Salisbury may serve as an example of the Humanism of the mid twelfth century. He had a number of pertinent things to say on the burning problems of the day. A short survey of his leading ideas should not lead to the assumption that he was one of the isolated *littérateurs* of the time who gave strong support to the papal-hierocratic thesis. Next to him there were the canon lawyers who, in their glosses, tracts, and *summae,* treated of the same question, quite apart from the many other non-juristic writers, such as St Bernard of Clairvaux, Hugh of St Victor, Honorius (sometimes called of Autun, sometimes of Augsburg), Gerhoh of Reichersberg, and a host of others, not to omit such distinguished thinkers as St Anselm and Gilbert Crispin, and so on. But John of Salisbury deserves a short summary of his views, and not the least reason for including him here is that his main work, the *Policraticus,* exercised considerable influence right down to the sixteenth century. The author's name soon came to be forgotten, and the title of his work was taken as the name of the author. Apart from the consideration of his influence, he also justifies a few remarks, because of his practical sense, his width of outlook and classical learning, and because he was a contemporary of Thomas Becket in his fight against the king, Henry II, a fight which in many ways touched upon the basic elements of the by then developed hierocratic thesis.

Soaked as he was in ancient and Roman cultural elements, John of Salisbury operated with the concept of the all-embracing *Respublica christiana,* the Christian commonwealth, which he equated with the 'Latin world' and which was to him nothing but the corporate and visible union of all Christians. Because it was essential to his system of thought that the soul ruled the body, he had no difficulty in transferring the allegory to the field of public government, which explained without effort why John of Salisbury was so anxious about the law as the force that kept the Christian commonwealth together.* He advocated, accordingly, that in the creation of the law by the prince the priesthood should be given a hearing, because they alone, according to him, were qualified to pronounce upon the essential ingredients of the law. For to him law could be none other than a rule of conduct based upon the Christian faith, and who else but the priesthood was qualified to say whether a proposed legal measure was in consonance with the faith or not. As he said, thereby expressing the teleological principle in classic form, 'the whole function of the laws is religious and holy'. The law was the vehicle of government which meant authoritative guidance and direction of an organized body: and his commonwealth was Christian. John did not separate 'politics' from 'religion'.

The unitary idea presupposed unitary headship of the Christian body corporate, and this head was for John the pope, set over the nations and kingdoms, from whose judgement there was no exemption either in regard to person or to matter. The papal law demanded unconditional obedience. As we have already seen,† he held that the prince received from sacerdotal hands the power to wield the sword, whilst the overriding authority remained with the priesthood. In a sense, therefore, the prince could be likened, John says, to a 'slaughterer', because one of his main tasks – we know that this was originally St Paul's and Isidore's doctrine – was the suppression of evil. It was for this reason that the Ruler was instituted by divinity, and, if he governed in order to realize this purpose, he was indeed 'the image of divinity'. For, he said, 'the will of the king' – the material ingredient of the law within a theocratic form of government – 'depends on the law of God', since law to be law was 'the gift of God' and 'the image of the divine will'. The law must, for John, embody the idea of justice, but this was to him an exclusively Christian concept, the contents of which were known only to those specially qualified. (In the thirteenth century most of these ideas were propounded with considerable sharpness by Bishop Grosse-teste of Lincoln). The tyrannical prince was a perversion of the Christian king, John held, because he governed in precisely the opposite way to that in which the Christian prince was supposed to govern: he became 'the image of the devil'. Since he was a scourge of the Christian people, he may well be killed by the subjects, John said, but in another place he advocated praying for the conversion of the tyrant. Both suggestions – tyrannicide and prayers – seem to be clear in-dications of the difficulties which the theocratic king presented to a man of John's calibre. As long as the king was the source of the law, and the 'will of the prince' imparted binding char-acter to the laws, no constitutional device was at hand to re-move the tyrant by means of the law. The recourse to force or prayers was an involuntary admission of the shortcomings of the theocratic kingship. (Thomas Aquinas in the following cen-tury had exactly the same difficulties in dealing with the tyrant.)

St Paul had in a number of letters employed the simile of the human body to explain his own ideas. The simile was to show the intimate connexion between the various parts of the human body which were directed 'by the spirit of the Lord'. Each part of the body had its own peculiar function, but no part functioned for its own sake, but for the sake of the whole body. This integrated functionalism was the principle of divi-sion of labour which rested upon the unity of purpose and could be explained only on teleological terms. This organo-logical conception of society exercised great influence in the Middle Ages, and in John of Salisbury it reached its climax.

Thereby the working of the descending theory of government could be demonstrated, and this quite especially because the 'soul' of the body corporate was the prince. John carried his organological thesis to its logical conclusion: the senate as the advisory body of the prince was compared to the heart, whilst the eyes, ears, tongues of the body corporate were represented by the judges and provincial governors, etc., the peasants resembled the feet of the community, the stomach was likened to the fisc, that is, the treasury that fed the officers, and so on. But, and this is important enough to state it explicitly, nowhere in his system was there any indication that the subjects of the prince had any right against him. John did insist that the prince's duty was to care for his subjects, and especially 'the feebler' members (St Paul, I Corinthians xii, 22) should receive the prince's attention; the subjects also could express their wishes and suggestions and so on to the prince, but all this was still a long way from ascribing to the subjects any autonomous rights. The notion of the subject precluded conceptually the emergence of any politological theme that he had rights (as well as duties).

As indicated, John of Salisbury was only one of the many who had expounded the hierocratic thesis of government in the twelfth century. It may be advisable to conclude this chapter with a specimen of late thirteenth-century writing which may well be taken as representing the advanced hierocratic ideology. Giles of Rome (Egidius Romanus) is on several counts worth a few remarks. His tract *On Ecclesiastical Power* was written at the time when the ferocious conflict between the pope and the French king was at its height; he was well trained in both canon law and philosophy, author of some notable works on philosophy and theology; he was an eminent member of the Augustinian Order and had earlier been tutor to Philip IV of France; his book reflects papal doctrine rather well.

The aim of the book of Giles of Rome was to prove that the pope had sovereignty (here called 'supremacy') over the whole of the world, concerning everyone and everything, and that consequently princes (in no wise different from the ecclesiastics) were subjects of the pope; furthermore, that all sacerdotal and regal powers were located in the pope by virtue of his plenitude of power. Unless subjected to him, no power was legitimately exercised. In themselves these statements were far from being new, but what gave the book its complexion were the arguments employed to arrive at these conclusions. His central idea was that of *dominium*, by which he did not so much mean property, but governance or lordship. The term, he said, was derived from *dominus,* denoting the superiority of one person over another, and the abstract notion of *dominium* expressed this *superior–inferior* relationship in the realm of theory. 'Lordship' might take the form of property in the narrow meaning of the term when material things were subjected to the lord, or it might take the far wider form of personal subjection of one man to another, in which latter case one could speak of governmental authority. For both it was essential that the exercise of power was lawful, that is, that there was a right to its exercise.

That right to governance or lordship could, for Giles, be obtained only through the working of the divine grace which became operational through the sacraments, above all, baptism. Hence the consequential thesis emerged that infidels could have neither legitimate property nor legitimate authority: what they had, they had unjustly and through usurpation. Governance or lordship could not be obtained by a mere inheritance (a merely carnal *generatio*) or by conquest, but solely by the efficacy of divine grace through regeneration, through re-birth in baptism. Power over infidels therefore belonged to the Christians, and above all to the pope. Here indeed Giles had an important model in Innocent IV a generation earlier, who had declared that every creature was to be subjected to 'the vicar of the Creator'. For as all things created by God were subjected to God, Giles said, the vicar of God on earth had (with certain restrictions) divine or celestial power.*

---

*'Just as God acts in governing all creatures, in the same way the supreme pontiff, God's vicar, acts in the governance of the Church and of the faithful.' He also said this: 'All men and all possessions are under the governance (*sub dominio*) of the Church, because the whole world and all who live in it, belong to the Church' (2.11).

Apart from that, an excommunicate person could have no legitimate property of his goods. Giles anchored this supreme authority in the Petrine binding and loosing powers.

By this manner of argument Giles was able to state that the pope had 'to institute the terrestrial power'. And from this followed the right to transfer kingdoms, to remove kings, and so on. The ancient principle of supreme authority and the consequential principle of division of labour were here put forward in the garb of supreme *dominium* held by the pope. The pope did not deal with temporal matters directly, but through the medium of the terrestrial power, though 'the primary and superior authority', that is, sovereignty, remained with the pope. 'The art of governing the people (by the terrestrial power) is in reality the art of managing material goods according to the disposition laid down by the ecclesiastical power.' The Two-Sword theory exemplified, according to Giles, that one had to distinguish between power as such and the execution or use of power. Power – that is, lordship – the pope alone had and this was always beneficial and good (according to Giles), because it came from God, but the execution in the hands of princes, might be good or bad, hence the need to direct and guide the princes to the proper use of power. It was understandable that Giles held the sacerdotal power to be *major* and the regal power *minor* which was merely the medieval view of expressing sovereignty. To him, in a sense, the pope was the real 'fount of power'; since no other power was more perfect, his might truly be called 'celestial'.

Just as God manages *(administrat)* corporeal things, so as to allow them their proper movements, in the same way the vicar of God should manage *(debet administrare)* the terrestrial and temporal powers, so as to permit them to exercise their proper office.

It would, nevertheless, be advisable, from the point of view of legal security, if the pope were to adhere to earlier papal pronouncements, Giles counselled, but it was also an axiom of his that the pope, just as God Himself, could set aside the laws, if this were justified by the situation. The laws of nature, he said, were sometimes put aside by God when working miracles, and similarly the pope as God's vicar was entitled and bound to put aside the positive law and go beyond it. No rigid rule could be laid down: the pope's jurisdiction was what Giles called flexible and adjustable (*flexibilis et casualis*). The concept of universal sovereignty Giles of Rome expressed thus:

To the terrestrial power the material and temporal things are committed, so that they could be dealt with directly by it in its execution of its office; but to the spiritual power were committed, as far as the principal governance goes, the primary and superior authority over all temporal things as well as over the whole world by right, though this is not the case *de facto*, because not all obey the gospel.

The hierocratic point of view, of which we have given a merely summary account, explains the papal preoccupation with the law. The body of the faithful to be led to its destined end was not merely a mystical or sacramental body, but one with definite earthly appurtenances, for on the life of the Christians in this world depended their life in the other world. If the corporate union of the Christians had been considered a merely mystical body, there would have been no need for a law, for a tribunal, for an organization. But as this body was viewed as an organic, governable body, it needed the law to direct its path – that, at least, was the standpoint of the papacy, which as a predominantly governmental institution insisted on the observance of its law, as any other governmental institution also did.

What the papal–hierocratic system made abundantly clear – and to a certain extent this also applied to any other theocratic government – was the pronounced relationship between law and faith. Faith in the institution and efficacy of the papal government – effective in this as well as in the other world – brought forth the law which in its turn regulated the faith itself and its individual articles. It was not for the subject to dispute or question the rightness or wrongness of the law or command: he had to obey. As Gregory I in the late sixth century said – and as it was often repeated – the decision of the superior, no matter whether just or unjust, was binding upon the faithful. In a curious way, and quite especially when the superior was held and claimed to act as God Himself would have acted, this doctrine was considered to reflect the view that one must obey God rather than man.

Consequently it was the distinction between office and person that imparted resilient strength to the hierocratic set of ideas. It is this impersonal, objective point of view which was reflected in the statement of Innocent III that it was no mere man but divinity itself that gave binding instructions through the law, or in the declaration of Boniface VIII (applying Proverbs viii, 15) that 'through the apostolic see princes govern . . . and kings rule'. The petrinity of the papal office, that is, the pope's possession of Christ's powers as vicar of Christ, excluded all considerations of a personal nature. The enforceability of a law resulted from its flowing from the office of the pope, and not from his person. And precisely because the papacy was an institution of government, its recourse to the law and jurisdiction is self-explanatory. No orderly government would ever be able to exist if the objective validity of its measures and decrees were to be dependent upon the subjective and personal character of the law-creating agency, that is, in this case whether the legislating pope was morally a good or bad man.

As far as the laws of logical reasoning went, this system of government could hardly be effectively assailed within the framework within which it worked. The actual historical process would show this. But as a result of the infiltration of, and influence exercised by, ideas which had little or nothing to do with the premisses upon which the papal edifice of governmental ideas was erected, the traditional, objective, de-personalized, office point of view was to give way to a personal, subjective, and human point of view – and when this came about, the papacy as a governmental institution was to suffer a diminution in its authority and standing. That was the period when it was no longer faith in the divine institution of the papacy, faith in the function of the pope as ethereal key bearer who could open and shut the gates to paradise (as Gregory IX on a memorable occasion had declared), when it was no longer faith in the function of the pope standing mid-way between God and man, but faith in the Bible, that is, faith in the individual's own ability to interpret the Bible. When that stage was reached, the days of the papal-hierocratic government became shorter and shorter. It was not so much the faith that had changed, as the point to which faith referred. The point of reference, in the hierocratic system, was the institution of the papacy as an organ of government. The point of reference in the later period was the Bible which the individual claimed to be perfectly capable of interpreting. The result was the emancipation of the subject and his release from the tutelage of the specifically qualified members of the Church. In the one case the faith directed itself to a visible, objective, external office; in the other it directed itself to an invisible, subjective, internal, and direct union with God through the Bible.

CHAPTER 5

THEOCRATIC AND FEUDAL KINGSHIP

I. THE SUBSTANCE OF ROYAL THEOCRACY

IN the preceding chapters the nature and character of theocratic kingship has figured prominently, since, conceptually, it was firmly embedded in the generally prevailing theocentric and ecclesiastical outlook. We have referred to the emergence of theocratic kingship in the seventh and eighth centuries, when the king, hitherto tied to the people, began to detach himself from those to whom originally he owed his position as leader. This detachment began in a visible and easily understandable form by the king's adopting the title of a 'King by the grace of God'. The king's title-deed lay not in the people's will, but in divinity. The thesis that kings ruled by divine grace was originally due to the influence of the Christian idea itself, or perhaps more accurately, of the Pauline doctrine 'What I am, I am by the grace of God'. The main features of this theocratic kingship (which in course of time was to turn divine grace into a divine right) have already been pointed out, above all, its structure as a descending form of government and the consequential function of the king as a sovereign.*

Kingly government was in the Middle Ages far more a matter of practice than the corresponding ecclesiastical government. Between the eighth and the eleventh centuries not a single writer on the royal side had made his appearance. That is, during precisely the period in which the hierocratic thesis made such significant strides, harnessing all the available literary and doctrinal material to its cause and building up its imposing ideological edifice, the royal government produced not a single work which would have set forth a well-argued royal thesis. On the contrary, the main features of the royal thesis were in actual fact constructed by ecclesiastics – witness the coronation rites, wholly the result of episcopal efforts, to which, paradoxically enough as it might well seem in retrospect, the

* See above, pp. 53ff. and 85f.

kings gave their full and unconditional support. The chancery personnel of the kings was overwhelmingly, if not exclusively, staffed by ecclesiastics, who, in the official royal documents, decrees, charters, and so on, spoke the king's mind which, however, on closer inspection was hardly distinguishable from their own. In the preambles to papal documents lengthy expositions of the papal thesis could often be found, expositions which were made in legal documents having legal force, but in the preambles to the royal documents the exposition of a royal thesis was scarce, brief, and in the overwhelming number of cases did not go beyond some theocratic commonplace statements. The point is that the royal side had no such programmatic blue-print as that which the ecclesiastical side possessed. Those whose 'natural' vocation it would have been to propound a royal blue-print, an educated laity, did not exist. It was all very well to insist upon the Bible and to emphasize the biblical background of theocratic kingship, to point out the numerous, if not innumerable, donations which the kings had made to ecclesiastical groups and individuals, but who was credited with a more authentic interpretation of the Bible, the unsophisticated king or the sophisticated pope?

Furthermore, before the eleventh century, although the king did have in practice a firm control over the clergy, notably the episcopacy, mainly through the operation of the proprietary church system, one is struck by the similar feature that no ideological justification of this system was undertaken. And when the assault came, and it came by confronting the practice with a highly developed theory, no doctrinal defence of the system was possible, because there was none. However much the royal-theocratic form of government was a matter of practice and unsophisticated religious reasoning, it was powerless in the face of a closely woven and integrated doctrine. Perhaps nothing characterizes the situation better than the reply which the pope gave to the – perfectly understandable – protestation of the king, the German Henry IV, in the midst of the Investiture Contest. The king protested that what he was doing was entirely in conformity with what all his predecessors had done and that his government was based upon the customs of his ancestors. To which the pope replied: 'The Lord did not say "I am custom", but the Lord said "I am the Truth".' Whatever the facts, whatever the history might have been, dwindled into insignificance when confronted by the Truth which the pope alone knew.

What the royal theocratic government made clear – and in this it was supported by ecclesiastical doctrine – was the sovereignty of the king over his subjects.* The structure of this sovereignty was in no wise different from that of the pope's. The king stood outside and above the people whom divinity had entrusted to his government. Consequently, there was no tribunal, no organ, no means to make the king responsible for his governmental measures and actions. He was above the law. 'No writ runs against the king'; and 'The king can do no wrong'. We have seen what difficulties a John of Salisbury had in dealing with this very point. Nor is it without interest to note that to this day the British Queen is still referred to as 'The Sovereign', which rather clearly mirrors medieval theocratic conceptions. On the other hand, whatever rights the subject people possessed, whatever offices they might occupy, whatever functions they might fulfil, they had as a matter of royal concession or royal grace (principle of concession). For just as the king was conceded or granted his power from God, so were the subjects conceded or granted their rights and powers from the king. The statement of James I could have been made in the Middle Ages, with perhaps more justification than when it was actually made:

We cannot (he said) with patience endure our *subjects* to use antimonarchic words to us, concerning their *liberties,* except that they subjoined that they were *granted* unto them by *grace* and *favour* of our predecessors.

Once this road was taken, there was – as we have seen – no obstacle to harness the idea of *Munt,* of supreme protection, to the royal theme itself, with the consequence that the people itself was put on the same level as a minor under age.† What

---

* See above, p. 88, for qualifications of the statement.
†Above, pp. 56f.

must be pointed out is that the people, not being considered fit, had no share in the creation of the law. The material ingredient of the law was not consent, but the will of the prince who, because of his divine appointment, announced the law to be obeyed by the subjects. This subjection to the king's laws was – at times – considerably strengthened by the subjects taking an oath of allegiance, whereby the duty of obedience was solemnly reinforced. That the people could make proposals, that they could supplicate for royal measures, has already been mentioned, and that the king, for reasons of practical expediency, was ill-advised to disregard them, was evident, but there was, within the theocratic framework of kingship, no legal means to force the king's hand. All was a matter of royal grace or concession. Did not the coronation texts say in so many words that the king was 'a mediator between God and the people'? The theocratic king's government was absolute, though we hasten to add that this was not the same as arbitrariness of government; nor could it set aside the divine law with impunity.

A commonly accepted doctrine was set forth in the *Dialogue of the Exchequer*, written at the time of the English Henry II. It stated that nobody and no one may presume to withstand a royal decree which had been made for the good of the peace. What the 'good of the peace' in concrete circumstances was, the king alone knew best, because he alone was charged with preserving and promoting the peace (the king's peace). The people were not considered fit enough to know what was in their best interests and for the good of the peace. And in the following century we have the testimony of the French Louis IX who declared that because the king had plenitude of power – a significant borrowing from the papal field – his governance was unfettered *(liberum regimen),* unfettered, that is, by human laws and human agencies. To this extent, the *liberum regimen* was nothing but the concept of sovereignty in the king. In his function as law-giver the theocratic king stood indeed outside and above the law. He formed an estate of his own which was symbolically expressed by his sitting on the elevated throne.

The weaknesses of the theocratic kingship were obvious. As well as the necessary estrangement that took place between king and people, there was a further important factor. Because, vocationally, the king protested that he was under God's law and that his judicial decisions and decrees did not contravene divine law, his flanks, so to speak, were constantly exposed to the intervention by those who, also vocationally, were considered to be the expositors of God's will and the divine law. Sometimes their intervention was not effective, but this depended on the prevailing circumstances and the human element, not on doctrine. The autonomous standing which the king's theocratic government was to show was considerably diluted in the very act that made him the king, in the coronation service. Here the draftsmen had taken great pains to show that the king received the divine grace of his kingship through the medium of the episcopal officers: it was they who administered the sacrament (or sacramental) of royal unction. In the very act of his becoming 'the Lord's anointed', the episcopacy, as the transmitting organs of divine grace, proved themselves as the mediators of the divine will and thus sandwiched themselves between God and the king. The theoretical possibility of ecclesiastical jurisdiction over the king always existed within the theocratic framework. Henry IV in the eleventh century reiterated and protested that, as he was 'the Lord's anointed', he was immune from ecclesiastical jurisdiction: by the very same argument Gregory VII deprived him of his kingship and excommunicated him. Furthermore, in the conferment of the sword, the symbol of physical strength, the mediatory role of the bishops was pointed up. And the accompanying prayer-texts leave no room for doubt about the meaning of this conferment. Similar observations could be made about the formulae accompanying the actual crowning of the king. Nor did the texts (amply supplemented as time went on) during the service omit to drive home the teleological view of the king's functions: he had received, as the texts repeated, his royal power for the sake of defending Holy Church. The king's becoming an ecclesiastical person had at least as many disadvantages as it had advantages. Kingship was, as often as not, a vocational, if not an occupational, hazard.

In this context the significance of medieval royal elections is important. In strictest theory royal elections in the Middle Ages had not the meaning customarily attached to elections. The result of choosing a king was that he was designated to the already existing royal office. With the office itself, the electors themselves had nothing to do: they could neither modify nor change the substance, the scope, or the nature of the office or in any way touch it. The office of kingship was not in the gift of the 'electors' (just as the office of the pope was not in the gift of the electing cardinals, or the office of a bishop in the gift of the electing cathedral chapter; etc.) which also explains why the electors could not legally take away the office from a king, since they had not conferred it on him. The office was divine, and, so to speak, laid up in heaven. Through the election no powers were conferred on the elected: he did not thereby become king. The 'election' signified the designation of the chosen candidate as a suitable person for the office of kingship which he received at the coronation, or, more precisely, at the anointing. The electors in theory presented the candidate for the office to be conferred by the officiating ecclesiastical hierarchy at the coronation service. For this reason, in fact, we read in the coronation texts that it was the bishops who had 'elected' the king during the coronation service. It was therefore no mere finesse that the king did not begin to act as king from the day of his 'election', but from the day of his coronation – that is, when the regnal years began to be reckoned – which was the practice down to the thirteenth century.

This theme of election as a designation also illuminates the continuous attempts to introduce hereditary kingship. That even a mere designation offered ample scope for intrigues, machinations, and bargaining, is evident. It is also evident that there could be a considerable time-lag between the 'election' and the constitutive act of the coronation. What therefore has to be borne in mind is that with the death of the king there also died the king's peace, the fount of all justice and the source of all law. The question which presented itself was this: where did power reside when there was a vacancy? The answer given was that the king's office and power returned to where it had come from: it reverted by escheat to divinity. There was created a vacuum by the death of the king which was not filled until the successor had been anointed. It was partly in order to shorten the interval between death and coronation, and partly to secure some form of continuity of government, that the idea of hereditary kingship always found favour, though, for reasons irrelevant to the development of governmental thought, the idea was frequently incapable of being put into practice.

II. THE DEFENCE OF THE THESIS

The fury of the Investiture Contest brought forth a number of writings which on the royal side attempted to refute the arguments advanced by the papal point of view. The target of the royal attacks was the papal plenitude of power derived from the papal interpretation of the Matthean passage,* whereby the thesis of papal monarchy, that is, of papal sovereignty over kings and emperors, was attempted to be translated into reality. This attempt at universal sovereignty (or in Gregory VII's expression the *regimen universale*) was bound to be resisted by the kings. How, then, did the royal side react? What arguments had the royal thesis with which to combat the hierocratic onslaught? It is here that the weaknesses of the royal theocratic position revealed themselves. The ideological position of the king was singularly tuned into the christocentric outlook of the Middle Ages, but it was also one which made it excruciatingly difficult to resist effectively those who had a professional monopoly of biblical interpretation and of all things connected with divinity and divine grace. Here we can but give a very brief summary of some of the views propounded.

The shattering character of the attack by the papal-hierocratic government on the sovereign status of the king is per-

*Above, p. 22.

haps difficult to appreciate in the modern age, because our ways of thinking are so different from those of the high Middle Ages. Above all, the modern age is familiar with the concept which would seem to make a conflict of this nature hardly possible, certainly in the form which it took. That concept of the modern age was not there – the concept of the State as a self-sufficient, autonomous, juristic body of citizens. It was precisely this which the royal side was groping for but could not find, because it had not the equipment and the tools to construct it. What there was, was a kingdom *(regnum)* and a priesthood *(sacerdotium)*, but both were parts of one and the same body, the Church. The concept of the State was as far removed from the mind of the high Middle Ages as the steam-engine and electricity. Because the Church consisted of clergy and laity, the papal-hierocratic standpoint had a comparatively easy passage in driving home its tenets: it was the Church that mattered and at its head stood the successor of St Peter and vicar of Christ who Himself had founded the Church, of which a kingdom was merely a part. But this concept of the Church made the defence and assertion of royal sovereignty *vis-à-vis* the pope exceedingly difficult.

The side most intimately affected by the hierocratic measures was that of the German king. Henry IV did not, as it is said so often, fight a battle of Church versus State. If he had been able to do so, his position would have been immeasurably stronger, and the conflict would in all likelihood never have occurred. On the contrary, he fought it on the then only available basis, that is, on the level of kingship and priesthood. What the royal side objected to was the assertion of monarchic sovereignty by the pope. Henry IV and his followers believed that this assertion was not based on the Bible or any doctrine, but amounted to a usurpation of powers by the pope. Hence the royal side advanced the argument that Christ had established a duality of governing authority over the Christian body in the persons of the pope and the king. In order to buttress this novel argument of a dualism of government, the allegory of the two swords was introduced, though it should be noted that the meaning of this Henrician allegory was fundamentally different from that which it was to become in the hands of Bernard of Clairvaux two generations afterwards.* It is perhaps best to quote the important statement of Henry IV, made in March 1076:

He (Gregory VII) usurped for himself the kingdom and the priesthood without God's sanction, despising God's holy ordinance which willed essentially that they – namely the kingdom and the priesthood – should remain not in the hands of one, but, as two, in the hands of two. For the Saviour Himself, during His passion, intimated that this was the meaning of the typical sufficiency of the two swords. For when it was said to Him 'Behold, Lord, here are two swords' He answered 'It is enough', meaning thereby that a duality is sufficient, that a spiritual and a carnal sword were to be wielded in the Church, and by them every evil will be cut off.

What in the final resort the introduction of the concept of dualism as an anti-papal panacea signified was the division of supreme authority, the splitting up of the concept of monarchy itself. According to the anti-papal dualist thesis the single and undivided sovereignty of the pope was, so to speak, to be halved. But it is evident that thereby the traditional concept of royal monarchy itself was to be halved, for whilst hitherto the king could justifiably claim to have had, in practice, true sovereignty in his kingdom, he now admitted that the pope too had some sovereignty, that is, over the so-called spiritual matters, whereas the king asserted sovereignty over temporal matters.

It is clear that this dualism – introduced as a weapon against the inflated hierocratic ideology – showed all the features of a rear-guard action. The basic justification of the dualist theory was the assertion that the temporal itself was autonomous, and because this was so, the king himself, dealing on his own admission only with the temporal, was also autonomous. Whether this was feasible or practical is not to be discussed here. The questions that did obtrude were what, in a thoroughly soaked christocentric milieu, were the criteria by which the 'temporal' could be separated from the 'spiritual' and, above all, who was to draw the line of demarcation?

* See above, p. 110.

The efforts made by the best brains in the succeeding age to find a criterion by which the one could be distinguished from the other proved futile, especially since the circle of issues under papal jurisdiction became ever wider: matters which in some remote way were concerned with a 'spiritual' affair were no longer temporal; for instance, questions arising out of dowry were spiritual causes, because connected with matrimony. The ascription of autonomous character to the 'temporal' by the royal side certainly signified an advance in thought, but, considering the intellectual temper of the time, was this ascription of autonomy convincing enough to destroy the Pauline views concerning the secular, visible, corporeal, that is, the temporal, and on which in fact the Gregorian assertions of sovereignty rested? Over and above this consideration there was the operation of papal jurisdiction 'by reason of sin' and 'after the examination of certain causes' (*certis causis inspectis*).

The royal theory of dualism, first advanced by Henry IV, nevertheless exercised great attraction. The publicists of the late eleventh century took it up and tried to buttress it. A typical example is the author of the tract *On the Preservation of the Unity of the Church*, who assailed the papal-hierocratic theory of the Petrine plenitude of power. He maintained that the papal thesis rested upon an erroneous interpretation of the Matthean text, for Christ's commission to Peter was not comprehensive. The binding and loosing concerned 'only those things which are fit to be bound and which it is expedient be loosed'. But the author did not give any specific definition of those things which should not be bound and loosed by the pope. What he obviously had in mind was a curtailment of the papal jurisdictional power. The pope, according to him, was not, on the basis of the Petrine commission, entitled to issue laws which affected a king. What the pope could do was exhort, counsel, advise the king, but by no means issue binding instructions in the shape of the law. Further, no pope had a right to excommunicate or depose a king, because 'he, having no superior, cannot be judged by anyone'. The author contended that by disregarding his essentially limited power the pope had arrogated to himself a function which was not his, thereby not just duplicating and trebling the swords (cf. Ezekiel xxi, 14) but multiplying the swords. According to the author the exercise of papal sovereign power resulted in untold harm, in evil, scandals, and civil wars. By issuing laws which were not in his competency, and thereby usurping royal power, the pope had become the destroyer of the unity of the Church. Hence the author proposed a dual form of government. Though no doubt putting his finger on the vital point of the nature of Petrine powers, he could no more than any one else in the royal camp fix the limits of the Petrine monarchy.

This attempt at de-mundanizing the papal monarchy by restricting the pope's legislative powers was nothing less than the attempt to find an autonomous basis for the king's monarchy, however much it was now confined to 'temporal' matters. The search for this basis was the search for the idea of the State which the writers, with the means at their disposal, could not find. What was required was a basis that had nothing to do with the whole christocentric cluster of ideas, and that desideratum could not come about until the thirteenth century, when the days of the king 'by the grace of God' were also numbered. Whether it was paradoxical or not, the fact remains that it was the firm adherence to a royal theocracy which had landed the Christian kings of the Middle Ages into such great difficulties with the ecclesiastical powers.

The dualist thesis of government also suggested the conception of a dual vicariate of Christ. This was the logical development which we witness in the official Staufen governmental ideology, evidenced by the Emperor Frederick I in the twelfth century. Christ, he maintained, was both king and priest. His royal function was vicariously in the hands of the emperor, His priestly function in those of the pope. Moreover, because the pope was only the priestly vicar of Christ, he had no power to issue laws. Once again we find that the de-mundanizing of the papal government was the aim of the exponents of this point of view, for, as Frederick I said, 'the holy laws of the emperors and the good customs of our predecessors' were the only basis of governing the empire: the pope had no right to interfere in the government of kings or emperors. Proper governmental authority was denied to the pope, who might well admonish the emperor, but was not entitled to subject him or his empire to papal laws and jurisdiction. The papal insistence on government – and government could be conceived only by means of the law – was at the root of anti-papal writings and official attacks on the papacy carried out by the adherents of the dualist programme.

The pattern which, at least in the empire, provided a basis for denying the pope his law-creating function was the Roman law. It became from the late eleventh century onwards the reservoir for royal and imperial ideology against the papacy. It was in fact the already mentioned Peter Crassus of Ravenna who, writing still during the Investiture Contest in the eighties of the eleventh century, was the first to operate with the Roman law, especially with the *Code*, and to use it for buttressing the royal side. Peter Crassus in fact made the Roman law part of the science of government. For him the crime of Gregory VII lay precisely in this, that he had set aside the sacred laws of the emperors by arrogating to himself the function of a lawgiver which was entirely alien to the conception of the papacy. Gregory in fact disregarded divine justice, which Peter Crassus found embodied in the imperial 'sacred' laws. What however also gives the tract its particular interest is the sharp division he made between the clergy and the laymen. As to the former, he conceded that they might be ruled by the pope as their lawgiver. The latter could be governed only by the imperial laws. There was, he said, 'a double set of laws', one applicable to the clerics, the other to the laity. He constructed a kind of dualist government, not by relying on the distinction between 'temporal' and 'spiritual' matters, but by advocating the civil laws as the laws for the laity primarily, and the canon or ecclesiastical laws for the clerics exclusively. Because the civil laws were given by God through the mouthpiece of the emperor, they had, however, to be obeyed also by the clergy, and it was precisely through wilfully and contemptuously disregarding the civil laws that the papacy emerged as the disturber of peace.

Probably influenced by the feudal position of bishops and clerics, there were a number of writers who, in order to retain the monarchic sovereignty of the king, concentrated attention on the material possessions, such as the estates, with which the bishops were enfeoffed. What these writers aimed at was the separation of the ecclesiastical office from the ecclesiastical possessions. It will be recalled that one of the topical points of the conflict was the investiture of bishops and clerics by the king (or lay lord) with their clerical office and their possessions. Office and benefice were conferred by the king. Now this group of writers tried to oppose papal governmental power in regard to the actual possessions which were termed, significantly enough, regalian rights. They belonged to the king in his function as king and were inseparably bound up with his kingship. These regalian rights were consequently termed inalienable, that is, the king was not entitled to dispose of them in any way. Whilst it was admitted that the king had no right to confer ecclesiastical offices, this group of writers insisted with all the greater emphasis that the regalian rights were solely the king's, and that a cleric invested with them had during his tenancy merely a usufruct of the goods. The regalian rights were defined in February 1111 thus:

> Cities, duchies, markgravates, countships, mints, tolls, customs, markets, hundredcourts, manors, soldiery, and fortifications.

Although the cleric was invested with these rights, the king remained the owner. The sovereignty of the king rested therefore on these material possessions. This point of view – originally suggested in the eleventh century by Guido of Ferrara – seems not only an eminently practical point of view, but also one that might well have been made the basis of constructive governmental thought: one might well detect in this thesis some embryonic elements of a concept of the State. The practical complexion of this theory was responsible for its adoption in the various agreements which concluded the great contest.

Although in the aggregate the royal publicists no less than the official standpoints presented quite trenchant criticisms of the papal-hierocratic ideology, they nevertheless never attained their opponent's logical consistency. Part of the explanation was theocratic kingship itself. Part of the explanation was also the very character of the conflicts between pope and king. It was a conflict centred in the realm of pure ideas which very largely betrayed the paternity of the papacy; and the papacy was bound up, in the Middle Ages, with the Christian idea itself. No other organization or institution had so long a memory as the papacy had: in its ideological storehouse, in the Registers and Archives, was found – or, if necessary, could be found – the *pièce justificative* for any governmental action or thesis. And the German kings who, for a time, had to bear the brunt of the papal-hierocratic attacks, had not even a capital, let alone orderly archives. The real strength of the kings lay indeed in 'the old customs', old usages, old practices, which had grown up without much ideological buttressing and argumentation, but this strength could easily turn into weakness if the embarrassing question was put: 'By what authority?' We recall the disarming reply of the pope to the king's protestations about tradition and custom. In an ideological conflict it was ideology that counted, and not custom. The royal side only began to argue and to reason out its function when it had long been overtaken by the ideology of its opponents.

It seems clear that the imperial side was at a still greater disadvantage than the royal side. Both the genesis and the actual history of the Western Emperor of the Romans had shown that he was the intellectual offspring of papal conceptions.* He was made and unmade by the pope. Again, whilst since the ninth century the papacy had erected a rather elaborate ideological edifice concerning Roman emperorship and had managed to embody its main governmental ingredients in the coronation rites, there was no corresponding development of an ideology on the emperor's side. When confronted by the mature papal ideology and the vast arsenal of ideology and historical precedent, not to forget the unmistakable liturgical symbolism, the imperial side was forced to argue entirely on the ground that was chosen by the pope and mapped out by

*Above, pp. 93f.

him, and that ground was, in fact and in theory, of the pope's own making. The imperial side represented by the twelfth- and thirteenth-century Staufen official and semi-official declarations, argued (1) that, by electing the German king, the princes thereby gave the king a title-deed to Roman emperorship; and (2) that the coronation to be performed by the pope was a mere formality; it was declaratory and not constitutive. Accordingly, the imperial standpoint was that the German king had a right to be crowned by the pope, and this was expressed by the novel term of *imperatura* which he had by virtue of his election as 'King of the Romans': the German princes therefore could demand the imperial coronation by the pope as a matter of right. The papal point of view that the conferment of the imperial crown was an 'apostolic favour' and a good deed was brushed aside. They went even so far as to say that the papal standpoint was 'an unheard-of audacity' – this was said to Innocent III by the Staufen side in 1199 and 1201 – because there was no superior judge who could sit in judgement over the elected candidate. If they were to admit the pope as a judge in imperial elections and affairs, they would thereby assist in the pope's arrogation of powers, which they strenuously denied. For such an intervention would amount to interference, because he would thereby 'meddle in secular matters'. These Staufen views did not become law until 1338, when the imperial law was passed (*Licet Juris*), according to which the mere election of the German king made him Emperor of the Romans without any antecedent examination and approval by the pope. But, when that law was passed, the empire had lost its importance for at least two generations; and the popes were sitting in Avignon, not in Rome.

The paucity of publicistic writings on behalf of the emperor's rights and functions was one more significant feature of the twelfth and thirteenth centuries. It is true that the civilians in the Italian Universities were laymen, but they addressed a somewhat restricted public, who in any case were already tuned in to the descending theme of government. Although they put forward arguments which were later to be shown of great value, at the time they were hardly applicable, as, for instance, the argument based upon the Roman law *lex regia*, according to which the Roman people had, at one time, possessed all power, which they transferred to the emperor. Again, this could have served, as it was to serve later, for the construction of an ascending theory of government, but in view of the actual making of the medieval emperor of the Romans it would have stood no chance of persuading anyone. Nevertheless, it was on the basis of this *lex regia* that the thesis was advanced that the seven German princes who elected the king (to become Emperor of the Romans), acted on behalf of the Germans (who, by some strange transposition, took the place of the Roman people mentioned in the *lex regia*). The standpoint of Frederick II, the ablest of the Staufen dynasty, illustrated the poverty and paucity of arguments which the imperial side was able to throw against the hierocratic assault by Gregory IX and Innocent IV (1239–45). In passionate appeals to the whole of Christendom, Frederick II, ably assisted by Peter de Vinea and Thaddaeus of Suessa, charged the pope with perversion of justice and abuse of power, and demanded that the pope should stand his trial before a general council, because this represented the whole Church, from which the pope had his power. In other words, the imperial side operated with the ascending theory of government, as far as the pope was concerned, but the emperor made it equally clear that he himself was not accountable to anyone, because he derived his powers directly from God: to him only the descending theory was applicable. This kind of argument would seem to show into what an acutely difficult position the imperial side had been manoeuvred by the hierocratic ideology.

III. KINGSHIP IN ENGLAND AND CONSTITUTIONALISM

IF the test of any theory on government is whether it is capable of leading to a development which is reflected in a constitution, the theocratic-descending theory of government cannot pass the test. If indeed the ruler, be he pope, king, or emperor, formed an estate of his own, was in every respect sovereign, stood above the law, and if on the other hand, the members of the community were merely his subjects who had no share in government or in the making of the law, but received the law as a 'gift of God' through the mouth of the king, it transcends human ingenuity to devise a constitutional scheme by which the subjects could put fetters on the exercise of the monarchic-sovereign will of the Ruler. Within that ideology it was conceptually impossible to limit the function of the Ruler by establishing controls, measures, and checks on the sovereign. From the point of view of evolution, the theocratic thesis can, without fear of contradiction, be stigmatized as barren. Its own conceptual rigidity and inflexibility barred the way to its becoming the bearer of a development leading to constitutionalism. And that surely was and is the test of any 'political' theory – whether or not it is capable of being moulded into the frame of a constitution. Once the function of the Ruler as an estate of his own was crystallized, that was the end of any development. The only way left open was that of revolution. However logically, flawlessly, and symmetrically constructed the theocratic theory was, it was a thesis that took little account of the human elements which necessarily entered into actual government. It was as if government moved entirely within the precincts of concepts and abstractions, and not within the realm of human society with all its earthly concreteness and multifarious diversities of man's own all-too-human ambitions, volitions, and prejudices. The theocratic-descending theory was the attempt to subject reality to a mere concept.

The medieval corrective to royal theocracy was the king's function as a feudal overlord. There were few kings who did not combine both functions, that is, the theocratic and the feudal. It is one of the chief defects of current expositions on medieval kingship to speak of 'the king' without realizing that that medieval king embodied both the functions of a theocratic Ruler and of a feudal overlord. So far we have considered the theocratic king, but from a practical point of view, especially from that of development of 'political' theory, the feudal side was considerably more important. The feudal function of the king was diametrically opposed to his theocratic function, and in this respect the medieval king was an amphibious being, for according to the latter function it was his will that created law and in its exercise he was unimpeded and independent, whilst according to the former it was the implied or explicit consent of the feudal tenants-in-chief to the law of the king which was the constitutive element. This entailed that the king had to proceed by consultation and agreement with the other parties in the feudal contract. The feudal link between king and vassals (for brevity's sake the barons) was in reality a contract, and, once this is properly appreciated, the fundamentally different character of feudal kingship emerges. In this function the king did not stand outside and above the community, but was in every respect a member of it; hence within this structure there was no margin for the sovereign display of the prince's will. It seems advisable to call attention to this dichotomy within the medieval king, a dichotomy which brooked no compromise: as so often in medieval history and in medieval thought one is faced with a basic contradiction, even affecting so vital an institution as kingship itself.

As Sir Henry Maine pointed out a long time ago, feudal society was governed by the law of contract. Indeed, none was clearer on that point than the English Henry Bracton, one of the king's justices in the mid thirteenth century, who declared that the feudal contract created a legal bond between lord and vassal. This legal bond not only made it possible to conceive of the king as a member of the feudal community, but also made possible the operation of consent in regard to those measures which affected both parts of the contract. The law that regulated the interests of both parts was a mutual agreement between the king and his barons. The essential nature of a contract was that both parts to it had to become active: for the keeping of a contract two were (and are) necessary. The further consequence was that there was the possibility of cancelling, that is, repudiating the contract (the so-called *diffidatio*) if the one party had failed to act in conformity with the contract; for instance, if disloyalty were involved. None of these features was applicable to a theocratic kingship, for it was precisely because of its very essence that there was no contract between king and community, since the latter was entrusted to him by divinity. The very point at which theocratic kingship virtually came to grief was that of resistance to the king who had turned out to be a tyrant. That difficulty was prevented by feudal kingship: feudal law itself had provided for this contingency. This feudal side of kingship had an extraordinary innate strength, tenacity, and resilience, but also showed flexibility and adjustability. It was of native growth, man-made and adaptable to the needs of the time, always ready to take account of the reality of a given situation. The contrast to theocratic kingship was indeed startling. Here an intensely practical kind of arrangement, there speculation and theory that came more and more under the accumulated weight of First Principles, Dogmas, and Authority.

The feudal side of the king made him, as it were, human, but what is of immediate historical interest is that the practice of feudal government proved itself an important harbinger and incubator of ideas which later could be developed on the basis of a theoretically conceived populist or ascending theory of government. Here, within the feudal function of kingship, law, as the vehicle of government, was arrived at by counsel and consent, hence by cooperation leading to team work. Law was a joint effort between king and barons. It is, at the same time, also understandable that any king conscious of this dilemma into which the double function had put him tried to minimize the feudal functions and stress his theocratic position, for here he was free and unhampered. Which side eventually prevailed, depended not so much on theory, as on the actuality and the circumstances of a situation. In general it would be true to say that, the more skilful the king was in handling his theocratic function, and the less vigilant the baronage was in asserting and maintaining their rights, the better the king could play on the theocratic keyboard and produce sometimes dazzling effects. It is furthermore true that, the more the king was able to stress his theocratic function, the less there was a possibility of developing constitutionalism. The road from the theocratic *point d'appui* leading to constitutionalism was bloodstained and signposted by revolution. The road to constitutionalism from the feudal *point d'appui* was characterized by debates, compromise – by evolution. And that also seems at least part of the explanation for the divergent constitutional developments in England and France.

The English development from the early thirteenth century onwards showed the preponderance of the feudal function of the king at the expense of his theocratic function. King John had not the ability, skill, and resources which had enabled his predecessors, notably Henry II, to whittle down their feudal obligations. John handled the delicate mechanics of theocratic kingship so clumsily that he aroused opposition culminating in open hostility of the barons. It was not so much that he as theocratic king set aside the law – there was no tribunal which could call him to account on this score – as the manner of his government and the extent and multitude of his exactions, disseizins, outlawry, etc. It was the over-use, not a misuse, of his monarchic powers which brought the opposition into the open. To this must be added the effects of the loss of Normandy, the ecclesiastical interdict, and the lost battle at Bouvines. John indeed seemed to show to his contemporaries to what lengths a theocratic government could in fact go, but what made him virtually invulnerable was his status as 'the Lord's anointed' and the powerful doctrinal background. On the other hand, the barons were ill-equipped to put their thoughts into learned books or tracts. A literary source of the early years of the thirteenth century, the so-called 'Laws of the English' (*Leges Anglorum*), had pointed out that the king should not rely on Roman law (for which reliance there were increasing signs), but on 'the law of Britain', and that 'he should choose the law with the help of the barons'. What the anonymous author wished to emphasize was that the king should govern less on his theocratic and more on his feudal basis. The only means by which the king could be restricted was in theory and in fact through the machinery which the feudal function of the king provided. To a very large extent Magna Carta was the application of feudal principles of government: the spring months of 1215 afforded perhaps the last opportunity of fetching the king back into his feudal mould.

The 39th chapter of Magna Carta has always been taken as one of fundamental importance, and rightly so. It was a clause which in its main elements went back to a feudal law issued by the German King Conrad II, in 1036, but which was adjusted to the exigencies of the time.

No freeman shall be captured and imprisoned or disseized or outlawed or exiled or in any case harmed, except by a legitimate court of his peers and by the law of the land.

The significance of the clause lay in that in the cases mentioned a properly constituted court was to apply the law of the land.*

The law of the land – and this was the crucial step taken by the baronage on the basis of the feudal functions of kingship – was not that law which the king had issued, but that law which was approved by both the king and the barons, and which was the result of the working of the feudal contract, which was a joint effort; in other words, a law that was common to him and the barons. The term 'law of the land' was the thirteenth-century expression for the (later) common law of England. As such, the law of the land referred to that body of rules, not necessarily written, which had its deep roots in native feudalism, hence the preponderance of land law (property, tenure, succession, etc.) and which derived its material ingredients from the implicit or explicit consent of both king and barons. From the point of view of legal-historical development no less than from that of governmental thought, the concept of the law of the land was a very important step, since it signified the third great system of law in medieval Europe: next to Roman law, next to canon law, there was the feudally based English

* The Latin term *judicium* used in the clause did not mean in contemporary jurisprudence judgment, but tribunal, court; the contemporary term for judgment was *sententia* (sentence). Further, the employment of *vel* was conjunctive, not disjunctive; when the framers wished to say 'or', they invariably said *aut*. When they joined capture and imprisonment, they also employed *vel*, because they were two actions which flowed into one: imprisonment presupposes capture, and so does the application of the law of the land presuppose a tribunal, a court, because somebody must apply the law.

'law of the land', the predecessor of the common law. And, precisely because it was a native law, it had all the appurtenances of its feudal progenitor – flexibility, adjustability, and resilience. By the second half of the fourteenth century one could hear voices maintaining that 'the law of the land was made in parliament by the king and the spiritual and temporal lords and the whole community of the realm.'

Indeed, as Maitland once said, it was the tyranny of John which had turned the baronial right of joining in legislation into reality. That the idea of consent was ever alive in the minds of the barons emerged vividly in the great assembly held at Merton twenty years after Magna Carta. Here was debated the question of whether or not the son born outside wedlock but whose parents subsequently married and had another son was the first-born, and therefore, on the principle of primogeniture, could inherit. Feudal law was clear: the illegitimately born son remained so and was unable to inherit. Roman law, and, following it, canon law, held the opposite, namely that by subsequent marriage he became automatically legitimate. The bishops, led by Grosseteste of Lincoln, clamoured for the adoption of the Romano-canonical law, to which the barons gave the unambiguous reply: We do not want to change the law of England, because, they added, this was used and approved. In other words, consent was withheld from the proposed change of the law.

That the barons were perfectly aware of the impossibility of bringing a theocratic king to book was compellingly shown by the so-called security clause of Magna Carta, which, attempting to create some sort of constitutional machinery for the future, nowhere referred to the king's coronation oath or promises. That constitutional machinery devised for the eventuality of a defaulting king presupposed that he was part of the feudal community, for only in this capacity could he be 'got at', and never in that of a theocratic Ruler. No writ runs against the king. The exemption of the person of the king from the envisaged punitive measures was the strongest possible endorsement which the incipient 'common law' could give to the theocratic king himself.

The further development based on Magna Carta belongs to constitutional history, but it may here be said that there emerged in the course of the thirteenth century the idea of 'the communalty of the realm' consisting of king and barons, with the consequence that matters pertaining to it had to be treated by both parties. It was a further consequence that, as Bracton informs us, law was to be made by both parties, and, because the king was part of the law-creative process, he could not unilaterally set the law aside. What Magna Carta expressed in chapter 39 was contained in Bracton's famous statement: 'The king was to be under God and the law.' He was equally unambiguous in his statement that the laws could neither be changed nor annulled without the common consent of those with whose counsel and consent they had, in the first instance, been issued. According to Bracton, in so far as the king was the vicar of God, he had the duty to make his subjects observe the laws and thereby preserve the peace: for this reason he had received the sword at the coronation.

Propitious circumstances made the application of feudal principles feasible in England and thereby initiated a constitutional development which was to impress itself upon subsequent centuries. Of quite especial significance was the resultant development of parliament. The feudal assembly had, as McIlwain has expressed it, melted into a national parliament, with the consequence that the feudal *quid pro quo* turned into a grant made by the representatives of the community in return for the royal assent to their petitions. Of perhaps even greater significance was that law as a joint effort was *made* and not given by the king, and made it was by the king and the barons or other corporate body (parliament). This is particularly important in view of the very significant addition to the coronation promises of Edward II in 1308. The new clause of Edward II's promise embodied the ideological and consequently constitutional development of the thirteenth century since Magna Carta. Because the law was made jointly by the king and the community of the realm, the latter had a right to see the law enforced. The unilateral non-observance of the law by the king was prevented by his promise to uphold and protect the laws and rightful customs which the community of the realm will have chosen (i.e. to be upheld and protected by him).

Indeed, Bracton's view that the king was under the law was reproduced in the coronation promise of 1308. Because the subjects of a theocratic king had no share in the law given to them by their sovereign, they had therefore no legal possibility to force the king to observe his own laws. But because the community of the realm had a share in the creation of the law, they had become partners of the law-creative process and could thus force the king to observe it. In the solemn and originally so theocratically conceived coronation rite, the community of the realm was given a standing.

But that is not all. The development of the abstract concept of the Crown seems intimately connected with the feudal conception of society that embraced both the king (in his feudal capacity) and the feudal tenants-in-chief. The Crown was to all intents and purposes the kingdom itself. Seen thus, the corporeal diadem, the crown, symbolized the incorporeal, legal bond which united king and kingdom. In the concept of the Crown a permanent habitat for the king was found. The Crown did not consist of the community alone nor of the king alone, but of both: it was the two which made up the Crown. Edward I, protesting to the pope about some papal demands, wrote that he could

do nothing that touches the diadem of the realm without having first consulted the prelates and barons.

From here one can understand why the Roman law adage 'What touches all must be approved by all' could easily be accommodated in the governmental thought of the late thirteenth century. Moreover, the organic conception of society exercised, once again, its peculiar attraction when, in the fourteenth century, the bishop of Exeter declared that the substance of the nature of the Crown is found in the king as head and the peers as members. The concept of the Crown proved itself of great value as a buffer, because it could be, as indeed it was, invoked as a shield by the king and the community; a variety of charges could be brought under its heading, both against the king for neglecting to protect the Crown, and against anyone else for infringing its rights. Above all, the Crown served as a perfect bulwark against papal demands: papal provisions could be attacked as being contrary to the interests of the Crown, and in fact any papal claim could be rejected on that score – the very shield which, we shall see presently, the French king did not have.

The practical application of the feudal theory of kingship in England also accounted for the development of representation. This idea was no strange bedfellow of feudalism itself, but what is important to bear in mind is that the preparation of the soil by the prevalent feudal notions powerfully assisted the easy absorption of contemporary continental political ideas, without any of the otherwise severe repercussions which the influence of the ascending-populist ideas would have had upon a purely theocratic government. The statement by Chief Justice Thorpe in 1365 that 'Parliament represents the body of all the realm' could be squared with the most advanced populist ideas current on the Continent. The debt which the English constitution owed to feudal principles of government is very great indeed. The attempted implementation of the populist-ascending idea of government in a country ruled by a determined theocratic government could have no other result than revolution, whilst the application of feudal ideas of government provided a platform of evolution. As far as English kingship was concerned, the wings of the theocratic king were clipped, and clipped they were by the practical application of feudal principles. The king was saved, despite himself. One of the effects of this strongly developed feudal kingship was that, despite periodic attempts to introduce it, Roman law never gained much practical importance in England. Of course, in efficiency and speed, the English royal government could not compare with those governments on the Continent which were predominantly theocratic. This was based on an ideology from which the last ounce of logical argument was squeezed and which made the king appear, so to speak, chromium-plated and his government streamlined;

the predominant feudal kingship in England was a cumbersome, heavy, and creaking machine which had to work with the consent and counsel of magnates and barons, which had none of the gleaming appurtenances of theocratic kingship, but which supplied the basis of a constitutional development exercising influence far beyond the confines of the constitution itself and far beyond the medieval period.

In contrast to the English scene, both French and German kingship relied heavily on the exercise of theocratic functions. French kingship was ostensibly tilted towards its theocratic side which had, for understandable reasons, been bolstered up both by king and pope and also the French episcopacy. The holy oil with which Clovis in the late fifth century was supposed to have been baptized served as a particularly strong factor with which to express the uniqueness of French theocratic kingship. None of the other kings had that distinction which he had. His oil was, as it were, brought down straight from heaven, whilst all other kings had to go to the chemist's shop. He was 'the most Christian king' of Europe who possessed so-called thaumaturgical, i.e. miracle-working and healing powers by which the royal *mystique* was considerably fostered. The French kings were also called 'the holy kings of France'. On the other hand, for a number of reasons, the feudal baronage of France did not present a common front and did not pursue a common policy. The accentuation of theocratic kingship was exemplified by the king's issuing his laws on the basis of the 'royal plenitude of power', by the Roman laws – though not under their proper name – exercising an incomparably greater influence upon the government in France than in England, by the adjustment of the royal coronation orders in which even the last pale remnant of a populist kingship (the Recognition) was cut out, by the frequent characterization of the king as 'king and priest', and by the personnel of the royal curia which was overwhelmingly staffed by professional jurists, which meant that they were experts in Roman law. The contemporary of Bracton in France, the eminent jurist Beaumanoir, writing in vernacular French, declared that, for a law to be valid, there was no need for a king to have the great council in attendance, because, as the jurist added, 'whatever pleases the prince should be held as law'. It was, furthermore, significant that the very term and concept of *souverain* was used by Beaumanoir in fixing the position of the king: the king, he said, was *souverain* over all barons, and for this reason he could make orders for the common good and profit as it pleased him. It is, consequently, not surprising that the idea of the king's being an emperor in his realm – *rex in regno suo est imperator* – was voiced several times in thirteenth-century France: since the sum-total of all sovereign rights was held to have been present in the (ancient) Roman emperor, the formula well expressed the theme of sovereignty in the language with which all the French jurists were familiar, in that of Roman law. The French king was also credited with having 'all the laws in his breast'.

The pronounced theocratic conception of French kingship made the French king particularly vulnerable to papal interventions, which the English kings at the turn of the thirteenth and fourteenth centuries were able to ward off by shielding themselves behind the Crown. The great conflict between Boniface VIII and Philip IV at the very time touched off a whole spate of publicistic literature strongly arguing on behalf of the king's rights *vis-à-vis* the pope. The tracts were partly written by the king's ministers and partly anonymously by Masters of the University of Paris. The participation of the educated laymen is noteworthy. Since feudal kingship was so weakly developed in France, the argumentation was bound to proceed on the level of theocratic kingship. Perhaps one of the ablest defences put up for the king was that in the *Disputation between a Clerk and a Knight,* conducted in dialogue form. Once again the argument centred in the papal plenitude of power and the comprehensive law-creative power of the pope, which indeed had just been proclaimed with aggressive vigour by Boniface VIII. The knight (who is obviously meant to have the better of the argument) concentrated on the sovereign power of the pope and denied that Christ ever had intended the pope to have any such powers as those claimed for and by him. The knight's chief theme was that dominion was a pre-

supposition for making the law, but the pope had no dominion,* for he was no more than a spiritual Ruler to whom the
law should be repugnant. This was the old opposition to the
pope as law-giver, and the author of the tract did not give
the clerk much chance to argue on this. His only concession
was the assertion of papal jurisdiction in cases of sin.

Surely, sir, it cannot be denied that the Church has jurisdiction
over sin, and, since this is so, this jurisdiction relates to justice and
injustice, but if the latter concerned temporal matters, it is clear that
the pope is judge over these matters.

This argument was not really answered by the knight, who was
made to retort that, if the pope were a superior in everything,
this would be an absurdity: it was nonsense and cannot be
proved by Scripture. The knight then goes over to the attack
by emphasizing what great protection the clerks enjoyed in the
kingdom.

Whilst the kings fight risking their lives and property, in order to
defend you, you lie in the shade and dine luxuriously – then, you
may indeed call yourselves lords, whilst kings and princes are your
slaves.

Old ground was traversed again, though this time with characteristic French punch and sting.

Another tract of this time warrants a few remarks. It was
also a short tract, also anonymous, though it is not unlikely
that Pierre de Flotte, one of the king's ministers, was its author.
It has no title – or the title has been lost – but begins: 'Before
there were any clerics (*Antiquam essent clerici*) the French
king was the guardian of the realm.' The significant feature
of this tract was that it attempted to supplant the ideological
superiority of the clergy by a chronological priority of the
king, and, above all, by roundly declaring that as members of
the kingdom they had certain duties which they could not
escape. He insisted that everyone was to do his share in the
promoting of the common good, but if the clergy refused to
pay taxes – and it will be remembered that the conflict between
pope and king was over clerical taxation – they abused their

* Cf. above, p. 125, for another theory of dominion.

position, for, instead of helping those who needed financial contributions for the sake of the public good, they feasted and lived a sumptuous life. Moreover, by not paying taxes they exposed themselves to the charge of high treason, the crime of *lèse majesté*.

No doubt, the underlying assumptions of this tract breathed a new spirit that upon closer analysis would reveal the infiltration of a good deal of new philosophy of law and the State. It was this new philosophy which was so dexterously (and yet paradoxically) harnessed by the French king against the papacy: and the result was a resounding victory over the pope. The significance of this last-mentioned tract lay precisely in that its author considered the clerics as citizens of the State that had existed before there were any clerics, and for this reason they had to contribute to the maintenance of the State, even if only by paying taxes. It was the incipient idea of the State which the French writers of the early fourteenth century manipulated and which was responsible for the profound changes which were to come about in all matters affecting the government: it was the period in which the idea of the State emerged and with it also political thought proper. In order to explain this, it is necessary to review briefly the impact of Aristotelian ideas in the late thirteenth century.

CHAPTER 6

THE REVIVAL OF ARISTOTLE AND ITS BACKGROUND

I. PRACTICAL MANIFESTATIONS OF THE ASCENDING THESIS

THE influence of Aristotle from the second half of the thirteenth century onwards wrought a transmutation in thought that amounts to a conceptual revolution. In fact and in theory the Aristotelian avalanche in the thirteenth century marks the watershed between the Middle Ages and the modern period. The question that confronts us here is this: given the strength of the theocratic-descending form of government in the Middle Ages and the kind of Christianity that underlay the prevalent governmental conceptions, how is one to explain the – by any standards – rapid advance of Aristotelian ideas? No theory, however consistent or convincing it may be, can have much hope of being accepted if the soil for its acceptance is not prepared. In order to explain why Aristotle so quickly captured the attention of thinkers and also partly of governments, it is necessary to refer, however briefly, to some popular features of medieval social life. It was in the preparation of the soil for the receptivity of Aristotelian ideas that the manifestations of a practical medieval populism became historically significant. Without them, it would be hard to explain why the ancient philosopher caused the conceptual revolution that followed.

However much the theocratic-descending theory of government was loudly, officially and unofficially, proclaimed as the only form of government compatible with Christian beliefs, the lower regions of society in many respects acted in a manner which did little to implement any of the basic principles of descending governments. On the contrary, even the few records we have about the activities of the people far below the vision of those sitting on elevated thrones show that they carried on what can only be termed as a natural way of conducting affairs. Yet the Rulers themselves, precisely because their contacts with the people were so few, did not take much cognizance of what was going on 'down below'. Nor did their activities attract the attention of learned writers. And yet, if a closer study were made of the 'ordinary' way of life of the 'lower' sections of the populace, it would be found that they acted very much on the ascending principles of government, which, from a universal-historical standpoint, seems to be more germane, if also not more natural, to the unsophisticated than the highly complex and intellectual descending theory of government. The manner in which the lower strata of society managed their own affairs is significant as a vital bridge between properly medieval ideas of government and the more modern political theory. In the lower reaches of society one can detect the actual harbingers of the theoretical and abstract political theses with which the modern age is familiar. Where a feudal kind of government was practised, it too, for the reasons indicated in the last chapter, considerably prepared the ground for the new orientation.

There in the lower regions one finds very much in evidence the popular association, which was not the result of any highfalutin theory and speculation; these numberless associations, unions, fraternities, communities, colleges, and so on, appeared as the answer to a natural urge of men to combine themselves into larger units. They pursued, partly, aims of self-preservation, partly, what would nowadays be called mutual insurances, partly, sectional interests – but, whatever their aim, the unions provided, so to speak, a shelter for the individual. But the organization and structure of these associations was based on the ascending theory of government: it was they, the members themselves, who managed their own affairs. The unions were populist enclaves within a theocratically governed kingdom. For instance, the village communities regulated their own affairs without any direction 'from above': times of ploughing, harvesting, and fallowing were fixed by the village community itself, which also arranged for the policing of the fields. Water supply, utilization of pastoral lands, the use to be made of rivers, wells, brooks, etc., compensation for damage to crops by cattle or fire, for damage to woods by unlicensed timbering, and so on, were subjects of regulations made by the community itself. The same applied to quarries, smithies, tileries, potteries, where working conditions were fixed. The mechanics by which the 'officers' of the village community came to be created were simple enough, and yet, incontrovertibly, proved the ever active urge to self-government. The mayor no less than the other 'functionaries' were elected by a community small enough to dispense with any idea of representation. Precisely because they had no aspirations towards 'great matters of State' they remained unnoticed by the governments.

With still greater force these considerations applied to the government of towns. Though a town to become 'free' had to have a royal charter, the government of the town was conducted entirely on the principle of the ascending theory. The very existence of a town council seems to be a pointer towards the implementation of the theory. Apart from that, there were numerous leagues of towns combining themselves for particular purposes, especially in northern Italy, and the beginning of the thirteenth century showed how carefully the process of electing town officials was regulated. England, too, offers excellent examples of how, for instance, at Ipswich in the early years of the thirteenth century the community of the borough itself elected their own bailiffs and the twelve sworn capital port men. Similarly, the proliferation of guilds and fraternities in the towns was a sign of the ineradicable urge of men to govern themselves. They were to all intents and purposes autonomous bodies and it makes very little difference whether they were guilds of artisans, merchants, or journeymen. What is clear is that the idea of consent was here very much in evidence. Again, there was no theoretical discussion, but all the more practice. It is also against this background that one can understand the prevalence of customary law in the medieval period. The very existence of customary law was in fact proof of the efficacy of the popular will which could be, as indeed it was, viewed* as tacit consent manifesting itself in practices and usages.

* See below, p. 215.

A critical analysis of the practice of the descending theory indicates that, despite its fundamental thesis, the 'people' (in whatever sense the term may be taken) were a necessary part of its implementation. For instance, to further his programme, Gregory VII appealed to the lay masses to boycott the services of married clerics; before him the German Conrad II had appealed to low-ranking forces in Italy. In the twelfth and thirteenth centuries we find appeals issued by popes and emperors to the masses, above all, in the matter of the crusades. What these instances made clear was that the descending governments had to enrol the support of wide masses, and to this extent implicitly acknowledged that their own fundamental theory somehow relied on popular support, that is, on the consent of the populace. Governments needed the cooperation of the masses, and cooperation presupposed consent and agreement with the programme. The crusades were large-scale movements of masses in the pursuit of an ideological programme. It is readily understandable that, when once the multitudes are called upon the plane, they are difficult to remove. Once again the paradox emerges, that is, that the multitudes were appealed to in order to serve theocratic governments. Because a number of 'freedoms' were conferred on the crusaders – exemption from civil debts and civil prosecutions, admittance to the papal 'family', etc. – the appetite of the people was whetted, and yet it was full of potential danger to the kind of government which this popular release was to support.

It is also from the standpoint of opposition that the amorphous multitudes assume importance in this context. There were on the one hand popular uprisings, local upheavals, and peasant revolts, and on the other hand there were the heretical sects which clearly manifested a spirit of populism: they were 'disobedient' to 'superior' command and showed that in their view the ecclesiastical hierarchy had disregarded what seemed to be fundamental tenets of Christianity; hence the battle-cry of a return to primitive Christianity and apostolic poverty. Once again, it was the ineradicable human urge to form one's own judgement and act upon it, a thesis that had since the fifth century been stigmatized by the 'establishment' as a sign of intellectual arrogance, because in the place of Authority was put the judgment of the heretics themselves. For the very concept of opposition embodied the right to condemn the thing opposed. The conduct of their own affairs revealed rather markedly populist elements: they assembled in 'conventicles', elected their own officers, and themselves appealed to the masses by itinerant preaching and provoking the 'establishment' to dispute with them in public. It was evident – the ferocious steps taken by theocratic governments against heretics bear it out – that, however amorphous, ill-organized, and scattered the heretical movements were, they were none the less dangerous and vicious manifestations of a spirit of independence. True, the attempted independence showed itself in religious terms, but, then, it was upon religious terms that the whole theocratic system rested and it was due to the recognition of the wider implications that the governments took such harsh measures against them. That they were denied the appellation of 'faithful' would in fact seem to accord with their own aims and intentions.

The papacy in particular (under Innocent III) was fully alive to the implications. The recognition of itinerant preachers by this pope implied that the multitude was to be reckoned with. The means which the Friars – the Dominicans and Franciscans – adopted were in fact those used by the heretics: to roam about in tattered clothing, to provoke public disputations, and do in general what the heretics had done, with this difference, that the Friars were to propound and preach orthodox doctrine. But what mattered was that the papacy was forced to take the multitudes seriously, and the Friars' movement was designed and promoted to deal with the multitudes which had emerged as a social factor. Once again, it was the towns which demanded increasing attention, for the large concentration of people within their walls facilitated and encouraged easy exchange of opinion and contact. Understandably, the Friars concentrated on the town populations. What is of immediate interest is that the Friars, especially the Dominicans, became thereby personally acquainted with the actuality of social life. It was no coincidence – on the contrary, it was historically conditioned – that it was the Dominicans who opened the thirteenth-century world to the welter of new ideas, and these were the ideas which were to imprint their stamp upon subsequent centuries.

II. INCIPIENT HUMANISM AND NATURAL SCIENCE

For a fuller appreciation of the background of the Aristotelian reception, some other features which in themselves had little to do with 'political' theories are relevant. There was the strong North Italian communal movement, significant because in the city-statutes the half-forgotten and ancient concept of the citizen (*civis*) was an operational instrument. Without much doctrinal elaboration the statutes took for granted the thesis of citizenship, the concept which was crucial to the ascending-populist theory. The point here was that in Italy familiarity with the Roman law (which was never lost) facilitated greatly the absorption of the concept of the citizen, of him who was autonomous and independent and who stood in such sharp contrast to the subject (the *sub/ditus*) that was a mere recipient of the laws given to him. The *popolo* as the aggregate of the citizens had succeeded in establishing its sovereignty. But the rest of Europe was not unfamiliar with the concept, since the inhabitants of every city were called *cives*, to whom the king addressed his charters. It is well to bear in mind that a perfectly harmless term, such as 'the citizen', greatly assisted the process by which this term could become the core of a significantly new theory: the linguistic usage of a term proved itself an important bridge between the medieval and indifferent meaning and the later pregnant substance of the citizen as the bearer of rights (and no longer the mere recipient of favours).

In the literary scene of the thirteenth century some significant changes also began to be discernible. Formerly the literary language was Latin: now from the thirteenth century onwards vernacular language came into its own, the language that was understood by the less literate and the less educated. Latin no longer seemed sufficient to express those feelings which mattered most: it was inadequate to give vent to the subtle modulations of human feelings. On the other hand, it was the very naturalness, the very humanity of the vernacular which, because it was natural, enabled the writer to convey the naturalness of human emotions and affections and to reveal psychological insights for which the Latin would have sounded banal. Latin was quite adequate for learned treatises, for abstract thought, for the mathematical scheme of logical and syllogistic deductions, but it was not the language of the ordinary human being. Latin was perfectly tuned in to the conceptual manner of argument with its algebraic equations, but it hardly ever reached the level of common humanity. Ordinary man thought in his own language, in his own vernacular, and his feelings could be expressed adequately in that language. The incipient subjectivism in the thirteenth century, the orientation towards the individual, stood in closest proximity to the rapidly rising vernacular literature.

In the thirteenth century respectable progress was also made in natural science. And, once observation and experiment as means of investigation came about, the scholastic method of inquiry, characterized by deduction from first principles,* had lost its monopolistic role. For observation and experiment worked on inductive principles, and they were concentrated on the phenomena of nature itself. Within this framework it was useless to rely on Authority because, so it was said in the late thirteenth century, this induced merely 'credulity' with which no useful investigations could be pursued. The Oxford naturalists of the thirteenth century were the equals of the medical scientists at Bologna and Montpelier. The significance of this development was that physical man himself, the *homo*, and not the Christian or the faithful, was the object of investigation. This somewhat radical departure from the accepted way of thinking explained the emergence of a new class of scholars who joined the company of the theologians and philosophers proper. What attracted the former was natural man as he was, and not the so-called re-born man, the baptized man, who alone had hitherto mattered. The monopoly of the theologian and philosopher who considered exclusively the Christian was

* See above, pp. 18, 120.

broken. The Christian man had now to share his limelight with the natural man, with him whom he was supposed to have supplanted.

In the visual arts the same manifestations of the creative spirit were discernible. Attention was focused upon the individual, upon man as he was in nature and in reality, and correspondingly less on 'the new creature', the Christian. Thirteenth-century sculpture and portraiture demonstrated this emphasis on the individual features, and the style has well been characterized as 'Gothic filled with the spirit of the Renaissance'. Early medieval portraiture and sculpture as well as manuscript illuminations presented mere types of man: it was to a large extent stereotyped portraiture, which showed hardly any individual features of the subject depicted. But now this abstract typified image – representing in truth no one human being in particular – began to give way to the portrayal of a human personality in all its substantial individuality and realistic concreteness. It was the individual trait that supplanted the objective, abstract norm which was to have been represented. What furthermore is noteworthy is that the attempt was made to paint a landscape as such: perhaps nothing illumines the medieval orientation towards the norm, towards an abstract image, better than the aversion from painting landscape itself. Again, in the thirteenth century this artistic genre came to be considered a worthwhile subject for the artist.

The searchlight in the thirteenth century was turned towards that part of the individual which had lain for so long in the shadow. We may recall that what mattered in all medieval thought was baptized man, the 'new creature' that was reborn as a result of the working of divine grace in baptism. The Christian had, so to speak, suppressed 'the man of nature', natural man as such, who by baptism was raised on to the level of a creature partaking in the divine attributes themselves. He became thereby a faithful who subordinated himself to the law given to him. As a Christian he stood on a level different from that of mere man. In widely differing fields throughout the thirteenth century a rather pronounced stress on Man himself, on the (Pauline) man of nature could be observed. It was as if a new continent had been discovered – the discovery of man's real nature – and a new subject-matter was revealed. With every justification has it been said that there was a Renaissance, a re-birth of the long-forgotten natural man. This re-birth of man, who had been for centuries overshadowed by the faithful Christian, had, as we shall presently see, far-reaching effects in the sphere of governmental science. The point of reference in the case of the Christian was his faith; in the case of the natural man it was his humanity. The two – man and Christian – began from the thirteenth century onwards to correspond to different categories altogether. What applied to the one need not necessarily apply to the other. The vacuum which the re-born man (the Christian) had left was filled: natural man was awakened from the slumber of centuries.

It is against the backcloth of the various manifestations of the human spirit (literature, poetry, the arts, natural science, etc.) that the impact of Aristotle becomes more easily understandable. The intellectual soil was ready for the fertilization with Aristotelian ideas, and this applies with particular force to the sphere of public government. In vital respects Aristotle provided the theory for what was observed in practice.

III. ARISTOTELIAN PRINCIPLES

The impact of Aristotle's theories of government revolutionized the thinking concerned with basic conceptions of society and its government, and in fact produced such a radical change that we are still not in the position to grasp its extent fully (H. Mitteis). The one-sided, speculative, monolithic thesis of society and government was to find a perfect complement. There were three quite distinct phases in the development of Aristotle's reception: (1) hostility towards him; (2) the accommodation of his doctrine within the Christian framework; (3) his gradual release from the Christian garb.

The main tenets of Aristotle, as far as they are relevant to our topic, should be briefly set out. His doctrine culminated in the view of the State as the supreme community of citizens, which was a product of nature, the result of the working of the laws of nature, and not the result of any agreement, contract, or convention, or, still less, of any specific act of foundation. And the laws of nature which brought forth the State were to Aristotle germane to man himself. He was born with them and they determined him to live in a self-sufficient, independent, autonomous community, the State, without which man could not exist – only beasts and gods could – and within which he could achieve his own perfection. Man was by nature a political animal. The State to him was the consummation of all other natural unions, such as the family, the village, the town, etc. Two essential things here were the natural growth of the State from below, that is, a community that was constituted by all the other smaller communities, and the naturalism of the State. Both features were vital points, and particularly the latter.

Aristotle's thought was pervaded by the idea of nature as the driving force, which was conceived in teleological terms: 'Nature does nothing superfluous', or 'Nature behaves as if it foresaw the future', or 'Nature does nothing in vain', were some of his often recurring statements which, with their strong teleological bias, could hardly fail to fall on receptive ears – and yet, what a difference there was between his and the traditional teleology: the laws of nature determined man's thinking and reasoning capacity. The hallmark of animals was their blind obedience to their natural proclivities: the hallmark of man was the employment of his will and reason by which the laws of nature were to be expressed, and the reasoned transformation of the laws of nature into a common will was the hallmark of man's State. Right and wrong were determined by man's insight into, and understanding of, what nature itself demanded. Man's reasoned will was therefore indissolubly linked with his nature. The fixation of right and wrong, of which animals were incapable, was the result of man's reasoning power. Consequently, nature working through the vehicle of human will and reasoning not only brought forth the State, but also determined its path. Since nature willed 'the good', Aristotle argued, and since the State was the supreme expression of all human associations, it followed that the State aimed at the highest good.

The instrument by which this aim could be achieved was, for Aristotle, the law, that is, the articulated will of nature pronounced by the citizens. The statement of Aristotle that

the principle that the multitude ought to be supreme rather than the few best could be satisfactorily proved,

has always been hailed as a most important thesis of Aristotelian thought (Oncken, Pohlenz, Knauss, E. Meyer, etc.). In other words, the popular assembly was the 'sovereign' ('supreme' in Aristotle's diction) which aimed at the promotion of the common good. The citizens possessed the natural right to partake in administration and the government of the State, their State. It was the autonomous character of the State which he stressed, or in his own words:

He who has power to take part in the deliberative or judicial administration of the State is said by us to be a citizen of the State, and generally speaking *a State is a body of citizens sufficing for the purposes of life.*

There was, however, according to Aristotle, a conceptual difference between man and the citizen.

It is evident that the good citizen need not necessarily possess the virtue which makes him a good man,

though in an ideal State there would be no distinction. The citizen operated on principles which belonged to the political and legal order, whilst man operated on norms pertaining to ethics. The good citizen was he who, according to the constitution, fulfils the demands made by the political order; the good man fulfils the demands made by a moral code. (A saint therefore could be a good man, but a bad citizen.) This sharp conceptual contradistinction between man and citizen was to be of crucial importance: it broke down the monolithic structure, it broke down the oneness and the 'totalitarian' or wholeness point of view, and considered the individual person from at least two angles, the political and the moral. And, when once the implications of this dichotomy were understood, the consequences also followed: first, the separation of the Christian from the citizen, and from man; and later ensued the further categorization into social, economic, cultural, etc. norms, each with its own set of principles. It was nothing but the atomization of man's activities.

The Aristotelian State grew and was subjected to the principles of natural evolution. It took account of the multifariousness and variations and diversities of the human-natural development. The contrast to the prevailing christocentric theme is so obvious that no comment is called for: the Church as the all-embracing body of lay and clerics was founded and instituted by a specific act of divinity. The contrast between the two points of view, as far as they related to government, can be expressed thus: the one governmental system, the descending, derived its substance from a principle, from a norm laid down by an a-natural organ, aiming at unity and uniformity; the other, ascending, started from the multiformity of natural manifestations and took them as the basis of its thesis. The one system related to the other world (life in this world was merely preparatory); the other system related to this world alone which was its goal.

There were nevertheless considerable obstacles to the influence of Aristotle, whose works had become available in the early thirteenth century. His *Politics* on which the above sketch is based, contained the application of his general philosophical and ethical theses: it was impossible to accept the one without the other. His was a system, and not just a conglomeration of disparate elements: his work was hewn of one stone. There was possible either total acceptance or total rejection. Another difficulty was that his works had become available through Jewish and Arabic versions, and not in the original text. Also a number of his presuppositions appeared quite unacceptable, as, for instance, his views on the continuity of evolution and his theme of causality, thereby precluding any view on the absolute beginning of the world, hence on the divine creation of the universe. Moreover, this theory of causality excluded the working of miracles, because to him every event had to have a traceable cause accessible to human reasoning. Nor could Aristotle's view on immortality be easily reconciled with the Christian view on the immortality of the soul. What he conceived by nature by no means corresponded to the traditional (Augustinian) view on nature. True enough, Jewish and Arabic thinkers had to face the same difficulties, which they resolved by separating theology from philosophy, but this was not a way that commended itself to Christian writers, according to whom philosophy was the 'handmaid' of theology (St Anselm), understandably enough if the totalitarian or wholeness point of view of Christian thought in the Middle Ages is taken into account. That the papacy opposed the study of Aristotle, especially of his *Metaphysics* and his *Physics*, was understandable, and especially so at Paris, where Averroistic, that is Arabic, teachings of Aristotle had caused a considerable stir.

Gregory IX forbade therefore the study of Aristotelian works at Paris, until his works 'were examined and purified'. The Dominican Friars suggested themselves as the most suitable to undertake the work, and it was the triumvirate of the Flemish William of Moerbeke, the German Albert the Great, and the Neapolitan Thomas Aquinas, which undertook this gigantic task. The translation provided by Moerbeke proved itself a worthwhile text upon which subsequent writers could draw. It is perhaps particularly significant that when Moerbeke came to the Greek term *politheuesthai** in Aristotle's *Politics* he had to coin a new Latin term, since – most significantly – there was no Latin word available for what Aristotle had wished to convey, and Moerbeke chose *politizare*, admittedly a clumsy and inelegant word, but one which indicated the meaning underlying the word. It was, as far as can be ascertained, the first time that a particular human activity was seen to have a particular political content. And it should also be kept in mind that through Moerbeke's translation there also began the triumphant career of other concepts and terms – for instance, *politicus* (political) or *politia* (government) – with which his contemporary world had not been familiar.

It is illuminating to see how the concept of natural law was viewed before Aristotle exercised influence. In general, in the traditional lore both the idea of nature and of natural law

* The term meant 'to act as a citizen', or 'to take an active part in public affairs'.

were speculative theorems and were parts of the whole Christian cosmology. Hence the treatment which the concepts received was embedded in the web and incrustations of the prevalent Christian outlook. But the great publicist writers of the eleventh century did not operate with nature or natural law, although Isidore of Seville in the early seventh century had tried to give a definition of the concept of natural law. Gratian, who has attracted our attention in a different context, presented the common doctrine of natural law concisely when he declared that 'the natural law was that law which was contained in the Old and New Testaments, according to which everyone was enjoined not to do to others what he did not wish to be done to himself'. Clearly, for him, natural law stood in closest possible proximity to divine law, and hence he also considered that natural law 'began with the creation of the rational creature' by God. This natural law was not the law of nature, but the law of God. It had little to do with observable phenomena; man himself was not the creation of nature, but of God. Natural and ecclesiastical laws were, in this system, conceived to flow from the divine will; hence also, from this point of view, the understandable claim of the papacy to rule non-Christians, because they were divine creations.

In its essence the natural law conception of the twelfth century was no more than the doctrine of St Augustine presented in summary form. His views, too, were closely linked with the idea of creation and culminated in the purely abstract theme that 'nature' signified the original and uncontaminated state which a thing had through its divine creation. Whatever evil a thing may have was nothing to do with its nature, and was against it. Evil was to him a perversion of the natural order, because 'nature' did not contain anything evil. Hence man's original natural state was that of innocence, knowing neither evil nor death. 'God did not create death' the Old Testament had declared, and therefore St Augustine held that death was contrary to the 'laws of nature'. It was the Fall which vitiated the true nature of man, who thereby became warped. What appeared natural in man, according to St Augustine, that is, growth, decay, death, passions, etc., was, when measured by the divine order of things, against his nature. What could restore man's true nature, was the divine grace, and through Christ this restoration, this re-birth or renascence, could be effected – and then neither mortality nor misery nor sin nor evil would come about. From these premises one can perhaps understand how St Augustine arrived at the equality of men, community of property, brotherly love, and so on. It would also seem explicable why this view on nature and natural law did not lend itself to much practical application or theoretical elaboration. It was a pure abstraction that was divorced from what was commonly considered nature.

It was advisable to draw especial attention to that intellectual ferment of the twelfth century, because it effectively prepared the ground which was to be fertilized by Aristotelian doctrines in the following century. And the ease with which Aristotle influenced thirteenth-century thought was assisted further by the study of Roman law which contained Ulpian's definition of natural law: it is that law which nature taught all animals (hence not only mankind). Ulpian, one of the classical Roman jurists, also explained that the term *natura* was derived from *nasci* (i.e. to be born or framed by nature). This was an important signpost: the concept of nature was linked with growth, with evolution, and would not seem easily compatible with the rigid and static Augustinian point of view. This somewhat more 'natural' point of view began to influence also non-jurists, such as John of Salisbury, and the jurisprudential preparation was to exercise more and more influence. Apart from the facts which engendered the absorption of Aristotle's political theories, there was also a not inconsiderable doctrinal preparation, conditioned by the exuberance of jurisprudence in the twelfth and thirteenth centuries.

CHAPTER 7

THE NEW ORIENTATION

I. THOMISM

THE accommodation of the ancient philosopher to Christian cosmology appeared as one of the urgent tasks in the thirteenth century. Now that his works were available in competent translations the 'Great Synthesis' appeared as a feasible undertaking: it was begun by the Dominican Albert the Great and accomplished by his pupil, Thomas Aquinas. It is certainly true that, as one of the eminent experts on Thomas has said, no one before and no one after the thirteenth century had studied Aristotle as thoroughly as Thomas had done.* Indeed, the masterly elaboration of Aristotelian ideas and their weaving into the Christian set of ideas presupposed a mind of quite extraordinary width, perception, and depth. The power of his intellect produced a fusion of Christian and Aristotelian themes 'which entailed an infinity of nice distinctions in accommodating a pagan philosophy to Christian cosmology'.† Thomas created a synthesis of disparate and irreconcilable elements, which appeared to deprive Aristotelianism of those ingredients which, from a theocentric point of view, were considered harmful. The effect of this synthesis was that Aristotle could now be fully accepted as part of the contemporary intellectual setting – indeed, one can with every justification speak of Thomism as Christian Aristotelianism‡ within the present context.

The evolutionary concept of nature, physical reality, or actual being (as opposed to an idealized postulate) was Aristotle's basic idea. Frequently enough Thomas referred to the element of growth in nature which he also explained by the same etymology as Ulpian had done long before him, whence Thomas maintained the idea of physical generation of the living organism, and hence of physical birth. In closest dependence on Aristotle he told his readers that the idea of motion was inherent in nature which could be observed in moving bodies, for they must have an 'intrinsic beginning' in them-

* M. Grabmann.   † McIlwain.   ‡ Grabmann.

selves. His concept of nature was no different from Aristotle's:
it designated birth, growth, decay. This 'naturalistic' way of
thinking – observable, at the very time Thomas wrote, in many
other departments to which reference has already been made
– was nevertheless a new departure in purely philosophical
thought. In fact, the idea of nature as an element that contained its own force and its own principles of operation became
a most important instrument in Thomas's system of thought,
which enabled him to declare that this or that phenomenon
was 'according to nature', 'above nature', 'contrary to nature',
and so on. Setting out from the (originally Aristotelian) premisses, Thomas had no difficulty in applying them to society and
its government. The Aristotelian teleology regarding the operations of nature and the idea of the State as a product of
nature reappeared in the Thomist system; and so did the
Aristotelian definition of man as a 'political animal', which
Thomas improved by designating man also as a social animal,
so that his definition was expanded to man being 'a political
and social animal'. This refinement of man as a being which
was also a social animal Thomas derived from the ancient
(pagan) writer Macrobius who wrote at the end of the fourth
century. The concept of man as a political animal signified
the entry of the 'political' into contemporary vocabulary and
thought-processes. Thinking in 'political' terms became a new
mental category.

What, however, is of immediate interest is that, for Thomas,
man and Christian were conceptually different notions. Man
was a natural product, and as such demanded attention. His
naturalness was his hallmark, and as member of human
society he was a social animal. This emphasis on man, on the
homo, brought forth the Thomist conception of *humanitas*
which he considered to be the essential being of man himself.
The conception of *humanity* was not in the least original with
Thomas – Roman law was perfectly familiar with it, and so
were theologians who had discussed the humanity of Christ;
shortly before him the idea of humanity was employed by
Frederick II in his famous constitutions of Melfi (1231). But,
then, there were few terms in the whole Thomist edifice which

had no pedigree: this is indeed one of the secrets of success, that is, to employ more or less well-known terminology and yet to fill it with contents different from the accepted meaning. For nothing facilitates the progress of a new theory better than familiarity with its terminology, however much a familiar term may thereby have changed its meaning. This observation applies to the Thomist *humanitas* and his concept of man. Neither of these (and other concepts, we shall presently meet) was new: each was familiar, and yet the meaning he gave to them did not entirely correspond to the commonly accepted one.

The complement of man in organized society was the citizen. The citizen was man writ large. The citizen was, to Thomas, no longer the subject, the *sub/ditus*, who simply had to obey superior authority. It was Aristotle's definition of a citizen as one who partook in government which supplied the solvent and which made possible the release of the (inferior) subject from (superior) authority. For, we recall, sharing in government was precisely what was denied to the subject, nor had he any share in the making of the law which was given to him. The important point here is that Thomas, by absorbing Aristotle's ideas, effected in the public sphere not so much a metamorphosis of the subject as the re-birth of the citizen who since classical times had been hibernating. It is impossible to exaggerate the significance of the emergence of the concept of citizen: his re-birth was to be of crucial importance. That the 'new' concept made rapid headway cannot, in view of the historical situation, cause any surprise. Moreover the distinction drawn by Aristotle between man and the citizen reappeared in Thomas's system:

It sometimes happens (he said) that someone is a *good citizen* who has not the quality according to which someone is also a *good man,* from which follows that the quality according to whether someone is a good man or a good citizen is not the same.

The significance of this statement does not need any comment. It was the denial of what for want of a better term we have called the totalitarian point of view. It was a major step forward towards a new orientation. What applied to the one need not necessarily apply to the other. The citizen – political man – answered the description of a being different from mere man. Thereby the spectre of splitting up man's activities begins to be discernible and herewith the subjection of man to different sets of norms and postulates (political, religious, moral, economic, etc.).

Thomas Aquinas began not only to re-introduce, in theory, the concept of the citizen (as distinct from the subject), but also – and on the same Aristotelian basis – to introduce political science proper. *Scientia politica* to him was knowledge concerning the government of the State, which he called *civitas* or *civilitas*. In fact, both these concepts were intrinsically linked in Thomas's mind. Political science was to him the science of government as far as it related to the natural product, the State. As such it was primarily concerned with practical matters, and not with speculation. It was what he called *operativa*, that is, a science concerning itself with the actual doing of things and with putting theories into practice. Contrariwise, political science was not a science that merely recognized things without doing anything about them. And the basis of this 'operative science' was natural-human reason with which man was endowed by nature. This became the pivotal point in his system. This human reason received its direction and orientation from concrete experience which, he said, was especially noticeable 'in the natural things' as well as 'in moral matters'. Still more important, political science had its working principles within itself – it needed no outside agency to make it work – and hence he called political science the most practical as well as the most fundamental and 'architectonic' of all the sciences, 'aiming as it did at the perfect good in human affairs'. The birth of political science at once brought forth its human and practical character: it was human experience that counted and the observation of the natural–human elements, because political science, as he stressed, was part of the *human* sciences and therefore 'aimed at imitating nature'. Reality as it is, and not as it ought to be, was for Thomas the keynote of the new science. This realistic approach emerged in his statement, for instance, that 'the law can rightly be changed because of the changes of men's conditions, according to which different laws are required'. This indeed was a breeze of fresh air.

The introduction of a further new concept, that of the 'political government' (*regimen politicum*), was closely related to the premisses upon which Thomas worked. Perhaps the easiest way in which the full meaning of 'political government' can be understood is to contrast it with its opposite, which was the 'regal government' (*regimen regale*). In fact the two chief theories of government and law were pretty clearly stated in these two notions. The 'regal government', i.e. the theocratic form of government, Thomas considered to be characterized by the king's possessing 'full powers' and by his unaccountability for his governmental actions: this is, as we know, the traditional medieval king. But opposed to this was the 'political government', which for Thomas existed when the Ruler had his powers circumscribed according to the laws of the State. This ruler, hedged in as he was by the laws of the State – or as Thomas said in a different context 'restricted by positive law' – had little in common with the theocratic Ruler. On the contrary, Thomas very clearly approached the ascending or populist theory, and this quite especially when he spoke of the *status popularis* in connexion with democracy and 'the will of the people'. His definition of democracy left little to be desired: here operated the will of the people, because 'from the members of the people the leaders can be elected and their election belongs to the people'. And at once the principle of representation emerged: the leader 'personifies' the State, so that it can be said that 'what the Ruler of the State does, the State itself is said to do'. For practical purposes Thomas held that a mixture of a political and regal government would be the most suitable.

The advance made by Thomas is so great that any commentary seems superfluous. What had not existed before, a political science, had come into being. Something more must be said about Thomas's concept of the State. It was this which had not existed in men's minds, and it was this which could only come about when Aristotelian ideas were absorbed and his political theory was made the basis of further elaboration. Thomas held that it was man's 'natural instinct' which brought forth the State, that is, organized human society. Consequently, to Thomas, the State was a product of nature and therefore followed the laws of nature. It was 'natural reason which urges' this human association, and for the working of the State no divine or supra-natural elements were necessary, because it had all the laws of its own operation within itself. Since 'nature leaves nothing imperfect', Thomas called the State a perfect community and also 'the most perfect human association'. What generations of writers and governments had been seeking was now found in the simple application of the concept of nature. The State was, in a word, a natural thing, and herewith the conceptual gulf between it and the Church was opened up: the latter had nothing to do with nature, because it was founded or instituted by divinity. The State was a natural product; the Church a supra-natural product.

Thomas's definition of the State – 'the State is nothing but the congregation of men'* brought into clear relief its essential difference to its supra-natural counterpart, the Church, which was 'the congregation of the faithful'. This was the dichotomy between man and the faithful Christian. The State was a matter for man or the citizen only: it had neither in its origin nor in its working anything to do with any ecclesiastical authority. Being a natural product, it pursued aims which were inherent in its natural essence, and that aim was the well-being, the welfare, of its members. This aim could be guaranteed only if the State was independent, and self-sufficient. The State stood on its own feet, was still a living organism, and not yet an abstraction which it was later to become. Once again, Thomas did not invent the terminology – everyone was familiar with the term *civitas* – but what he did was to give the term a new meaning, and the success of a new theory is assured if it employs familiar terminology. To Thomas the State was a *corpus politicum et morale*, a body politic with moral

Civitas est nonnisi congregatio hominum.

179

ends which took into account the social habits and customs of its citizens. The Church on the other hand was a mystical body (*corpus mysticum*). Thomas gave back to the thirteenth-century world the ancient and yet forgotten concept of the State: it was a human body politic, in which indeed the accent lay on the human, that is, natural qualifications of its citizens.

Thomas's legal theory reflected these ideas. The enacted law, or what he called by the still novel term 'positive law', was derived from natural law, if it was to be law, that is, an enforceable rule. He stated explicitly that the force of the human positive law depended upon its correspondence with natural law, and in other passages he declared that positive law was determined by natural law. This standpoint is easily explicable. Since the State itself was a product of nature, its laws too must be derived from nature. The laws of the State were to Thomas the channels through which the natural law found articulate expression. What, however, was equally important to him was the view – intimately linked with the Christian theme – that divine law did not do away with human positive law, provided it was based on natural reason. To him all law was 'the rule and measure of human actions' and the ultimate source of all law was the eternal law of God, which was not so much a law as divine reason and intellect governing the universe. Every living creature had 'the impression of the divine light'.

According to Thomas, the point that distinguished the rational creature from the irrational was the former's ability to reason and therefore to perceive the eternal law of God, that is, the divine ordering of things. Man, through natural law, shared in the eternal law of God and consequently was, by employing his natural reasoning faculties, in a position to know evil and to know good. 'The impression of the divine light in us' propels this natural law that is implanted in us, and this natural law enabled man 'to be in possession of the natural principles of his actions'. In a different place he held that 'natural law was nothing less than the participation of the

rational creature in the eternal law'. This important statement explained his insistence that human law should not be
at variance with natural law, otherwise human law would be
a perversion or a corruption of the very idea of law as a means
of ordering life. His definition of law was

an ordinance of human reason for the common good, and the right
to ordain anything for the common good belongs either to the whole
community or to someone who acts in the place of the people;
therefore, the authority to establish a law pertains either to the
whole multitude or to a public person who has the care of the multitude.

The passage shows the teleological view he had of law (that
is, his view of its purpose), but it also shows that his definition
of law was applicable to both the populist and theocratic
theories of government. Nor was he any less explicit about the
enforceability of law – the hallmark of any law properly so
called – when he declared that the enforceable character of the
law consisted in the power to compel.

The ability to compel is possessed by the multitude (people) or
by a public person who has the right to inflict penalties (in case of
non-observance), and for this reason he alone can make laws.

The considerable space that Thomas devoted to the theory
of law can be explained by the function which he attributed
to the laws: they were the means by which the aim of society
could be achieved.

This sketch of the Thomist view on law should have clarified the specifically Christian ingredients of his ideas. But so far
we have concentrated on the 'natural' aspects of his theory,
which is, so to speak, only one half of it. The other half consisted of the supra-natural elements, and both halves must be
taken together for an adequate understanding of Thomist
theses. For he himself considered at all stages of his mature
writing that there were always two levels on which any discussion on political topics ought to proceed. This two-tier
system was indeed an imperative necessity if the Aristotelian
welter of ideas was to be accommodated within the Christian

structure. The traditional gulf between nature and grace was bridged by Thomas. There was no ambiguity in his thought about the efficacy of nature itself and of natural law – both did and could operate without any revelation or grace or divine assistance, because they followed their own inherent laws and these latter had nothing to do with grace. But – and this was the great step forward – whilst in the traditional doctrine there was a sharp contrast between nature and grace, in fact a very real dichotomy, with Thomas there was none of it: with him contrast and dichotomy gave way to a hierarchy of different orders, so that the two opposites were to be seen as two hierarchically differently placed orders, the one the natural, the other the supra-natural. Hence, so far from being hostile to each other, nature and grace were to be viewed as complementary. This was the meaning of the often quoted statement of Thomas that 'grace does not do away with nature but perfects it'.*

We can perhaps best grasp the advance in thought if we recall the hitherto prevailing doctrine that the miraculous effects of baptism resulted in doing away with the 'man of nature' and in bringing about 'a new creature'. Now with Thomas grace was not seen as an element which did away with nature, but on the contrary perfected it: grace was complementary to nature. Though there must be differently operating principles in nature and grace, these principles were not opposed to each other, but merely worked on two different levels. There was, Thomas said, a double ordering of things (*duplex ordo in rebus*), one was the natural, the other the supra-natural. The conceptual element which enabled him to view both the natural and supra-natural as two hierarchically different orders was his notion that God was the author of nature, that God was the supreme regent of the created world. In this conception lay, at least partly, the secret of his accom-

---

Gratia non tollit naturam sed perficit. It should however be pointed out that exactly a century earlier John of Salisbury in his *Metalogicus* (1.1) had a statement (which has not attracted attention at all) which clearly pointed to the same conclusion: 'Grace brings nature to fruition' (*naturam fecundat gratia*), but John of Salisbury said no more about it.

plishing the task of accommodating Aristotle to Christian principles. By not postulating a dichotomy but by creating two complementary stages (or hierarchical orders), he achieved a reconciliation and harmony where there was previously hostility. The inflexible contrast between nature and grace gave way to a more flexible and realistic dualism, a dualism consisting of nature and super-nature.

Corresponding to man (*homo* as such) in the individual sphere was the citizen in the public sphere, and each belonged to the natural order of things. The State itself was the congregation of the citizens, a product of nature. The complement in the supra-natural sphere was the faithful Christian, and the congregation of the faithful, the Church. Both the State and the Church were manifestations of the divine ordering of things, the former on the natural, the latter on the supra-natural level. This dualism – a natural body, the State, and a supra-natural body, the Church – entailed a quite drastic re-orientation in thinking which, understandably, jolted a number of Thomas's contemporaries still set in the traditional monolithic ways of thought. For instance, Thomas had no patience with the (old Isidorian) view on the effects of the Fall of man and the consequent justification of secular power, i.e. to repress evil: for Thomas the State was produced by nature and thus embedded in the divine order of things. Nor did Thomas have any words of condemnation for the States of the infidels or pagans: they exercised their authority legitimately, because their State was as much a product of nature as any other State was. The decisive point was that Thomism showed the conceptual existence of a human body politic, the State, a notion and an idea which had not been in men's minds before. For reasons which should be clear by now, a vacuum that had existed throughout the Middle Ages was now filled. The monopoly of the simple theocratic-descending theory of government and law was, at least conceptually, broken: the single pivot of an institutional foundation sufficed no longer. Thomas presented the thesis of divine working manifesting itself in nature and in revelation. The sole source of power was no longer Christ's statement to Peter, but could also be located in the natural community, the State. That this system was cosmic, is evident: it was applicable to non-Christian societies. The individual himself could be viewed from two angles, from the natural angle of man (and in the political field as citizen) and from the supra-natural angle of the faithful Christian.

Thomas taught, spoke, and wrote at the very time when the ascending theory of government and law had already found – as we have seen – permanent habitations in the numerous communities, guilds, colleges, associations, and so on, which practised what the Parisian master taught as a matter of doctrine. The ascending theory had already clearly manifested itself in many separate branches of intellectual and creative activities quite independently of each other – the incipient natural science and the arts had nothing in common; surgery and anatomy had nothing in common with the naturalism of the vernacular literature, and so forth. This was now supplemented by a theory in the field that was to become central to reflective man: the political field proper, and its science, which Thomas called architectonic. Admittedly, the Thomist system was a brittle synthesis which required rather delicate handling and which was by no means free from flaws, but there can be no gainsaying of its fructifying effects. The soil was ready for fertilization with these ideas, and quite especially as the most pronounced form of the descending theory of government, the papacy, had by that very time aroused a great deal of opposition if not hostility in many quarters. The Thomist synthesis provided also the ingredients of a full-scale attack on the very foundations upon which the traditional conception of society and its government rested. For it was all very well to insist, as Thomas did, on God as the author and creator of nature, but was it not possible to sever this link? It was barely a generation afterwards that this step of cutting the link between God and nature was taken. This appeared as the thesis that there was a natural law which was in any case valid and persuasive enough without any recourse to divinity, simply because the natural law was reasonable in itself. Indeed, the conclusion could be reached without undue effort that there was a natural law which would have existed if there were no God, and that it would be valid without any reference to divinity. Assuredly unwittingly, Thomas Aquinas opened the sluices to the fully-fledged attacks, first on the papacy, and then on any descending theory of government, attacks which were to usher in the age which had many of the appurtenances we like to call modern.

Note. It should perhaps be pointed out that the above sketch of Thomism, as far as it relates to our topic, is drawn mainly from the mature works, above all his *Summa Theologiae* and his commentary on Aristotle's *Politics,* which he wrote about two years before his death* and which reached Book III, lect. 6 only. In view of the quite incredibly high output it is not surprising that his earlier writings contain views which are difficult to reconcile with his mature opinions. It would have been miraculous if within his short span of life – he was barely forty-eight years when he died in 1274 – and within the enormous extent of his writings, there had been no inconsistencies. For instance, Boniface VIII's ending in *Unam sanctam* was a literal copying of Thomas's statement made in a small work and dedicated to Urban IV (1263).† In another work he held that in the pope Christ was corporeally present, hence the pope as a visible monarch combined both regal and sacerdotal powers, etc. The continuator of his commentaries on the *Politics,* his pupil at Paris and later bishop of Clermont, Peter of Auvergne, struck up quite radical naturalist chords, particularly in connexion with social and economic questions and problems connected with marriage. For instance, he held that, since the State had to be self-sufficient, it was imperative to limit the number of citizens, otherwise poverty would follow. Hence he advocated limitations in the size of families. Aristotle's suggestion of abortion was not endorsed, but in order to avoid over-population he suggested restrictions of procreation between the ages 37 and 55 with men and 18 to 37 with women, because then fewer children would be born. Beyond these age groups there should not be sexual intercourse with a view to procreation, but simply for the sake of health or for some other valid reason.

* Cf. M. Grabmann, '*Die mittelalterlichen Kommentare zur Politik des Aristoteles*', in *Sitzungsberichte München,* 1941, fasc. 10, p. 16.

† See above p. 115

II. THE UNIVERSAL STATE

The age of Thomas Aquinas was also the period in which the European importance of the empire visibly shrank. It had spent its energies in the death-struggle with the papacy, from which it was never to recover. True enough, the papacy also paid a very heavy price for its transient victory, but, for reasons irrelevant in this context, it disposed of greater resilience, and its decline was not so rapid or dramatic as the empire's. Even when, with the accession of Rudolph of Habsburg (1273), some semblance of order and peace was restored, the effects of the thirty years anarchy after the deposition (and excommunication) of Frederick II had left scars in the social fabric in Germany, Italy, Burgundy, no less than in Sicily, Hungary, and Poland. Thoughtful people began to ask questions about the justification of a universal Roman empire. Could it be justified at all? Why was there a universal empire? It was this kind of question which beset thinking men, and not without reason has this problem been called 'The problem of the Empire' (Cecil Woolf). That it vitally concerned the Germans is not difficult to understand. There are a number of tracts which appeared towards the end of the thirteenth and at the beginning of the fourteenth centuries and which gave the German answer to the problem. It cannot be said that these tracts greatly contributed to the development of political thought at the time. They were on the whole retrospective and introspective and did not put forward constructive plans. They did not reveal that the new learning had greatly exercised them.

For instance, Engelbert of Admont took great pains to show that the institution of the empire was both just and necessary. The reason for writing his tract *On the Origin and Purpose of the Roman Empire* was, as the preface tells us, that he had had a discussion with mature and learned men who questioned whether there was any need for it at all, now that the empire had proved itself a failure. He held that the empire was a factor that made for peace and justice in the world, provided that concord between it and the papacy could be established. This concord was necessary, he insisted, if the reign of Anti-Christ was to be prevented. This concept of the Anti-Christ in medieval writers always stood for disorder and the overthrow of established ways of life. The empire was also necessary for the propagation and defence of Christianity. He did admit that in the past the empire did not always achieve what it set out to do, but one could not expect perfect security in this world. Engelbert had no patience with those who asserted the uselessness, if not positive harm, of a Super-State, as the empire by definition was, because differences in language, customs, and race militated against this universal body politic. On the contrary, he maintained that all nations lived according to the natural law and employed those parts of the Roman law which were applicable to nations and kingdoms, from which thesis he concluded that all kings should be subjected to the Roman emperor. This universal ruler formed, for Engelbert, the apex of the pyramid, at the base of which stood the city, over it the kingdoms, and at the top the empire. This argument was not only the result of 'confusion of thought' (Gierke), but was also a rather superficial and incongruous argumentation based on slim acquaintance with Aristotle.

Written in the eighties of the thirteenth century, the tract of another German, Alexander of Roes, a canon of Cologne, arouses interest, because one finds in it a clear appreciation of the national tensions which came more and more to the fore. His plan was to provide a place for the three great nations on the Continent and thus reduce tensions. The occasion which prompted him to compose the tract was the election of the Frenchman Simon de Brion as Pope Martin IV in 1281. Alexander had joined the household of the Cardinal James of Colonna, who took part in the election at Viterbo. When Alexander found, at the mass said during the conclave, that, in the Roman missal which a papal functionary had put at his disposal, prayers for the emperor were expunged, he was provoked to wrath, which did not abate in the least when during the subsequent papal coronation at Orvieto he heard statements which were most displeasing and disconcerting to the German. He heard people say that the Germans should never have had the empire, because they were too barbarous, too undisciplined, and too domineering for this role; he also heard that the papal coronation was a real triumph for France and that, after all, Charlemagne was a Frenchman and that the Empire should belong to the French as the most excellent nation. It was this personal experience of Alexander which forced the pen into his hand and the outcome was the tract, which he called a *Memorandum* (*Memoriale*). Its purpose was to warn the world against the upheaval of which he had noticed unmistakable signs. All the old order, all that the world had treasured, was in danger of being overthrown. The Cologne canon made use of a good deal of his historical and biblical knowledge to show that it was God's will that the Germans were the rightful leaders of the world and should continue to be so, but he made some concessions to the other two nations. The Romans or Italians, he suggested, rightfully possessed the papacy, whilst the French had scholarship which was equally necessary for the well-being of Christendom. The University of Paris, the *studium* par excellence, was to be the third pillar upon which Western civilization (in the thirteenth century) was to rest. The proper ordering within Christendom was therefore that the Germans continued to govern it, whilst the religious leadership should be in Italian, and intellectual leadership in French, hands. This, Alexander protested, was the divine plan of saving Christendom from the Anti-Christ. He did not deny some independence to France, but it was part of a larger whole and as such had to take its place within a wider framework. On no account should France be allowed to stretch its hand out to imperial power or, which would be nearly as bad, to arrogate itself the papacy, for this would be a grave disturbance of the divinely willed order. 'In these three, papacy, empire, scholarship, as in the three elements of soul, body, and spirit, the holy catholic church lives, prospers, and grows.' Externally, too, 'the building of the Church could become perfect only when all three – the foundation, the walls, and the roof – were firm.'* These German answers to the problem of the empire did not excel either in profundity or in constructive thought, although Alexander's was illustrative of German sentiments,

* Cf. I Thessalonians, v,23.

with their appeal to Providence and to tradition; but whatever arguments the Germans employed, the result was always the same: the government concerning Christian Europe, world-monarchy as understood at the time, was to be theirs.*

'The Italian answer' to the problem of empire, Dante's *Monarchia*, occupies a very special place. It was more than a merely Italian answer and less than an idealized universal monarchy in poetic transfiguration. It was once again, and above all, a tract which was prompted by the exigencies of the time and exhibited all the traces of a period when the new had not yet quite arrived and the old not yet quite disappeared. It was looking backward, and yet also forward. It was both retrospective and prospective; or, seen differently, it was in part an answer to present needs, but it also contained a philosophy of politics. One might go further and say that while purporting merely to answer a concrete problem, he presented a philosophy of politics. It was the fruit of long deliberations on the part of a layman who was politically active as well as an exile. And all experience proves that banishment and exile sharpen political consciousness and stimulate creative thought as perhaps nothing else does. For, by brooding over the past, the exile looks into the future: whether the future belongs to him, is conquered or is merely influenced by him, is as often as not a matter of pure chance. Although Dante's claim in the preface – the work was written in the early years of the fourteenth century – that 'the knowledge of temporal monarchy is most important and least explored' and 'has been attempted by none', has caused some misapprehension, there is nevertheless a good deal of truth in his statement, that is, in regard to the ideas underlying his conception of universal monarchy. The work is divided into three books, and each deals with a particular point relative to his main theme. It seems best to give a short synopsis and then to sketch the underlying principles.

The themes of the three books are: (1) Was a universal

* It is perhaps not without significance that more than seventy manuscripts of this tract are still extant, which shows what demand there was for it; apart from this, there were numerous German translations from the original Latin.

monarchy justified? (2) Did the Roman people rightfully acquire the office of monarchy? and (3) Was the monarchic office derived immediately from God? As to the first question, Dante held that the well-being of the world and the conditions of human welfare were best served by a universal monarch, because he alone was in a position to guarantee the quiet and tranquillity of peace. The one Ruler was also the proper authority to secure unity of mankind. Standing as he did above the turmoil of petty princes, the universal monarch was an authority to whom recourse could always be had. 'Since the one (prince) may not take cognizance of what concerns the other (prince), the one not being subject to the other, for a peer has no rule over his peers, there must needs be a third with wider jurisdiction who is prince over both, within the compass of his right.' The argument which appeared to weigh most with Dante was that of justice as wielded by the universal monarch:

The monarch has naught that he can desire, for his jurisdiction is bounded by the ocean alone, which is not the case with other princes, since their principalities are bounded by others ... whence it follows that the monarch may be the purest subject of justice among mortals.

Nor could greed corrupt the monarch's judgement, since he had already everything that any mortal might wish. But apart from this, Dante considered, it was a matter of experience that 'what is capable of being done by one should be done by one and not by more than one'. These, and many other detailed statements and considerations, can be explained by the stark reality which confronted the world in Dante's time: Italy herself torn by internecine strife, so many of the hitherto unquestioned premisses being questioned, the lack of authority in public matters, the shortsightedness and egoism of rising potentates, and above all the national kings.

The remedy for all these ills Dante sought to find in the universal monarch. It may, however, be open to doubt whether his conception of a world monarch was in fact identical with the traditional concept of the (German) Roman emperor. To Dante that world monarch was not so much a governor in the customary sense as a coordinating organ endowed with coercive force, and therefore standing above and aside from the kings and other rulers who in actual fact had to do the governing. In some ways Dante's concept of world monarchy had some semblance with the papal monarchy, as it was originally conceived, and yet in other ways it was an early and premature attempt to nip the incipient concept of national sovereignty in the bud. Indeed, Dante's contemporary conditions were not unlike those of later times which produced organs and institutions dealing with matters which were of utmost concern to thinking men. But whilst in modern times* the answer to the question of the basic location of power and of the origin of political institutions does not present insuperable difficulties, and whereas means suggest themselves for creating such organs or institutions, no such readily available means existed in the early fourteenth century.

It was this last-mentioned difficulty which explains the second and third books of the *Monarchia*. For there remained nothing for Dante but to fall back on the obvious historical model, that is, the Romans. His arguments in this context could not make much impression on his contemporaries, for they operated on a typical medieval *petitio principii*. His conclusion was that the Romans had earned the empire – what no doubt fascinated Dante was the idea of the *pax Romana* and all its consequences, real or imaginary, through the judgment of God. It was, furthermore, and perhaps above all, nature which had made the Roman people rightfully possess world monarchy. 'And what nature has ordained, it is right to observe.' This could, in Dante's opinion, be demonstrated by the history of Rome: 'The Roman people was ordained by nature to command.' And consequently he could say that 'nature has ordained in the world a place and a people for universal command'. That the Roman empire was a legitimate universal monarchy followed also, so Dante reasoned, from the fact that Christ had suffered under Pilate, the emperor's vicar – an argument which betrayed traces of the Augustinian teleology of history.

* One has but to think of the League of Nations or the United Nations and the numerous agencies of international law.

One may suspect that this discussion of the Romans as legitimate holders of universal rulership was really only a preliminary to the question treated in the third book, whether the emperor was directly instituted by God. This he answered in the most affirmative sense. The supra-national authority of the universal monarch was a necessity to Dante (as he had tried to show in the first book), and this necessity now in the third book becomes a natural necessity. Once having taken this stand – which was no more than applied Thomism – there was no reason at all for any papal rights over the emperor's authority, and still less need for the making of the emperor by the pope. As he said, 'what is received from nature, is received from God', with the consequence that the emperor's authority was autonomous and independent of the papacy. Dante made this application of Thomism quite clear when he declared – in refuting the well-worn sun–moon allegory of the hierocratic party – that 'as to its *existence* the moon is in no way dependent on the sun' because the moon had its own motions, its own motor, its own operations. 'But with respect to the moon's *better* operation it does receive something from the sun, to wit, abundance of light by the receipt of which it operates with more virtue.' This was the Dantesque expression of the Thomist view that 'grace does not do away with nature, but perfects it', which is here utilized for the question of imperial authority. Continuing Dante stated: 'In the same way I say that the temporal power does not receive its being from the spiritual nor its authority', though for the better working the former could well profit from the 'light of grace which the blessing of the chief priest infuses into it'.

This standpoint of Dante's made it obvious that he had little patience with the usual hierocratic arguments. With an elegance and economy of words which only barely hide his withering contempt he brushes these hierocratic points aside; he is particularly acid about the canonists as the professional upholders of hierocratic principles: 'strangers and ignorant of all theology and philosophy ... volubly maintaining that the traditions of the Church are the foundation of the faith'. The idea of nature and natural law enabled Dante to dismiss the hierocratic papal plenitude of power, for 'with respect to natural operations, the successor of Peter has no divine powers'. The universal monarch, being a product of nature, was not created by the pope, 'since God could not in any way commit the power of creating (to the pope)'. The Donation of Constantine came in for a particularly severe handling by Dante, and so did the Two-Sword allegory and historical precedents, the latter 'amount to precisely nothing, for the usurpation of a right does not create a right'. Since the basis of Dante's thought was the natural conception of universal rulership and since his thesis was nothing but Thomism applied to the universal monarch, the sentence ending the work, which has caused so much misunderstanding, was nothing but the Thomist theme of nature and grace:

Let Caesar therefore observe that reverence to Peter which a first-born son ought to observe to a father, so that, illuminated by the light of paternal grace, he may with greater power irradiate the world over which he is set by him who is Ruler of all things.

Behind Dante's concrete solution there were several important general ideas underlying the tract. Dante set forth an unadulterated dualism of government – that the book was put on the papal Index of prohibited books where it remained until 1908, cannot cause much surprise – and in so doing he advanced political philosophy quite considerably. What the anti-hierocratic writers and governments, what the Salian and Staufen emperors could not achieve, Dante could, and he could because he had been given the natural tools, the tools which had become available since the Aristotelian absorption and the Thomist synthesis. Because they were unaware of it, the earlier anti-hierocratic thinkers left out the essential thing which Dante supplied: in natural things the pope's writ did not run, only in supra-natural ones. The earlier opponents could not book any success against the hierocratic party, because they spoke the same language, used the same Bible and the same similes, and worked with the same patristic equipment as their opponents did. The chief reason for their failure appears to be that their attempts at restricting the papal

plenitude of power always operated with biblical and theological arguments, and never with the natural order of things. In
some ways they thereby unwittingly subscribed to their opponent's thesis. The Thomist-inspired Dantesque principle of a
double ordering of things put the whole cluster of apparently
insoluble problems into a different light.

Dante did conceive of mankind as one unit, not made up
of Christians only, but also of Moslems, Jews, and pagans.
It was this body which he termed 'the human race', or simply
humanity (*humanitas*), or perhaps most significantly the human
State, the *humana civilitas* ; none of these terms was unfamiliar
to contemporaries. Perhaps nothing showed the advance made
by Dante better than a comparison of the meaning of his
civilitas with that of, say, John of Salisbury 150 years earlier.
John, steeped in classical culture, attributed to it the meaning
of civility or politeness or humane approach, whereas with
Dante the term meant the human race, mankind itself, in which
the accent lay on the citizens who composed it. And this *civilitas* was of natural origin where the natural laws of operation
were effective. The supra-natural complement was the body
of the faithful, the Church, *christianitas* itself. The double
ordering of things could not manifest itself better. The *christianitas* was 'not an effect of nature', hence different norms,
different modes of operation, different sets of principles were
applicable. Man pursued therefore a twofold aim, as a citizen
a this-worldly, as a Christian an other-worldly, end, the one
natural, the other supra-natural. In fact, we detect in Dante
the Thomist thesis that God's operations could be observed in
nature as well as in revelation. Dante's system was catholic,
and not specifically Christian. 'Humanity' and 'Christianity'
were two different conceptions. Above all, rulership was no
longer an issue or a result of the working of grace, but of
nature. Government belonged to the natural entity, the *humana
civilitas*. In this scheme of things there was nothing that could
be 'mediated' by the priests – the human State had everything
it needed for its working.

The humanizing, not to say, humanistic features of Dante's
tract emerge with all desirable clarity from his considerations

of human liberty and the exercise of the human will. The hall-mark of man he found in his intellectual powers, which were the guide and rule of all human matters and which presupposed the exercise of free will, in itself conditioned by the liberty of man 'which is the greatest gift God conferred on human nature'. Liberty alone assured for Dante that man would achieve felicity on this earth, because only that was free that existed for its own sake, and not for the sake of something or somebody else. The pursuit of human ends based as they were on the natural insight of man himself, in other words, the pursuit of humanity for its own sake – and not for the sake of some other-worldly aim – was Dante's theme. And that human activity which pursued these human ends Dante called *politizare*, that is, acting in a political manner with the aim of achieving human happiness. It was the unostentatious, unspeculative doing which mattered – 'our present matter (he said in the beginning of his book) is not primarily concerned with thinking, but with doing' – because it aimed at the practical realization of all the potentialities of humanity and man himself, for 'the function of any right government is to see that men exist for their own sakes'. Government in other words was service to the people – the government was 'the minister (servant) of all' (*minister omnium*). The significance of this term can be gathered best when it is compared with the traditional designation of the ruler as 'a minister of God'. Dante's thesis culminated in the release of humanity from Christianity, in the release of the human element from its specifically Christian incrustations. Man was re-born. He himself had once again become, after so many centuries, the pivot of *civic* life, and was thereby recognized as fully capable of mastering and shaping his own fate.

III. TERRITORIAL SOVEREIGNTY

The new orientation can further be exemplified by the development of the concept of the incipient State sovereignty. In one way this could also be regarded as an answer to the problem of the empire, though not quite in the sense in which the theoreticians envisaged it, and in another way this 'answer' was, paradoxically enough, the very thing against which Dante had protested. But this time it was no mere theory, it was stark legal reality which set the tone.

Throughout the latter part of the thirteenth century the principle was voiced in France that 'the king was an emperor in his realm'.* The meaning attached to it was that within his kingdom the king was sovereign, and this idea could be expressed suitably only in the language of the Roman law, according to which the emperor was the supreme, 'superior' authority. When first voiced, the principle had exclusive domestic application. It was to point up the sovereign status of the king *vis-à-vis* other potentates in France, and above all to stress that no appeal from his court to any other court in France was allowed: what pleases the prince has the force of law.

Apparently quite independently of the French development, there emerged a very similar body of opinion in the kingdom of Sicily, also in the latter half of the thirteenth century. It was here the jurists and scholars of the University of Naples – notably Marinus and Andreas de Isernia teaching between the sixties and the nineties – who put forward a thesis which yielded a result not dissimilar to the point of view advocated in France. To these scholars the (Sicilian) king was a 'monarch' in every sense of the term. Because his government was exercised over the territory of his kingdom, his laws could not display any force outside the confines of his territory, but inside the territorial confines were so fully operative that nobody could interfere with his government. They called this monarch 'free', precisely because he was unrestricted in the exercise of his authority within the boundaries of his kingdom. The Sicilian jurists argued mainly on the basis of the Roman law and its enactments concerning the territorially limited powers of a judge's jurisdiction: † for instance, no Roman judge could summon anyone from the district of another judge. These jurists concluded that the Sicilian king was excluded also from

*Above, p. 156.

† A feature similar to the ecclesiastical diocesan structure in which no bishop could issue orders which had effects outside his diocese.

the jurisdiction of the emperor, holding as they did that his authority was similarly restricted to territorial confines. Consequently no king could commit high treason against the emperor, because he was not a subject: both were 'sovereign' within their territories. But high treason presupposed that it was committed by a subject against 'superior majesty'. Apart from this, the conclusion was also implicit that an appeal from the king's decision or law to the court of another king or of an emperor was not permissible.

These views were soon to be put to the test, and the case which triggered off the final development combining the French and Sicilian theories became classic. The case itself was simple enough. On the occasion of his Italian campaign the Emperor Henry VII (in 1312) met not only military resistance by the forces of the king of Sicily, Robert the Wise, but also a situation in the towns which made it clear to him that the Sicilian king bore the entire responsibility for the hostility. Henry charged the king with high treason committed against him as emperor in that he had incited the Lombards and Tuscans to revolt against him, that he had concluded treaties of assistance with the rebel leaders and that he had expelled the German-imperial administration in Northern Italy. King Robert was summoned before the imperial tribunal at Pisa to stand his trial.* The king ignored the summons, did not appear, and in his absence was condemned for the crime of *lèse majesté*. The juristic problem was this: was the emperor by law entitled to take steps against the king? Could, above all, a king be summoned by the emperor before his court? Since the kingdom of Sicily was nominally a fief of the papacy, Robert submitted the case to the pope, who himself consulted a number of eminent jurists on the problem. Clement V (1305–14), in one of the most influential decrees the papacy had issued, officially and solemnly endorsed the point of view which was hitherto merely a doctrine, that a king was sovereign, that he could not be cited before a tribunal of any other king, not even before that of an emperor, and that as king he could not commit high treason against another king, because he was no subject.

*12 September 1312.

The matter was dealt with in the papal decree *Pastoralis cura* of 1313. In it the territorial conception was prominent. The pope laid down as a matter of law that a king could not be summoned by anyone, including the emperor, because the king was resident in his own kingdom, had his ordinary domicile there, and hence not even the emperor had any 'superiority' (sovereignty) over the king on territorial grounds. The exercise of public power was territorially confined and there was no organ that could legitimately exercise jurisdiction beyond that territory, with the consequence that one Ruler could not issue a summons against another. Hence also a king who was superior (sovereign) could not possibly commit high treason against another Ruler, since no Ruler was the subject of another Ruler. Pope Clement V's decree was significant in that (1) it was the first legal expression of the concept of territorial sovereignty, and (2) perhaps paradoxically, the universality of the emperor's rule, upon which the papacy had always laid so much stress, was denied: the emperor exercised no more than a territorially limited government.* There is no need to dwell on the all too obvious implications of this papal standpoint: it undercut the medieval idea of universality and set in its place the individual sovereign kings as lords who, indeed, could do within their kingdoms as it pleased them. The Roman law with its hallowed 'what pleases the prince, has the force of law' was also brought to play its part in a context, and for purposes for which it was certainly not originally intended. What was domestically, that is, in the territory of a kingdom, laid down or done by a Ruler was removed from the jurisdiction of another Ruler. That was the reason why the pope repeatedly stressed that the king had never left his kingdom and continued to reside within it and that, even if the accusations were true, there was no legal means of bringing him to book. The ideological and legal development at the turn of the thirteenth and fourteenth cen-

*According to earlier papal conceptions every king (who in this context was sometimes called a 'kingling' (*regulus*)) was subjected, at least *de jure*, to the emperor, a point vigorously made little more than ten years earlier by Boniface VIII: the French king should recognize that he was *de jure* subjected to imperial authority.

turies marked the beginning of the concept of State sovereignty, that is, of the State's own and exclusive competence to do what 'it pleases to do'. The development in the public sphere corresponded to that in the individual sphere: here, as there, the process of atomization took its course.

CHAPTER 8

THE SOVEREIGNTY OF THE PEOPLE

I. POPULAR BASIS OF THE RULER'S POWER

LESS than a generation after the death of Thomas Aquinas the fructifying effects of his stimulating theses could be observed. He himself had no opportunity of expressing himself on the concrete problems which engaged other writers of the time. We have already referred to the spate of publicistic literature which was occasioned by the bitter and acrimonious conflict between the pope and the French king, Philip IV.* It was this kind of ideological battle which prompted contemporaries to think out again, and to go back to, the fundamental questions of authority, law, and so on. But this time, and in contrast to the publicistic literature of the Investiture Contest in the late eleventh century,† the thinkers and writers had been given the tools with which the papal claims could be rejected and stigmatized as papal pretensions and interferences. The tools came from Aristotle's and Thomas's intellectual armoury.

One of the important and influential men who applied Aristotle and Thomas was John of Paris, a Dominican, who – like his great brother Dominican – lectured at the University of Paris. In the very early years of the fourteenth century he wrote a short tract, entitled *On Royal and Papal Power*. John of Paris was not so much a philosopher or theologian as what would nowadays be called a political scientist. Advancing political science proper, his book was an intelligent application of Thomist theories to reality, observable and concrete in his day. What characterized the book was its concise and trenchant argumentation, its lucid and unambiguous statements, and a comparative freedom from accumulating supporting authorities. With the help of Thomist principles he aimed to demonstrate the autonomous character of the kingdom.

The tract plunged straight into the crucial matter and dealt in its very beginning with the exposition of man and the State,

* See above, p. 156.   † Cf. above, pp. 116ff.

200

an exposition that was based on Thomist conceptions of nature and natural law. Man he defined as 'a political and social animal', and the eventual source of the government of the kingdom he found in natural law. This differed little from Thomas, but John went further when in the immediately following chapter he juxtaposed the Church to his concept of the kingdom. The Church to him was a mystical body pure and simple – a concept that had come more and more in evidence in the thirteenth century – and as such contrasted sharply with the natural body politic. Since the Church was purely mystical, its ministers had similarly purely sacramental functions. Negatively expressed, the Church was, for John of Paris, no organic, juristic body in the traditional sense: it could not, he held, legitimately intervene in the mundane life of the citizens themselves or issue orders to rulers. Quite the contrary was true: the sole function of ecclesiastical ministers was the administration of the sacraments to the faithful. John thus sharply distinguished between the natural body politic and the supranatural mystical body of Christ, the former held together by the bonds which nature itself had forged, the latter by the bond of faith which had nothing to do with nature. Consequently, by virtue of its natural origin, the State pursued purely natural ends: although nature was of God, it had nothing to do with the ecclesiastical hierarchy. The task of the king's government was to provide the means for the realization of the ends germane to the State; it had no qualification to lead the faithful to the supra-natural end. This was, after all, merely a spelling-out of Thomist theses.

The significance of the fundamental divergence between the natural and supra-natural entities lay in their respective operations. Being supra-natural, the Church needed not to take into account any of the natural divergencies which obtained between various countries and regions, nor was there any need for the Church to pay particular attention to the natural features, conditioned as they were by geography, climate, and language. The teachings of the Church could indeed be absolute, precisely because they did not deal with natural, but only with supra-natural matters. No limits could be set to the preaching by word which could safely disregard all the differences created by nature. On the other hand, John was very insistent on these limitations which nature imposed upon the government of the State. Whilst the keynote of the Church was absoluteness, the keynote of the State was relativity, for, as he said, what was good for the one community need not be so for others. There were different modes of living which justified different political institutions (*diversae politiae*). There was no such a thing as the right way of life for everyone, because natural conditions had in fact created different modes of living, and having been created by nature they must be 'right'. Modesty, enjoined by natural limitations, was the hallmark of the State. It was, he said, comparatively easy for the Church to demand the absolute and the unity of faith, for 'it is easier to employ the word than to use the hand', a statement indicative of a wholesome realism and also reminiscent of the retort which Peter de Flotte, one of the king's ministers, made to the pope; 'Your power is verbal, ours is real.'

The significance of the advance made by this tract lay in that the temporal could be equated with the natural, and the spiritual with the supra-natural. These were old nomenclatures: within the prevailing 'totalitarian' standpoint the dividing line between the temporal and the spiritual could never be found: generations of the ablest and most discriminating writers racked their brains to discover what constituted the line of demarcation – a futile beginning at best, and worthless mental gymnastics at the worst. But now the introduction of the concepts of the natural and supra-natural made the distinction a feasible undertaking. Since the temporal could be equated with the natural, it could indeed be said that it was autonomous, because it lived, so to speak, on its own laws which were those of nature. Moreover, it pursued its own end. In the previous doctrine the temporal was merely an adjunct of an auxiliary character to the spiritual; now the temporal became autonomous and important in its own right. The previous doctrine, which he did so much to demolish, John dubbed as 'a rustic and raw argument', no doubt a courageous statement in view of the official papal doctrine. It was no less courageous of him to brush aside the papal thesis of the plenitude of power and declare it a 'frivolous argument'. In the State, which he called a political community, ecclesiastical laws did not display any validity. Clerics were mere instructors of the faith and morals. They had no right to intervene – or rather interfere – in the possessions of laymen, for their property was acquired by their own labour, industry, and diligence, with the consequence that they had thereby obtained true dominion over their goods. In practice this meant that not even the pope had a right to place burdens on lay property by taxation or tenths and the like. This was a far cry from the traditional thesis that property was an issue of grace* and therefore within papal jurisdiction. What John wished to express was the distinction between the (enforceable law and (unenforceable) morals: clerics could give counsel and exhort the faithful, but coercive power they had none.

Since the political community, the State, was a natural product and since God had created the whole nature, the government in the State was eventually also traceable to God, but more immediately to the people. John was emphatic in asserting that there was no link between the Church and the State, for the king's power was derived from God through the election by the people. Still more articulate was the thesis of the people's sovereignty in his statement that the king came into power 'by the will of the people' (*rex est a populi voluntate*). The king's function was to preserve the social order, to improve living conditions within the kingdom, in short, to provide for the necessities of a good civic life. This thesis was a quite considerable advance on Thomism as well as a radical departure from the traditional descending theory of government. Here indeed we approach the proper ascending-populist theory of government. For John also transferred this theory to the prelates of the Church, who received their power 'from the electing or consenting people'. And the pope's governmental powers could be taken away by the people, because the material ingredient in the pope's power was the consent of the faithful and that consent could be withdrawn in the case of the pope's

*Above, p. 113.

203

ineptitude, insanity, uselessness, or for any reason that the people considered relevant. The underlying idea of John was that power could be acquired only with the consent of those who were to be governed. Just as the king was elected by the people, in the same way he could be deprived of his power by the people: the deposition of the king was a matter for the people. The old Pauline thesis that the prince did not bear the sword without cause was now turned upside down: he possessed the sword so as to ward off with it any interference by clerics. This was the origin of the French proceedings known as *appel comme d'abus*, which was an appeal from the ecclesiastical court to the king's court (or to parliament) for alleged abuse of clerical power (in some ways it could be likened to the English contempt of court). This procedure was in force until 1905. Lastly, according to John the pope was entitled to excommunicate a faithful Christian, but this had no effects in civil life. The interference by clerics in civic matters would, he held, lead to the destruction of the State.

John of Paris did not invent any new ideas or principles, but logically followed up the theses laid down by his great master. They proved themselves eminently reasonable and plausible. Few literary products exhibited the kind of intellectual chastity and integrity which characterized John's tract. To impugn the old established theories required courage of a quite extraordinary degree: John had to battle against an entrenched traditionalism and habits of thought which culminated in the virtually sacrosanct position of the pope: his theories might well have appeared revolutionary. That he was suspected of heresy, we know from a notice of the Inquisitor Bernard Gui, who also informs us that John died in 1306 at Bordeaux on the way to the papal curia, where he was to expect definitive sentence for heresy.

II. THE PEOPLE AS SOVEREIGN LEGISLATOR

As long as nature and the natural law were conceived to be manifestations of divinity, a formidable bar to the fully-fledged autonomy of the citizen and of the State was erected.

This was indeed the weakness of Thomism: because natural law was in the last resort still linked with divinity, there was always the more or less remote possibility of a clerical intervention. And, when once the initial shock of Thomism had been absorbed, it could still be said that the citizen and the faithful Christian were two sides of the same coin.

If the thesis of the citizen's and the State's full autonomy were to be constructed, a radical operation was needed. That radical operation was performed by Marsiglio of Padua. He was a student at Padua University – which in the late thirteenth century was 'infested' with Aristotelian teachings – and he also read medicine and studied 'nature' under an 'egregious teacher' whose identity is disputed. At one time or another he seems to have taken lower orders and became in course of time rector of the University of Paris, and it was in that seat of learning (in which Thomas Aquinas and John of Paris also wrote their works) that he composed his work *The Defender of the Peace* which was destined to become most influential. The book was finished on 24 June 1324 and soon afterwards became the subject of inquisitorial proceedings. Marsiglio and his assistant John of Jandun were declared heretics by the pope at Avignon in 1327: they were called 'the sons of the devil', 'the sons of Belial', 'pestiferous men', whilst a later pope, Clement VI, in 1343 called them 'the worst ever of the heretics'. Curial attempts to have Marsiglio extradited by the imperial court to which he had fled, failed.

The title of the work was to indicate its purpose. The intention of Marsiglio was to show how 'peace and tranquillity' could be achieved. Because this presupposed the examination of some general principles he devoted the first part of the book to them, in order to show in the second part why it was that peace was disturbed and who the disturber really was. Here we can but give a short summary of his views: his book comprises in the modern edition more than 600 closely printed pages. He set out from the axiom that the link between nature and God was a matter of faith, and not a matter capable of rational proof. For, as he said, political science had modest aims, and it was not the business of the political scientist to inquire how natural things had come about: he had to operate with nature in its empirical and observable sense in so far as it affected human government. He cast aside anything that had no rational explanation and held that speculations about the wherefrom and whereto of nature prevented a correct appreciation of the physical laws relating to human society and its government. It was furthermore impossible to prove by rational means that there was an eternal bliss or, for that matter, any life beyond this world. In any case none of all this was demonstrable and all of it was based on 'credulity without reason'. There was no evidence that God had instituted a human government. The essential point to note with Marsiglio was that the natural and the supra-natural had assumed full autonomy and that, as far as civil government was concerned, they had nothing in common. 'Nature and supernature became two completely separate realms, and a proposition which was false in one could be perfectly true in the other'.* Consequently, there was no attempt in his system to reconcile the two. What mattered to him was the natural body politic pure and simple. His approach to political matters was very much in the line expected of a natural scientist of the fourteenth century.

The Marsilian State was an end in itself: it had its own value and was incapable of being 'improved' (as the Thomists had it) by bringing divine grace to bear upon it. The stage was reached in which the 'congregation of the citizens' (the *universitas civium*) had assumed full autonomy. The former congregation of the faithful (*universitas fidelium*) was to give way to the mundane, earthly citizens' body, the State, as the one and only public body that lived on its own laws and on its own inner substance. It was for Marsiglio a body which was self-sufficient and therefore a 'perfect congregation', a definition which echoed the Thomist standpoint. The state was composed of citizens only, and it did not matter whether they were Christians. The constitutive element of the State was the citizen pure and simple. Of course, neither the term citizen nor the term congregation was in any way new, but what was new was the meaning attached to the combination of the two.

* Wilks.

His thesis of the citizens as constituent members of the State had important consequences. Previously, the concept of the faithful Christian embraced both lay and cleric, who in their aggregate constituted the Church, but it was the cleric by virtue of his special qualification who set the tone. Now the concept of the citizen also came to embrace both the cleric and the layman, but in their function as citizens there was no difference: each had the same standing. It was only logical that the thesis of a numerical or quantitative majority emerged in the place of the hitherto practised qualitative principle: since every citizen had the same value, no distinction in quality could be made, and there remained only counting by heads.*

Marsiglio would not have been a medieval political writer if he had not focused attention upon the law as the crucial matter of political science. In fact, one can go as far as to say that his theory of law was the pivot of his political doctrine. Law to him – as to anyone else – was an enforceable precept. The question was, who or what conferred enforceable character on the law? How was it that a rule became endowed with enforceability? The descending-theocratic theory of government and law had no difficulty in answering the question: it was the will of the Ruler who, because of the divine derivation of his powers, could enforce his will, provided always that the subjects had the required faith. But an answer on this level was not available to Marsiglio, for to him it was axiomatic that, since law was the force which ordered and regulated the humans living in the State, it was the 'humans' themselves, the citizens, who infused enforceable character into rules of conduct. Hence the laws derived their enforceable character from the will of the people. The law was not *given* to them by some specially qualified officer, but *made* by them themselves. The totality of all the citizens Marsiglio termed therefore the 'human legislator', to distinguish it clearly from any divine law-giver. The

*He himself advocated nevertheless the combination of the two principles. The first time that the numerical principle of majority was applied was in the papal election decree of 1179: all the cardinals were the electors and, since no distinction between them (as regards 'merit, zeal, and authority') could be made, counting by heads alone was possible (two-third majority).

material ingredient of the law was the will of the human legislator, and herewith emerged not only the vital element of consent of the citizens, but also the citizen in his full maturity and
autonomy, who himself was the law-maker. The concept of the
subject (*sub/ditus*) now began to recede into the background.
'Citizen' and 'subject' denoted in fact two entirely different
governmental systems.

What the citizenhood (the human legislator) was concerned
with was to order its own life autonomously through its laws.
Life in the next world, Marsiglio said, may be quite important,
but the citizens as citizens were not concerned with it. For the
function of the laws was to provide 'good living' in this life
and world, that is, they aimed at the human well-being of all
citizens. For this reason also the citizens were best qualified
to make their own laws, because they knew best what they
wished to achieve. Marsiglio's was an unadulterated ascending-populist theory of government and law. Since the people
itself fixed what was just and what was unjust, it followed
for him that the contents of justice were not the same in every
society or region. The keynote of relativity once again confronts us. Most significantly, he stressed that there was no one
above the people: the people, the citizenhood (or the human
legislator) was 'superior', that is sovereign, since there was no
authority outside or above it. The citizenhood had become its
own superior, its own sovereign. Marsiglio went even so far
as to say that plenitude of power belonged to the people, thus
using a notion from the opposite camp to make clear his own
principles. In brief, the primary function of the citizenhood
was to make the law, because the law was the vehicle by which
the end of the citizens' society could be achieved. That he
thereby also achieved quite effortlessly the dividing line between law and morals seemed evident: morals had no enforceable character, because not willed by the citizenhood, and, if
willed by the citizens, it ceased to be a moral precept and became law. Marsiglio's human law had in itself no moral overtones and offered no short-cut to the achievement of salvation,
nor did it embody eternal truths. Law was solely a matter for

the citizens: it was in the law that they expressed their desire of how to shape public order and life.

Not only could the citizens make laws on any matter they wished but they also could institute any kind of government they preferred. Of what kind this government was – monarchic, republican, etc. – was of little concern to Marsiglio, provided that original power remained located in the citizenhood. Once again he used traditional terminology by declaring that the human legislator *conceded* power to the government: the old concession principle was now turned upside down.* What functions the citizens conceded to the government, which he called 'the principal part of the State', depended on the constitution which the citizens had chosen, and that constitution was, evidently, a law which he called the form of the State (*forma*). The function of the government was executive or instrumental: it acted within the framework of the constitutional law made by the citizens.

Although the legislator as the primary and proper cause of the State must determine which persons must exercise what offices, the execution of such matters, as also of all other legal provisions, is commanded or, as the case may be, prohibited by the principal part of the State.

The government remained always, however, responsible to the people, from which it originally had its powers. The removal of the government for transgressing the constitutional law under which it took office was expressly provided for by Marsiglio. Moreover, the government might be elected for life or for a number of years, it might include several persons or only one – all this depended upon the people's will. The government, according to Marsiglio, was to put into practice what the citizenhood would have done if it had had to act: the day-to-day routine governmental work, the necessary laws and decrees and ordinances were to come from the government as the 'principal part of the State'. The government was the instrument of the people's will. The great significance of this stand-

* Cf. above, p. 132.

point lay in that it did away with the vital theocratic principle, according to which the office of the ruler was, so to speak, laid up in heaven; it was for this reason that the electors could not modify or alter the substance of the office.* Here, however, the office was defined by the citizenhood itself, which could lay down, in the constitutional law, the extent and scope of the office: the office itself had once again been created by the sovereign people – the test of the ascending-populist thesis. And the office could understandably be taken away by those who had conferred it – a consequence which throws the contrast to the descending thesis into clear relief.

In characterizing the State as 'living nature' (*natura animata*) Marsiglio once again borrowed a terminology from the opposite camp, in which the ruler himself was spoken of as the 'living law' (*lex animata*). In his term of the State as 'living nature' he wished to bring out the essential naturalist basis of the State. It was – as Aristotle had taught him – through the promptings of nature that the State came into existence: it was the will of the citizens which made this natural body alive. His designation of the law as 'an eye composed of many eyes' (*oculus ex multis oculis*) seemed an excellent way of characterizing the law as a measure willed by the many, because they were mature enough to see what measures contributed to the well-being of their State. The distance between this doctrine and the antecedent one emerged also in this context: previously the law was called 'a gift of God',† and now it was on a thorough-going populist basis, 'an eye made up of many eyes'.

The clergy as such had in Marsiglio's system no powers beyond those of other citizens. He considered the function of the clergy as healers of souls and pure administrators of the sacraments: they might well admonish men; they could also paint in the gloomiest colours the horrors which awaited the sinners in the other world, but they could not exclude sinners from human society. As long as an offence was merely a sin, it was of no consequence to the State; the citizens became interested in sin only when it became a crime. The priests might declare

*Above, p. 135.   †Above, pp. 123, 146.

conduct as heresy, but this too had no effect in the State, unless and until the government made it a crime. If divine law was infringed, there was no earthly authority that could deal with it, because the judge was Christ alone. Of course, human law might well impose penalties for breaches of the divine law but then this was a matter for the human legislator and the divine law ceased to be a divine law and became a human law. Above all, the priests had no function to issue decrees or to make any judgments. What they did, for instance, in the confessional was no judgment at all. He poured scorn on the exercise of this 'internal jurisdiction':

A vicious or ignorant priest can lead to grave civil harm, since priests, through their authority as confessors, often have secret colloquies with women. And since women are easily misled, especially the young ones, whether virgin or married (as is clear from Genesis, ch.3, and as the apostle shows in I Timothy, ch.2: for Adam was not deceived, but the woman being deceived was in the transgression), it is clear that a vicious priest will easily be able to corrupt their morals and modesty.

Apart from this, a judgment of excommunication issued by any clerical officer could not have any effect in the civil sphere, for thereby

priests or groups of them can remove all states and governments from the rulers or kings who have them. For, when a ruler is excommunicated, the multitude subject to him will also be excommunicated, if it wishes to obey the excommunicate ruler, and thus the power of every ruler will be broken.

He was courageous enough to say that clerical jurisdiction was based partly on spurious documents, partly on wrong interpretations of the Bible, and partly on sheer usurpation by the papacy: and this was the real cause of disunity. The question of who disturbed the peace could easily be answered by Marsiglio: the pope and his claim to jurisdiction. 'They (the popes) worm themselves into others' rights, especially into those of the empire during vacancies, until they now claim jurisdiction over all subjects.' The extension of spiritual causes was a further reason for lack of peace in society. What was there spiritual, he asked, in an offence committed by clerics? They could borrow, buy, sell, mortgage, rob, rape, fornicate, swear false oaths, and so on, in no wise different from lay people, but were all these crimes spiritual matters, just because they happened to be committed by priests? There was no justification at all for any kind of ecclesiastical jurisdiction over clerics: they were citizens and had to stand their trial before the court of the people.

Let no one object that injuries by word of mouth or to property or to the person forbidden by secular law become spiritual acts when committed by priests and that their punishment does not belong to the secular ruler, for these acts are carnal and temporal.

But, since the clergy were special officers, it was for the citizenhood, that is, the State, to fix the amount of clergy allowed within the State, for they enjoyed many advantages which the State provided for them and they should therefore be kept in proportion to the number of citizens. What was called the primacy of the pope and his succession to St Peter was, for Marsiglio, a fairy tale, invented by the popes. In disputing the fact of succession he shrewdly alleged the scriptural lack of evidence; he also showed that he possessed a historical–critical mind when he pointed out the absence of any mentioning of Peter's sojourn at Rome in any record. It was, he said, only through an ignorant and superstitious laity, the willing compliance of kings and emperors, and the craftiness of the popes that the canon law could ever become a social factor at all. The remedy which he suggested was to do away with the papacy as an institution of government altogether, because it had no title-deed for it at all.

Marsiglio was emphatic that the ascending theory of government and law should, in the cause of peace, also be applied to the Church as the body of the faithful, so that the latter too might become real bearers of original power. The practical manner of implementing this was through the general council in which the whole of Christendom was to be represented. After all, if it was true that 'what touches all should be approved by all' in the State, it must also be true in the Church, in the body of Christians. Faith and its fixation was a matter that touched all Christians, and therefore their representation in a general council was justified. It was the Christian people – and this included the laity – who through the machinery of a general council with its lay representation were to elect the pope, fix his power, define the articles of the faith, and designate the ecclesiastical officers. Because of the working of the Holy Ghost in the general council, its decisions were infallible; the pope was as much subjected to error as any other Christian and could be deposed by the general council. The pope in other words became a member of the Church and was, so to speak, incorporated in it: he no longer formed an estate of his own, standing outside and above the Church in his function as governor.*

It certainly is difficult, in the twentieth century, to appreciate adequately the veritable reversal in political thinking which the Marsilian ideas effected, though on closer inspection a number of his points are still topical today. But what can readily be appreciated is the rapid advance in political thought since Aristotle had become available. It was little more than a generation since Thomas Aquinas had presented a synthesis. Marsiglio performed a surgical operation in which he excised from political doctrine Christian elements as irrelevant. Part of the explanation for the receptivity of the soil for Marsilian ideas could, paradoxically enough, be found in the institution which he had attacked so acrimoniously. The papacy had taxed the credulity of the faithful Christians to an astonishing degree, since every papal law, decree, or verdict was alleged to have been the divine word made manifest, and yet a comparison of papal – let alone episcopal – actions with these assertions was bound to kindle criticism and to produce a somewhat detached reaction amongst the faithful. Marsiglio's bitter recriminations against the popes could well be taken as an accusation that they had betrayed the Christian theme and had exploited the faith of their subjects. Two generations earlier these charges would have fallen flat, but in the fourteenth century they expressed what large sections of the populace in any case

* See above, pp. 28, 105n.

felt. Once again, a political theory is shown to be intimately linked with the actuality of a concrete situation. Man himself as an individual, or, as the member of the State, the citizen, had now been accorded his proper standing and fully emancipated from the tutelage of an earlier dispensation. Marsiglio's was the implicit belief in man's own natural capabilities to order his own affairs in his own State without recourse to divinity, the spokesmen of which had provided ample evidence for questioning their own system. There was no superior set above the State as the body of the citizens, just as there was no superior set above the Church understood as the body of the faithful: each was, in a word, sovereign.

III. THE CITY-STATE

The political doctrine of Marsiglio may profitably be supplemented by the theory which a contemporary of his, Bartolus of Sassoferrato, put forward. Bartolus was perhaps the greatest of all the medieval lawyers who expounded Roman law. He taught at Perugia, where he died in 1352, barely forty-three years old. It is interesting that Bartolus arrived on purely juristic grounds at virtually the same doctrine which Marsiglio had reached on philosophic grounds. Bartolus was in no wise influenced by the Paduan, of whom in all likelihood he had never heard. That is not to say, however, that Bartolus created a new doctrine out of nothing. What he did was to utilize certain already well-known Roman law texts and to construct the ascending thesis of government and law out of individual Roman law elements. The most important of these elements we have mentioned before: the concept of the citizen,* the concept of customary law,† and the so-called *lex regia*.‡

The achievement of Bartolus lay in that he combined all these three elements and thus presented a doctrine of the sovereignty of the people on the exclusive basis of Roman law. All civilian jurists – the Roman lawyers – had dealt with these concepts, but none had combined them and shown how they could be utilized in the service of the ascending

*Above, p. 164.   †Above, p. 161.   ‡Above, p. 145.

THE CITY-STATE

thesis. By demonstrating how these three elements were inter-related, Bartolus provided a theory of popular sovereignty for the practice of popular sovereignty observable in the North Italian cities at his time. The Roman citizen as represented in the Roman law *Digest* was in every sense a full bearer of rights and duties. Customary law was a law which resulted from con-tinuous practice and usage by the people itself. The *lex regia* was in reality a misnomer, as it never was a law: it was an ex-planation of the Roman jurist in the second century A.D. of the basis of the emperor's power. The explanation given was that the Roman people had possessed all public power but had trans-ferred it to the emperor. The *lex regia* was a construction to explain to the Romans in the second century how their emper-or had obtained his power. Although the civilian jurists of the twelfth and thirteenth centuries dealt with it, the common opinion was that this was an irrevocable grant made by the Romans,* although this opinion was as much a construction or a fiction as the *lex regia* itself was. For this juristic opinion there was no basis in the perfectly lucid and unambiguous wording of the text.

Practice in the North Italian cities appeared to lend support to the thesis contained in the *lex regia*, according to which the people had power. Bartolus argued that if the people could create customary law – and nobody ever doubted this – there was no reason to withhold from the people the right to make also statutory, that is, written, enacted law. The element which infused legal character to mere practices and usages was the consent of the people: it was a tacit consent of the people which created customary law. But what the people could do by tacit consent, Bartolus reasoned, they could also do by explicit consent, that is, to make statutes, written law. The difference between customary and statute law was merely in the way consent came to be expressed: in the one case it was tacit, in the other it was explicit. That people or citizenhood which

* It should be mentioned that there were instances in which the *lex regia* was made the programme of anti-hierocratic movements, the most notable being the attempt of Arnold of Brescia in the mid twelfth century in Rome to establish a government based on popular consent and will.

made its own laws was 'a free people' and could be compared to the Roman people which, according to the *lex regia*, originally had power. And a free people, Bartolus said, was that which recognized no superior, because it was its own 'superior', or, as he also had it: a free people was its own prince. What the French and Sicilian jurists had maintained by their view that 'the king in his kingdom is an emperor'* reappeared in Bartolus's thesis of the people itself as the prince (*civitas sibi princeps*). There it was the king's sovereignty, here it was the people's sovereignty, which was to be expressed by the Roman law term of *princeps*.

That 'free people' which had no superior and was its own sovereign, had, consequently, a government which belonged to the people. This Bartolus designated as *regimen ad populum*. And when government lay in the hands of the people the maxims and principles applicable to the monarchic-sovereign Ruler could be applied to the government of the people: the State – which Bartolus called the *civitas* – could legislate 'as it pleased'. What gave particular flavour to Bartolist doctrine was the idea of representation. According to him, the people in the popular assembly elected the Council, which was the governing body, and the Council represented the whole citizenhood, the State. It represented, as Bartolus very succinctly stated, 'the mind of the people' (*Concilium representat mentem populi*). It was entirely in the power of the people to confer as much authority on the Council as it wished: the Council's power could also be circumscribed or restricted; the decision whether the government should be elected for a specific time was also left to the people. Authority stemmed from the people, and not from a 'superior' authority. The function of the government was to issue such laws as were conducive to the public good and engendered the public interest (*utilitas publica*). It was no longer the superior insight of the Ruler which determined what was in the interests of the people, but the people itself was recognized as perfectly capable of forming its own judgement on what was in its interests, for at all times the

*Above, pp. 156, 196.

people retained control of the Council. Once again we meet the concession principle,* though in an inverted sense in that the people as the bearer of public rights and duties had conceded to the Council governmental powers. The Council itself proceeded on the principle of simple numerical majority and elected the chief officers of the State, who were divided by Bartolus into judicial, administrative, and financial officers. They were responsible to the government, whilst the government remained responsible to the State itself. The nature of the office was defined by the citizens themselves, who could prescribe its contents and also change them: the office was no longer laid up in heaven, but emanated from the people. Within this framework one could speak of elections in the proper meaning of the term.

With a few juristic strokes Bartolus provided within legal theory what Marsiglio had provided within political theory. To both it was axiomatic that there was no sovereign above the people. 'A free people is not subjected to anyone', Bartolus had declared. And with this the concept of the subject also vanished, since a free people knew no subjects, but only citizens. A practical application of this thesis could be observed very soon after Bartolus. Within the traditional doctrine the crime of 'high' treason was – in entire agreement with the underlying conceptions of the descending thesis – committed against the majesty of the Ruler; now this same crime was to become an offence committed against the people, because they had become 'superior', the sovereign. This indeed was the case in the Italy of the early fifteenth century. The State itself, in other words, was the proper object of treasonable activities, and no longer the Ruler. And a further fructifying effect of Bartolist juristic doctrine was the penetration into, and elaboration of, the concept of citizenship itself. This would indeed seem a major development, the last tremors of which were to be felt right down to modern times. The Bartolists distinguished between a natural citizenship, that is, a citizen naturally born within the State, and an acquired citizenship, a citizen

*Above, p. 132.

who by act of State could be made a citizen. Marriage was a condition which turned the 'foreign' wife into a citizen of the husband's State.

Some differences between Marsiglio and Bartolus should be pointed out. Bartolus's system was applicable to small states, that is, to small communities in which a real 'democracy' could work, whilst Marsiglio's was intended to be applicable to any community, large or small, because his was a philosophic system rather than a legal one; and that was also the reason why Bartolus, true Roman jurist as he was, still tried to maintain a *de jure* lordship of the emperor: on the basis of the Justinianean *Code* hardly any other view could have been expected. A real and basic difference between the two lay in the composition of the people, that is, who was a citizen. To both it was fundamental that a citizen was he who participated in the government of the State, and on Aristotelian premisses Marsiglio excluded from citizenship slaves, foreigners, women, and children. Bartolus, too, excluded these, his reason being that they were incapable of giving legally relevant consent, but he also excluded from citizenship clerics: he held that laity and clergy formed two separate sections, and what the one section decreed had no relevance for the other. His juristic conservatism apparently prevented him from taking the radical step which Marsiglio had taken. Despite the obvious advantages of the Bartolist system, there can be little doubt that the restricted concept of a citizen was, from the historical-ideological standpoint, a deficiency.

There is no need to stress the great advance which political theories had made in the course of the first half of the fourteenth century. The ascending thesis of government and law was no longer presented as a merely defensive measure but was shown to be capable of making a positive and constructive contribution to the solution of problems which had beset thinking men before, and were to beset them afterwards. It was both the sub-structure and super-structure of Marsiglio's system which made it impossible to disregard it. His theory of the people's sovereignty was bound to exercise the influence which it demanded, and with the means at the disposal of men in the fourteenth and fifteenth centuries there was very little that could, in substance, be added.

IV. CONCILIARISM

Although little could be added to the ascending thesis, the theory itself came by the early fifteenth century to be applied also to that body which at first sight would have seemed immune to it – the Church. The ascending thesis emerged as conciliarism, according to which the general council of the Church was 'superior' to the pope: sovereign power rested with the congregation of the faithful in their representative organ, the general council, and no longer with the pope, who in this scheme became a member of the Church and its officer.

That conciliarism won the day was not a historical freak or coincidence. It emerged as an answer to the problem of how to control the pope's monarchy. That the exercise of papal plenitude of power had become a problem by the mid fourteenth century, was fully recognized by the cardinals of the Roman Church (at that time residing at Avignon), who were the intimate counsellors of the pope and his electors. They had come to realize that the unfettered monarchic sovereignty of the pope was not always to the advantage of the Church. In order to restrict his sovereignty, they hit upon the idea (which indeed they borrowed from the practice prevailing in episcopal elections by the cathedral chapters) of the so-called papal electoral pacts. That is to say, whilst in conclave the cardinals formally agreed upon a number of points which he who was elected pope promised to carry out. The first attempt at establishing something approaching a constitutional monarchy of the pope was made on the occasion of the election of Innocent VI in 1352. This compact amongst the cardinals was sworn to by each of them and solemnly sealed in the presence of a notary.*

*In course of time these electoral pacts became lengthy and detailed lists of many points. The pacts continued to be concluded down to the sixteenth century. The pact of 1352, for instance, laid down the maximum number of cardinals to be elected (twenty); the college of cardinals was to give its consent to the creation of new cardinals; the cardinals had to consent to higher appointments in the papal state; nepotism was to be ended; etc.

It was an ingenious device but it never worked, because once elected the pope asserted the very thing which the pact was designed to restrict – his plenitude of power, not without declaring that the oath was taken by him as a cardinal and was hence no longer binding on him.

The events of April 1378 brought forth the problem of papal monarchy in stark reality. For the same college of cardinals had within a short time elected two popes, their reason being that their first choice (Urban VI) was totally unfit, if not insane. During the Great Schism which followed, and which was to last forty years, the problem of the pope's sovereignty became acute, especially when from 1409 there were three popes, each fulminating against the others, each deposing his rivals and excommunicating their followers. The period of the Great Schism provided the fertile soil upon which conciliarism grew and flourished. In conciliarism was seen the guarantee that a recurrence of this deplorable state of affairs would be prevented: the general conviction was that the source of all the trouble was the unfettered sovereign monarchy of the pope.

In its essence conciliarism was a combination of Marsilian and Bartolist theses with the canon lawyers' theory of corporations. The latter culminated in the view that the bishop and his chapter formed a corporation, that he was bound by the decision of the chapter, and that he could not act without its consent in any major matter. This theory was transferred to the pope, but then the question arose, what body should take the place of the cathedral chapter; was it the college of cardinals, or was it to be a much wider body? The cardinals, understandably perhaps, declared themselves for the first alternative, but they were confronted by a virtually unanimous opposition, which declared that the body to control the pope was a general council. It was at this juncture that Marsilian and Bartolist theses came into their own. The ascending thesis was to be ruthlessly applied to the government of the Church.

Accordingly, sovereignty – or, as it was called, 'superiority' – belonged to the whole body of Christians, and not to the pope. It was the whole Christian people – clerics and lay alike – to whom the crucial Matthean verses were said to apply. The principle of representation was to find its embodiment in the general council. It was to be the representative body of the whole Church or, as it was said on the model of Bartolus, 'the general council represents the whole catholic church'. A good deal of patristic lore was adduced to buttress the theory and the great councils of Christian antiquity were invoked as models. The most notable conciliarists were Cardinal Francis Zabarella, Jean Gerson from the University of Paris, Cardinal d'Ailly the bishop of Cambrai, and the German Dietrich of Niem. Their contention was that, since dogma and doctrine affected every Christian, the fixation of dogmatic and doctrinal points should not be left to one man, the pope, but was the business of the whole body of believers. 'What touches all must be approved by all' was readily at hand. The pope was to be bound to the decisions concerning faith. Infallibility belonged not to the Roman Church, still less to the pope, but to the general council. This organ had also to elect the officers of the Church, above all the pope, who remained responsible to the Council. The pope became incorporated into the Church and an officer charged with specific functions and tasks. How strongly this ascending thesis had in fact entrenched itself can be shown by the absence of any defender of the descending point of view in the late fourteenth and early fifteenth centuries. The significance of this development was that the doctrine developed and applied for just about 1,000 years came to be disavowed by thinking men. The pope, forming an estate of his own, standing outside and above the Church, changed into a member of the Church to which the ordinary corporation laws applied. Instead of distributing power downwards and conceding it to lower-placed officers, it was now the pope who was to receive power from below. Whilst previously the allegory of the 'head and members' was used, in papal doctrine, to demonstrate the directing function of the pope, this same allegory now in conciliar doctrine came to assist the process of the pope's 'incorporation' in the Church, since the head was said to belong to the body. Medieval allegories seem to have been double-edged weapons.

These theoretical views were given legal force in the decrees of the Council of Constance (1414–18), which ended the Schism. Two of these decrees are of particular interest. The one embodied the conciliarist theme proper: the Council representing the whole Church had received its power from Christ, and adherence to the decisions of the Council in matters of faith was enjoined upon everyone of whatever status or rank, even if of papal rank. The other decree concerned the pope's profession of faith: after his election every new pope was to promise to uphold inviolably and defend, if necessary with his life, the decrees of all the previous general councils. In practice this meant curtailment of the pope's legislative functions.

Once again the emergence of a political doctrine, as conciliarism indubitably was, was closely linked with the actuality of a situation. The ascending thesis of government gained at least a theoretical triumph in that quarter which seemed impregnable. How receptive the soil was for this thesis can perhaps best be gathered from the fact that it was churchmen in the highest possible positions who propagated the theory. Marsiglio and Bartolus could not have wished for greater success.

V. CONSERVATISM AND TRADITION

But conciliarism was to remain pure theory. Perhaps at no other time did the protagonists of a theory themselves do so little to implement their own theories as the conciliarists did. The intellectual climate was wholly favourable to them. There was in the early fifteenth century an increase of academically trained people, which meant in actual fact the spread of University education to the lower clergy and, above all, to the laity; new schools and colleges were founded, which also accounted for the expansion of the University population. The new theories had become fit and proper subjects to be taught and lectured upon: they had come to stay. Last, but certainly not least, the feature that explained so much of 'political' doctrine in the high Middle Ages, the institutionalized faith, diminished and was replaced by an intellectual radicalism which oftentimes went beyond the confines of the – as yet – permissible. And yet, despite all these circumstances, the fact remains that within a generation the pope had returned to the same position which he had before the troublous years: it was again the same sonorous chords of the papal monarchy and plenitude of power which resounded in the decrees and laws. How is one to explain this? The situation in the fifteenth century pre-portrays a good deal of subsequent history, and an explanation of this situation may assist the understanding of the ideological forces which were to be at work right down to the more recent period.

Conciliarism was abandoned by its own advocates. By the mid fifteenth century hardly any of the reputable conciliarist theoreticians were left; one by one they had drifted back to the traditional papal–monarchic point of view. Part of the explanation is that the conciliarists did little to change the constitution of the Church, although it was they themselves who with deafening insistence reiterated the idea that original power was located in the Christian people, which included of course the laymen. And yet no effort was made to turn the status of the layman from a merely passive into an active role. On the contrary, the layman was to remain in the receptive role into which traditional doctrine had cast him. In so far, conciliarism was a resuscitation of the old episcopalist theory:* under the cover of a progressive movement an old theme was presented in a new cloak. Laymen indeed could submit memoranda, make speeches, partake in debates, but they were debarred from voting, unless they fulfilled special qualifications, the most important being that they were legates of kings and princes. But they did not vote in their capacity as laymen, but as legates of the 'king by the grace of God'. The theocratic-descending standpoint entered by the back door. Apart from this, it was difficult to see how the principle of representation – so much propagated at the time – was in reality applied.

There can be no doubt that the relegation of the laymen to the role of mere spectators showed how little the conciliarists themselves cared in practice for the implementation of their own theory. 'What touches all, must be approved by all' was a persuasive theoretical slogan, but one missed its appearance

* See above, p. 108.

in practice. The Councils of the fifteenth century were, as heretofore, ecclesiastical assemblies. That there was a sufficient body of educated laymen in the fifteenth century becomes evident from a glance at University records. The lower clergy and the educated laymen were, so to speak, knocking at the gate, and were refused entry. But it was precisely these two classes to whom the reformers in the next century were to appeal so successfully. The responsibility of the conciliarists for the subsequent religious and political cataclysm was indeed great. They had not the courage of their conviction to transplant their own theories into reality. It was the amorphous multitude which first frightened them and then made them abandon their own position, only to retreat into the old papal–monarchic framework. Indeed, it was fear of the multitude – of the laity – which made the conciliarists join the 'Establishment' in which they found a secure bulwark against the rising tide of popular forces.

But similar considerations applied to the secular rulers, above all to the pronouncedly theocratic kings, who were equally prompted by the fear of the 'third estate'. For conciliarism was after all no more than an offshoot of the ascending thesis of government. It was not in the least surprising that in the course of the fifteenth century a number of concordats were concluded between popes and kings, notably that with the Emperor Frederick III (1448) which was of great influence. Evidently, whilst the papacy was affected by conciliarism, the kings were affected by its parent. In view of the enmity that existed in previous times between papacy and kings, their peaceful cooperation was certainly noteworthy: both parts agreed to quite substantial concessions. It would be naïve to think that, in contrast to earlier periods, there was no cause for friction between them, but theocratic Rulers saw themselves threatened by the same forces which threatened ecclesiastical institutions,* and they joined hands. Indeed, the exponents of the descending forms of government were understandably alarmed when, for instance, doctrines such as those of Wyclif were broadcast to

* Some of the speeches made in the German Diets, e.g. at Frankfurt (1446) or in ecclesiastical councils at the time, pointed out this danger.

the effect that the people (significantly enough called by him: *populares*) could make their lords responsible for their delicts. Later, the Bohemian John Hus expressed similar views. That their condemnation was decreed at Constance, with the effective help of the emperor, is not surprising. Often enough we have referred to the absence of any right of resistance to a tyrant within the descending theory of government. When Jean Petit, one of the Parisian Masters, in the early fifteenth century taught with singular directness that to kill a tyrant was not only licit and meritorious, but also a duty of the subjects,* the assembled conciliar wisdom at Constance stigmatized this view in a special decree as heretical, scandalous, and seditious: anyone holding it was to be treated as a heretic, because it was 'erroneous in faith and morals'. The significance of this theory was that the hallowed descending form of government had received a severe jolt, and the reaction to it was equally severe. Established authority had to be protected by all conceivable means. In brief, the ascending theory of government was seen as the real enemy of established order: but it was the governments of the established order which had the effective power in their hands.

The situation in the fifteenth century was a portent, and showed with remarkable clarity the strong forces which could be marshalled and aligned to retard the practical implementation of the theme of popular sovereignty. That much of this retarding process was also due to human inertia, torpor, and traditionalism, seems clear enough. There were additionally a number of conserving and preserving agencies which retarded the full operation of the ascending theme at a later period. The institutions themselves, whether ecclesiastical or royal, by the very fact that they were institutionalized organs of governments, were in course of time to become the bearers of – ideologically speaking – outmoded political ideas. They engendered their own ceremonies and ceremonial: one has but to think of the uninterrupted sequence of royal coronations, with their

---

* The case which touched off this doctrine was the murder of the Duke of Orleans on 23 November 1407; the murdered had amply proved that he was the personification of tyrannical evil.

strong emphasis on the divine derivation of royal power, to realize how much they assisted the retarding process: every prayer text, symbol, gesture was highly charged with theocratic elements. But thereby the ecclesiastical power itself was also considerably buttressed. 'Throne and altar' were the two symbols by which the established forms of government came in course of time to be expressed. Nor should the inhibiting effect of language be omitted in an attempt to explain why the practical application of the thesis of popular sovereignty took so long a time. Centuries-long usage of terms and of vocabulary which was originally coined and intended for quite different circumstances, the overtones and undertones created by the employment of specific theocratic notions, the mental associations which resulted from repeated use of certain terms – all these must be assessed, if one wishes to understand the slow historical progress by which the people came to be emancipated from 'sovereign' tutelage.

Whatever writers, thinkers, and *littérateurs* propounded, the paraphernalia of power were none the less in the hands of governments. On the other hand, the fact that the subjects were under the tutelage of their governments which 'benevolently' governed them as minors under age had some compensating features: the subject's main duty was to obey the sovereign. In obeying the law was seen the culmination of the subject's 'civic' duties, no doubt, a comfortable and comforting and soothing standpoint, but one that would not appear conducive to constitutional progress. The attempt to replace a descending form of government by the operation of the ascending thesis was bound to lead to revolution if the government was determined enough. It is interesting to see that during the French Revolution the term 'Citizen' became attached to the name itself and became, so to speak, a title: this feature was repeated after the Russian Revolution of 1917 when, again, the surname was to be prefixed by 'Citizen'. Perhaps nothing epitomizes the conflict between the ascending and descending views better than the corresponding concepts of citizen and subject. The constitutional conflicts and revolutions of the nineteenth century were conflicts between ideologies of medieval parentage.

A somewhat different picture emerges in communities in which not the theocratic, but the feudal kind of rulership was preponderant. Certainly, a government working on feudal principles could not hope to equal a theocratic government in glamour or efficiency. On the other hand, a feudal government was characterized by a slow, cumbersome process leading eventually to compromise between the two parties, the very thing which the theocratic view of government precluded. The king's feudal government made it possible for the vassals to take part in the machinery of government as of right, and therefore to take part in the making of the law. Law was a common effort. That was part of the reason why in the fourteenth century the new theories of popular sovereignty could find so easy an ingress into the English constitutional and political scene. It is indeed a fascinating feature of the English development in the later Middle Ages that the new theories were so easily accommodated without any reverberations. The explanation is that the soil was fertilized by feudal principles which were not dissimilar to those which the ascending theme had postulated. Certain rights were ascribed in practice to the members of the feudal community which they had, not as a result of concession or grant by the king, but by virtue of the simple fact that they were members of the feudal community. It did not need particular acumen at a later stage to look at these rights as natural rights with which man was born. One of the reasons for the immediate influence of the theories of, say, Locke, or, later, Blackstone, was that they fell on ground that had already been cultivated for their reception. It was again no coincidence that the English common law became in the seventeenth century the bulwark of the individual liberties against the (irrepressible) monarchic aspirations of the king, but that common law was in its genesis and working a law that had grown on the feudal soil since the twelfth century,* a law that was common to the king and the (feudal) community. The development of a theory of basic civic rights in the feudally soaked England was historically conditioned. The Declaration of Human Rights in Virginia (1776) revealed the historic pattern plainly.

*Above, pp. 150f.

Can one be surprised that the declaration of the French Constituante of 26 August 1789 on the inalienability of human rights created such havoc in France? The ground was not ready for this sort of thinking which was, as yet, no more than academic speculation: the influence of the antecedent legal and political ideology in France turned such far-reaching declarations into instruments of revolution, forcibly creating a new order which had no historic, social, or political roots in the past.

CHAPTER 9

CONCLUSION

MANY years ago Frederic William Maitland poured scorn on what he called 'aimless medievalism', the effort spent on the study of matters historically and ideologically quite irrelevant, if not trivial. The study of political ideas in the Middle Ages can never incur this charge of antiquarianism, because the governmental and political ideas dominant in the Middle Ages have created the very world which is ours. Our modern concepts, our modern institutions, our political obligations and constitutional ideas are either direct descendants of those in the Middle Ages, or have grown up in direct opposition to them. True, there are nowadays few manifestations of the descending thesis of government and law – though considerably more than one is perhaps inclined to admit – since it is the ascending thesis that holds sway, but to understand why and how the latter gained the ascendancy in long, protracted, and blood-letting conflicts, the inquiring mind will not remain satisfied with a descriptive statement of an organization or a constitution or institution, but will try to find out how they have become what they are.

The value of the study of medieval political ideas also shows the modern inquirer how ideas of government and politics came originally into being. One should appreciate that between the fifth and twelfth centuries, when vast stretches of the Continent were still uninhabited, a society grew up which had to learn the fundamentals, the very rudiments, of how to manipulate the ordering of public life. There were no 'historical' precedents; no possibilities of learning how to govern by imitation or by the mistakes of others; it was a young society which knew little of an outside world and which had to find its own means of doing the very things which other societies were to take for granted. That the political thought in the early and high Middle Ages was so strongly christocentric and biblically orientated is not difficult to explain: Christianity and the

Bible contained ready-made 'philosophies' from which a good deal of knowledge could be gathered for problems of government. That the West received both Christianity and the Bible in Latin shape explains the overwhelming Roman influence in the Middle Ages, Roman in both the pagan and ecclesiastical senses. What the study of medieval political ideas yields is a feature which is not frequently encountered in this field of inquiry, namely that whole governmental systems were exclusively based on an abstract idea, on programmatic blue-prints, on an abstract principle from which the last ounce of argument was squeezed out and doctrinally deduced. The legal and political system of the – in the high Middle Ages – prevalent theocratic-descending theory of government and law was the result of the overpowering might of an idea, the working of which demonstrated an aversion from, if not an opposition to, empirically reached conclusions and recognitions. That there were numerous items which astonish modern readers who, perhaps understandably, ask how this or that item could find such ready acceptance, should not dispense one from studying them, if for no other reason than to rediscover the principle of the rule of law, the principle upon which all political ideologies in the Middle Ages were agreed (but which today has not yet found universal acceptance). The avenues which led to this principle differed, but the instrumental concept was that of nature: first, nature was to be conquered by divine grace, then it was to serve as a model to be imitated, and – in modern times – it was again to be conquered (in a different field, and not by faith or grace, but) by the science of nature.

The label of antiquarianism can never be attached to the study of the history of political ideas. The history of political ideas not only promotes the understanding of how and why modern society has assumed the complexion it has – in itself assuredly a worthwhile task – but also demonstrates more convincingly and persuasively than any other study can hope to do, the differences between the various forms of government practised in different countries. That, for instance, Germany could produce the government which it had for twelve years under Hitler; that Italy could produce a government which

CONCLUSION

it had for twenty years under Mussolini; that Soviet Russia
could produce a government which it still has after nearly five
decades – not to mention other instances – was and is due to
the predominant but antecedent impact which political ideas
had upon the frame of mind of the populace: it was the slow
but steady attuning of the mind to specific responses which
created the historical situation, itself giving birth to sharply
accentuated political régimes. The idea of the *Obrigkeitsstaat*
in Germany was the historic–ideological premiss for what followed in the twentieth century, just as Byzantinism played a
similar role and function in Russia. On the other hand, the
role played by medieval feudalism in shaping what is called the
democratic form of government is still not fully appreciated.
Feudalism, feudal law, and feudal government were part of
the historical process, and yet have been relegated to dusty
shelves. A feudal kind of government was not a doctrinaire
matter, was not the effluence of some high-falutin principles
and dogmas, but was earth-bound, man-made, never removed
from practical exigencies, and therefore showing a resilience,
adjustability, and flexibility which no pure ideology could
match. That indeed is the explanation of the steadiness and
gradually progressive character of the democratic form of
government: it is rooted deep down in the historic soil, and
had experienced a historical evolution eventually stemming
from the native growth of feudal royal government. What the
study of the history of political ideas makes abundantly clear
is that historically conditioned ideas cannot fruitfully be trans-
planted on to a soil that has not been fertilized by the antecedent development. The French Revolution is one example;
the Weimar Constitution is another; and the sorry state of
some of the emerging non-European countries at the present
time would furnish further proof for the disastrous effects of
this artificial doctrinal insemination. After all, it is man himself
who has to manipulate political ideas, and this cannot be
achieved by a wholesale transfer of political ideologies to societies which are not prepared for them. In more than one way
can one say that the study of the history of political ideas is
the study of society and its government in its historic setting:

the study of medieval political ideas helps to explain the historical process in the Middle Ages and also offers a genetical
explanation of the present.

SELECT BIBLIOGRAPHY

GENERAL

Battaglia, F., *Lineamenti di storia delle dottrine politiche*, 2nd ed., Milan, 1952.

Carlyle, R. W. & A. J., *A History of Medieval Political Theory in the West*, 6 vols., W. Blackwood & Sons, Edinburgh, 1903–36.

Crump and Jacob (eds.), *The Legacy of the Middle Ages*, O.U.P., 1926.

Entrèves, A. P. d', *The Medieval Contribution to Political Thought: Thomas Aquinas, Marsilius of Padua, Richard Hooker*, O.U.P., 1939.

Gierke, O., *Political Theories of the Middle Age*, transl. by F. W. Maitland, repr. C.U.P., 1959.

Gilson, E., *Christian Philosophy in the Middle Ages*, Sheed & Ward, 1955.

Kantorowicz, E., *The King's Two Bodies*, Princeton, 1957.

Lagarde, G de., *La naissance de l'esprit laique au déclin du moyen âge*, 6 vols., 3rd ed., Paris, 1959–.

Lewis, E., *Medieval Political Ideas*, 2 vols., Routledge, 1954.

McIlwain, C. H., *The Growth of Political Thought in the West from the Greeks to the end of the Middle Ages*, repr. Macmillan, 1961.

Strauss, L., & Cropsey, J. (eds.), *A History of Political Philosophy*, Chicago, 1963.

Ullmann, W., *Principles of Government and Politics in the Middle Ages*, Methuen, 2nd ed. 1966.

1

LATE ROMAN EMPIRE: Lot, F., *La fin du monde antique et le début du moyen âge*, 2nd ed., Paris, 1948.

Jones, A. H. M., *The Later Roman Empire 284–602*, 4 vols. Blackwell Oxford, 1964.

PAPAL PRIMACY: Ullmann, W., 'Leo I and the theme of papal primacy' in *Journal of Theological Studies*, 1960, pp. 25 ff., 295 ff.

Ullmann, W., *The Growth of Papal Government in the Middle Ages*, 4th ed. Methuen, 1970, ch. I.

SELECT BIBLIOGRAPHY

RELATIONS BETWEEN ROME AND CONSTANTINOPLE: Gaudemet, J., *La Formation du droit séculier et du droit de l'église au IVᵉ et Vᵉ siècles*, Paris, 1957.

Ostrogorsky, G. A., *A History of the Byzantine State*, transl. Joan Hussey, Blackwell, Oxford, 1956.

Treitinger, G., *Die oströmische Reichs-und Kaiseridee*, 2nd ed. Darmstadt, 1956.

2

(a)

JUSTINIAN: *Corpus Iuris Civilis*, ed. Th. Mommsen & Krüger, repr. Berlin, 1928.

GREGORY I: Letters ed. P. Ewald & L. M. Hartmann in *Monumenta Germaniae Historica*, section: *Epistolae*, vols. I and II, Hanover, 1887–99.

MARCULF FORMULAE: ed. K. Zeumer in *Monumenta Germaniae Historica*, section: *Formulae*, Hanover, 1886; new critical edition with French translation by A. Uddholm, *Marculfi Formularum Libri Duo*, Uppsala, 1962.

LEGENDA S. SILVESTRI and DONATION OF CONSTANTINE: ed. C. B. Coleman, *Constantine the Great and Christianity*, New York, 1914; relevant parts of the Donation translated in H. Bettenson, *Documents of the Christian Church*, repr. O.U.P., 1956, pp. 135 ff.

(b)

Arquillière, H. X., *L'Augustinisme politique*, 2nd ed. Paris, 1955.
Folz, R., *L'Idée de l'empire du Vᵉ au XIVᵉ siècle*, Paris, 1957.
Ohnsorge, W., *Das Zweikaiserproblem*, Hildesheim, 1947.
Ullmann, W., *Growth* (as under I), ch. II.
Ullmann, W., *Principles* (as under GENERAL), part II.

3

(a)

PSEUDO-ISIDORE: ed. P. Hinschius, Berlin, 1861.
CORONATION ORDERS: (i) imperial: *Ordines coronationis imperialis*, ed. R. Elze, Hanover, 1960.
  (ii) royal: L. Wickham-Legg, *English Coronation Records*, Constable, 1901.
  (iii) *Liber regie capelle*, ed. W. Ullmann, Henry Bradshaw Society, vol. 91, 1961.

(b)

Davenport, E. H., *The False Decretals*, Blackwell, Oxford, 1916.

Schramm, P. E., *A History of the English Coronation*, O.U.P., 1937.

Stutz, U., 'The proprietary church', in *Medieval Germany 911–1250: Essays by German Historians*, ed. G. Barraclough, vol. II, Blackwell, Oxford, 1938.

Ullmann, W., 'The Bible and Principles of Government in the Middle Ages', in *Settimana di studio Spoleto*, Spoleto, 1963.

Ullmann, W., 'Reflections on the medieval empire', in *Transactions of Royal Historical Society*, 1964.

Ullmann, W., '*Der Souveränitätsgedanke in den mittelalterlichen Krönungsordines*', in *Festschrift für P. E. Schramm*, Wiesbaden, 1964.

4

(a)

GREGORY VII: *Register*, ed. E. Caspar, repr. Berlin, 1961.

INNOCENT III: *Register*, in J. P. Migne, *Patrologia Latina*, Paris, 1855, vols. 214–17.

GREGORY IX: *Register*, ed. L. Auvray, 4 vols. Paris, 1955.

INNOCENT IV: *Register*, ed. E. Berger, 4 vols. Paris, 1921.

CANON LAW: *Corpus Iuris Canonici*, ed. Ae. Friedberg, repr. Leipzig, 1956.

JOHN OF SALISBURY: *Policraticus*, ed. C. J. J. Webb, O.U.P., 1909; transl. by J. Dickinson, *The Statesman's Book*, New York, 1927.

GILES OF ROME (EGIDIUS ROMANUS): *De ecclesiastica potestate*, ed. R. Scholz, Weimar, 1929.

UNAM SANCTAM: transl. in Bettenson (as under 2 (a)), pp. 159 ff.

(b)

Knowles, D., *The Evolution of Medieval Thought*, Longmans, 1962.

Lea, H. C., *The Inquisition of the Middle Ages*, repr. Eyre & Spottiswoode, 1963, with a Historical Introduction by W. Ullmann.

Pacaut, M., *La Théocratie: l'église et le pouvoir au moyen âge*, Paris, 1957.

Poole, R. L., *Illustrations of Medieval Thought and Learning*, S.P.C.K., 1920.

Ullmann, W., *Growth* (as under 1), chs. IX–XIII.

Ullmann, W., *Principles* (as under GENERAL), Part I.

Voosen, E., *Papauté et pouvoir civil à l'époque de Grégoire VII*, Louvain, 1927.

SELECT BIBLIOGRAPHY

5

(a)

HENRY IV: Letters transl. in E. F. Henderson, *Select Historical Documents of the Middle Ages*, repr. Bohn Libr., Bell & Sons, 1927, pp. 366 ff.

DIALOGUE OF THE EXCHEQUER: ed. Ch. Johnson, Nelson, Edinburgh, 1950.

MAGNA CARTA: transl. by J. C. Dickinson, Historical Association Pamphlets (G. 31), 1954.

(b)

Bloch, M., *Feudal Society*, Engl. transl. Routledge, 1960.

Bloch, M., *Les Rois thaumaturges*, 2nd ed., Strasbourg, 1962.

Fawtier, R., *The Capetian Kings of France: Monarchy and Nation*, English transl., Macmillan, 1960.

Figgis, J. N., *The Divine Rights of Kings*, repr. New York, 1965, with an Introduction by G. R. Elton.

Howell, M., *Regalian Rights in Medieval England*, Athlone Press, Univ. London, 1961.

Jolliffe, J. E. A., *Angevin Kingship*, 2nd ed., A. & C. Black, 1963.

Kantorowicz, E., *The King's Two Bodies* (as under GENERAL), chs. IV and VII.

Kern, F., *Gottesgnadentum und Widerstandsrecht*, 3rd ed. by R. Buchner, Darmstadt, 1963; partial English transl. of the first edition (1914) by S. B. Chrimes, *Kingship and Law in the Middle Ages*, Blackwell, Oxford, 1939.

McIlwain, C. H., *Growth* (as under GENERAL), ch. VII.

McIlwain, C. H., *Constitutionalism: Ancient and Modern*, Ithaca, 1947.

Mitteis, H., *Lehensrecht und Staatsgewalt*, Weimar, 1933.

Mitteis, H., *Die deutsche Königswahl*, 2nd ed., Brno, 1943.

Miller, G. J. T., 'The position of the king in Bracton and Beaumanoir', in *Speculum*, 1956.

Painter, S., *Feudalism and Liberty*, Baltimore, 1961.

Pollock and Maitland, *A History of English Law*, 2nd ed., C.U.P. 1926.

Schulz, F., 'Bracton on Kingship', in *English Historical Review*, 1945.

Ullmann, W., Principles (as under GENERAL), Part II.

6

(a)

ARISTOTLE: *Politics*, transl. by B. Jowett, with an Introduction by H. W. C. Davis, repr. O.U.P., 1953.

AUGUSTINE: *City of God*, transl. in Loeb Classical Library, 1957.

(b)

Baynes, N., *The Political ideas of St Augustine's De civitate Dei*, Historical Association Pamphlet, 1936.

Combès, G., *La Doctrine politique de s.Augustin*, Paris, 1927.

Deane, H., *The Political and Social Ideas of St Augustine*, London and New York, 1963.

Entrèves, A. P. d', *Natural Law: an Introduction to Legal Philosophy*, repr. Hutchinson's Univ. Libr., 1960.

Gierke, O., *Natural Law and the Theory of Society*, with an Introduction by E. Barker, C.U.P., 1934.

Gilmore, M. P., *Argument from Roman Law in Political Thought 1200–1600*, Cambridge, Mass., 1941.

Grabowski, S. J., *The Church: an Introduction to the Theology of St Augustine*, St Louis, Mo., 1957.

Jones, W. J., *Historical Introduction to the Theory of Law*, O.U.P., 1940, especially ch. IV: 'The Law of Nature'.

Jolowicz, H. F., *Lectures on Jurisprudence*, ed. J. A. Jolowicz, Athlone Press, Univ. London, 1963.

Le Bras, G., '*Le Droit romain au service de la domination pontificale*', in *Review historique de droit français et étranger*, 1949.

Marrou, H., *St Augustine and his Influence through the Ages*, English transl., Longmans, 1957, with extracts from texts in translation.

7

(a)

ALEXANDER OF ROES: *Memoriale*, ed. and transl. (into German) by H. Grundmann and H. Heimpel, Weimar, 1949.

CLEMENT V: *Pastoralis Cura*, ed. in Clementinae, II. XI. 2, in Ae. Friedberg (as under 4 (a)), II. 1151–3.

DANTE: *Monarchia*, transl. D. Nicholl, London and New York, 1954.

THOMAS AQUINAS: *Selected Political Writings of St Thomas Aquinas*, ed. and transl. by A. P. d'Entrèves and J. G. Dawson, Blackwell, Oxford, 1948. *On Kingship*, transl. G. Phelan and I. T. Eschmann, Toronto, 1949.

(b)

Aubert, J. M., *Le Droit romain dans l'œuvre de s.Thomas*, Paris, 1955.

Davis, C. T., *Dante and the Idea of Rome*, O.U.P., 1957.

Entrèves, A. P. d', *Dante as a Political Thinker*, O.U.P., 1952.

Entrèves, A. P. d', *The Medieval Contribution* (as under GENERAL).

Eschmann, I. T., 'Studies on the notion of society in Thomas Aquinas', in *Medieval Studies*, 1946.

Eschmann, I. T., 'Thomistic Social Philosophy and the Theory of Original sin', in *Medieval Studies*, 1947.

Lottin, O., *Le Droit naturel chez s.Thomas d'Aquin et ses prédécesseurs*, Louvain, 1931.

Rivière, J., *Le Problème de l'église et de l'état au temps de Philippe le Bel*, Louvain, 1926.

Ullmann, W., 'The Development of the Medieval Idea of Sovereignty', in *English Historical Review*, 1949.

Ullmann, W., *Principles* (as under GENERAL), part III.

Wilks, M. J. *The Problem of Sovereignty in the later Middle Ages*, C.U.P., 1963.

Woolf, C. N. S., *Bartolus of Sassoferrato*, C.U.P., 1913.

8

(a)

JOHN OF PARIS: his tract ed. by J. Leclercq, *Jean de Paris et l'ecclésiologie du xiiie siècle*, Paris, 1942.

MARSIGLIO OF PADUA: *The Defender of Peace*, transl. by A. Gewirth, New York, 1959.

(b)

Gewirth, A., *Marsilius of Padua: The Defender of Peace*, vol. I, New York, 1951.

Tierney, B., *Foundations of Conciliar Theory*, C.U.P., 1955.

Ullmann, W., *The Origins of the Great Schism*, Burns Oates, 1948.

Ullmann. W., 'The Validity of the Papal Electoral Pacts', in *Ephemerides Juris Canonici*, 1956.

Ullmann, W., *'De Bartoli Sententia: Concilium representat mentem populi'*, in *Bartolo da Sassoferrato*, vol. II, Milan, 1962.

Wilks, M. J., *The Problem* (as under 7 (b)).

Wilks, M. J., 'Chaucer ... in Medieval Political Thought', in *Bulletin of the John Rylands Library*, 1962.

APPENDIX A

SUPPLEMENTARY BIBLIOGRAPHY

1

Relations between Rome and Constantinople:

Dvornik, F., *Byzance et la primauté romaine*, Paris, 1965.

Nelson, J. L., 'Gelasius I's doctrine of responsibility' in *Journal of Theological Studies*, xviii, 1967, 78 ff.

Rahner, H., *Kirche und Staat im frühen Christentum*, Munich, 1962.

2

(b)

Dölger, F., *Byzanz und die europäische Staatenwelt*, Darmstadt, 1964.

Ewig, E., 'Zum christlichen Königsgedanken im Frühmittelalter' in *Das Königtum*, ed. Th. Mayer, Darmstadt, 1965.

Wallace-Hadrill, M., 'The via regia of the Carolingian age' in *Trends in Medieval Political Thought*, ed. B. Smalley, Oxford, 1965.

3

(a)

Pontificale Romano-Germanicum, ed. C. Vogel and R. Elze, Rome, 1963.

(b)

Congar, Y., *L'ecclésiologie du haut moyen âge*, Paris, 1969.

Folz, R., *La naissance du saint-empire*, Paris, 1967.

Ullmann, W., *The Carolingian Renaissance and the idea of kingship*, London, 1969.

4

(b)

Costa, P., *Iurisdictio: semantica del potere politico nella pubblicistica medievale*, Milan, 1969.

Ullmann, W., 'The papacy as an institution of government in the middle ages' in *Studies in Church History*, ed. G. J. Cuming, London, 1965, ii. 78 ff.

5

(b)

Friedrich, C. J., *The philosophy of law in historical perspective*, repr. 1968.

Holt, C. J. *Magna Carta*, Cambridge, 1965.

APPENDIX A

6
(b)

Gregory, T., *L'idea di natura nella filosofia medievale*, Florence, 1965.

Markus, R. A., *Saeculum*, Cambridge, 1970.

Wilks, M. J., 'Roman empire and the christian state in the *De Civitate Dei*' in *Augustinus*, 1967, 489 ff.

7
(b)

Lachance, L., *L'humanisme de s. Thomas d'Aquin*, Paris, 1965.

Maffei, D., *Gli inizi dell'umanesimo giuridico*, Milan, 1966.

Ullmann, W., *The Individual and Society in the Middle Ages*, London, 1967.

8
(b)

Black, A., *Monarchy and Community*, Cambridge, 1970.

Oakley, *The Political Thought of Pierre d'Ailly*, Yale, 1964.

Sigmund, P. E., *Nicholas of Cusa and Medieval Political Thought*, Cambridge, Mass., 1964.

Wilks, M. J., 'The early Oxford Wyclif: papalist or nominalist?' in *Studies in Church History*, ed. G. J. Cuming, 1969, v, 69 ff.

APPENDIX B

ADDITIONAL BIBLIOGRAPHY

GENERAL

Coing, H. (ed.), *Handbuch der Quellen und Literatur der neueren europäischen Privatrechtsgeschichte*, I, Munich, 1973, especially the contributions by P. Weimar, pp. 129–59; N. Horn, pp. 261–364; and A. Wolf, pp. 517–799 (important for the effects of territorial sovereignty in the field of legislation).

Eichmann, E., *Quellen zur kirchlichen Rechtsgeschichte*, repr. Munich, 1968.

Paradisi, B., 'Il pensiero politico dei giuristi medievali' in *Storia delle idee politiche, economiche e sociali*, ed. Luigi Firpo, Turin, 1973, pp. 1–160.

Rotelli, E., and Schiera, P., *Lo stato moderno: dal medioevo all' età moderna*, Milan, 1971.

Ullmann, W., *Principles of Government and Politics in the Middle Ages*, 3rd ed., London, 1974.

Ullmann, W., *Law and Politics in the Middle Ages*, London, 1974.

1

(b)

Affeldt, W., *Die weltliche Gewalt in der Paulus Exegese: Römer 13. 1–7 in den Kommentaren der lateinischen Kirche bis zum Ende des 13. Jahrhunderts*, Göttingen, 1969.

Heggelbacher, O., *Vom römischen Recht zum christlichen Recht: juristische Elemente in den Schriften des sog. Ambrosiaster*, Freiburg, 1959.

Joannou, P.-P., *Die Ostkirche und die Cathedra Petri im 4. Jahrhundert*, Stuttgart, 1972.

Kreilkamp, 'Rome and Constantinople in the 5th century' in *The Jurist* xxxi, 1971, 319 ff.

Ullmann, W., *A Short History of the Papacy in the Middle Ages*, 2nd ed., London, 1974, chapters 1 and 2.

Ullmann, W., 'The cosmic theme of the Prima Clementis and its significance for the concept of Roman rulership' in *Studia Patristica*, xi, 1971, 93 ff.

2

(a)

New edition of the Donation of Constantine by H. Fuhrmann in *Monumenta Germaniae Historica: Fontes iuris germanici antiqui*, x, 1968 (though the editor's dating of the forgery is erroneous).

(b)

Anton, H. H., *Die Fürstenspiegel und Herrscherethos in der Karolinger-zeit*, Bonn, 1969.

King, P. D., *Law and Society in the Visigothic Kingdom*, Cambridge, 1972.

Kroeschell, K., 'Rechtsfindung; die mittelalterlichen Grundlagen einer modernen Vorstellung' in *Festschrift für Hermann Heimpel*, iii, Göttingen, 1972, pp. 498 ff. (Important in that it shows how little basis there is for the popular myth that in the Middle Ages law was not created or made, but 'found' or 'discovered'.)

Wallace-Hadrill, M., *Early Germanic Kingship in England and on the Continent*, Oxford, 1971.

3

(a)

Pontificale Romano-Germanicum, ed. C. Vogel and R. Elze i–iii, 1963–1972 (= *Studi e Testi*, ccxxvi–ccxxvii, 1963; cclxix, 1972).

Schimmelpfennig, B., *Die Zeremonienbücher der römischen Kurie im Mittelalter* Tübingen, 1973.

Schramm, P. E., *Kaiser, Könige und Päpste*, ii, Stuttgart, 1968, pp. 140 ff; (text of West-Frankish coronation orders, pp. 208 ff.); pp. 169 ff. (text of Anglo-Saxon orders, pp. 223–48).

(b)

Marchetto, A., *Episcopato e primato pontificio nelle decretali pseudo-isidoriane*, Rome, 1972.

Peters, E., *The Shadow-King: rex inutilis in medieval law and literature*, Princeton, 1970.

Spörl, J., 'Gedanken zum Widerstandsrecht und Tyrannenmord im Mittelalter' in *Widerstandsrecht und Grenzen der Staatsgewalt*, ed. B. Pfister et al., Munich, 1955, pp. 11 ff.

Ullmann, W., 'Schranken der Königsgewalt im Mittelalter' in *Hist. Jahrbuch*, xci, 1971, pp. 1 ff.

4

(b)

Bellamy, J. G., *The law of treason in England in the Middle Ages*, Cambridge, 1970.

Kuttner, S., 'Urban II and the doctrine of interpretation' in *Studia Gratiana*, xv, 1972, pp. 53 ff.

Smalley, B., *The Becket Conflict and the Schools*, Oxford, 1973.

Steenberghen, F. van, *La philosophie au XIIIe siècle*, Louvain-Paris, 1966, pp. 397 ff.

Ullmann, W., *Papst und König* (Salzburger Universitätsschriften, vol. iii, 1966, pp. 37 ff.

Ullmann, W., 'Von Canossa nach Pavia: zum Stukturwandel der Herrschafts-grundlagen im salischen und staufischen Zeitalter' in *Hist. Jahrbuch*, xciii, 1973 pp. 265 ff.

5

(b)

Baldwin, J. W., *Masters, Princes and Merchants*, Princeton, 1970.

Caenegem, R. van, *The Birth of the English Common Law*, Cambridge, 1973.

Ullmann, W., 'A Note on inalienability with Gregory VII' in *Studi Gregoriani*, ix, 1972 (= Memorial volume for G. B. Borino), pp. 115–40.

APPENDIX B

6

(b)

Michaud-Quantin, P., *Universitas: expréssions du mouvement communautaire dans le moyen âge latin*, Paris, 1970.

Wilks, M. J., 'St Augustine and the General Will' in *Studia Patristica*, ix, 1966, pp. 487 ff.

7

(a)

Best edition of Dante's *Monarchia*: P. G. Ricci, *Dante Alighieri: Monarchia*, Edizione nazionale, Milan, 1965.

(b)

Chenu, M. D., *Nature, Man and Society in the Twelfth Century*. transl. by J. Taylor and L. K. Little, Chicago, 1968.

Cheyette, E. L., 'The sovereign and the pirates' in *Speculum*, xlv, 1970, pp. 41 ff.

Cortese, E., *Il problema della sorvanità nel pensiero giuridico medioevale*, Milan, 1969.

Feenstra, R., 'Jean de Blanot et la formule Rex Franciae in regno suo princeps' in *Études dédiées à G. LeBras*, Paris, 1965, pp. 885 ff.

Limentani, U., *The mind of Dante*, Cambridge, 1965.

Löwe, H., *Von Cassiodor zu Dante*, Berlin, 1973, pp. 277 ff., 298 ff.

Ullmann, W., 'Dante's Monarchia as an illustration of a politico-religious renovatio' in *Festschrift f. Wilfried Zellar* (forthcoming).

Watt, J. A., 'Dante, Boniface VIII and the Pharisees' in *Studia Gratiana*, xv, 1972, pp. 201 ff.

Wolf, A., as above under 'General'.

8

(a)

The tract of John of Paris is now translated by J. A. Watt, *John of Paris on royal and papal power*, Toronto, 1971.

(b)

De Lagarde, G., *Le Defensor Pacis*, Paris, 1970.

Goudet, G., *Dante et la politique*, Paris, 1969.

Leff, G., *Paris and Oxford universities in the 13th and 14th centuries*, New York, 1968.

McGrade, A. S., *The political thought of William Ockham*, Cambridge, 1974.

Quillet, J., *La philosophie politique de Marsile de Padoue*, Paris, 1970.

Ullmann, W., 'Der Wiedergeburtsgedanke in der Staatslehre des Mittelalters' in *Aufstieg und Niedergang der römischen Welt*, ed. H. Temprini (forthcoming).

Wilks, M. J., 'Corporation and representation in the Defensor Pacis' in *Studia Gratiana*, xv, 1762, pp. 251 ff.

Wilks, M. J., 'Reformatio regni: Wyclif and Hus as leaders of religious protest movements' in *Studies in Church History*, ed. D. Baker, ix, Cambridge, 1972, pp. 109 ff.

APPENDIX C

SUPPLEMENTARY NOTE TO CHAPTER 3

THERE is some need to supplement the themes treated in Chapter 3, because the Carolingian Renaissance was not confined to the literary or cultural sphere, but went far deeper: it concerned a regeneration of the whole society, a rebirth of society, on the model of the rebirth of the individual through the act of baptism. Just as the individual had shed his natural characteristics and become a different being (above, p. 17), in the same way society, that is, the totality of all individuals, was to shed its Germanic past and historical and natural appurtenances by becoming an ecclesiological unit which was grounded in the idea that divinity itself had created it. The character of society was to be shaped in agreement with a particular doctrine, that is, the Christian norms and laws. This was the first attempt in Europe to refashion a whole society according to a programme and a blueprint: similar efforts were to be repeated throughout subsequent history and can still be observed to this very day on a global scale.

The consequences of this Carolingian idea of renaissance were very great indeed and concerned, amongst others, the following topics:

(1) Through the adoption by the king of the title 'King by the grace of God' (above pp. 53 ff.), the Ruler had opened the gates to ecclesiastical intervention, because the clerics alone were held qualified to pronounce on this religious issue of divine grace. Hence not only the clericalization of governmental ideas (above pp. 74 ff.), but also the development of the thesis that the Ruler was subjected to a higher law, that is, the divine law which was taken in a very wide sense and included also the ecclesiastical law. It was law interpreted by the ecclesiastics. The significance of this was that the always latent absolutism of theocratic kingship was nipped in the bud by making the king, in theory at least, obey a set of rules which were directly linked with the religious foundations of kingship voluntarily adopted by Western rulers. Furthermore, this higher or basic law was prior to the king himself and wholly independent of him. This problem of subjecting public government, including heads of States, ministers, etc., to a basic law, became, as is well known, a major issue after the Second World War, but was first seen within the context of theocratic kingship in the Frankish and post-Frankish ages. In other words, the idea of the rule of law which has been hailed as an achievement of the recent past, has a very distinguished ancestry in Frankish writers and governments.

(2) Precisely because the kingdom was not held to be of human,

natural, but of divine origin, the king was considered a trustee appointed by divinity for taking charge of the kingdom. Hence it was that because the kingdom was merely entrusted to the king, the idea of the king as a tutor of his kingdom emerged: he was called *tutor regni* from the mid-ninth down to the fifteenth centuries. Old-Germanic conceptions (the *Munt* understood as protection of the weak) could easily combine with the Roman idea of the *tuitio* according to which the tutor's sole concern was the well-being of the ward entrusted to his care. What practice and doctrine in the earlier Middle Ages evolved, was the transfer of the idea of guardianship or tutorship from the private realm to the public sphere. The place of the individual ward was taken by the collective ward, the kingdom. The significance of this development that began in the ninth century, was that in his function as a tutor the king was not allowed to alienate any goods or rights which belonged to the kingdom. Indeed, to sell, mortgage or in any way to diminish the legal status of the ward, would have made a mockery of the role of the tutor. And the same applied to the king: his tutorial function became an essential attribute of medieval kingship. This indeed was the origin of the highly important principle of inalienability (cf. above p. 142), according to which the ruler was not permitted to transfer or convey or donate, in a word, to alienate, any of the so-called regalian or crown rights. The preservation, if not augmentation of these public rights was one of the main duties of the king which he solemnly promised to fulfil at his coronation. The papal decretal of Honorius III in 1220 (*Intellecto*) did not, therefore, state any new law, but merely clarified a state of affairs that had existed since the early ninth century. Moreover, it was only on this basis that the efficacy of the forged Donation of Constantine could be assailed.

(3) This tutorial function of the king with its sequel of inalienability, was based not only on the Germanic *Munt* and the Roman *tuitio*, but also (and this too is not usually recognized) on the doctrine of St Paul set forth in his letter to the Galatians (iv. 1–2) and its interpretation by patristic writers (St Jerome, St Augustine, etc.). And with the penetration into the Pauline texture there also came about a further fusion between Roman and Christian ideas which resulted in the view that the kingdom was, in law, placed on the level of a minor under age (cf. above, p. 56): just as the minor under age lacked the legal ability to order and manage his own affairs, in the same way the kingdom was held incapable of so doing – which consideration only went to strengthen the need for a tutor, and that tutor was found in the king. It stands to reason that this conception strongly militated against the degeneration of medieval kingship into unbridled absolutism. In the high Middle

Ages there was no one who would not have viewed the *res publica*, the *regnum*, etc., as a minor under age that needed a tutor: it was the universally accepted standpoint.

(4) The consequence of this point of view was that the king's function as a superior and the individuals making up the kingdom as inferiors were thereby greatly buttressed. Precisely because theocratic kingship was sanctioned by the ecclesiastics – different rules and consequences applied to feudal kingship (above pp. 146 ff.) – this situation made it much more difficult to develop the idea of any inherent, autonomous rights belonging to the individuals: the ideological change of the individual from a subject to a citizen as one endowed with autonomous, independent rights, found a strong resistance in the centuries-old tradition and later petrification of the view that the kingdom and its members were in public law mere minors who needed the guiding hand of a tutor in the person of the king: before this release of the king's subjects from tutelage (in the literal meaning of the term) could be constitutionally effected, a great deal of blood was to flow in numerous revolutions, some of which we have witnessed in our own days.

(5) The idea of renaissance was also applied to the king himself: he was reborn through having received the sacrament of royal unction at the hands of the bishops: he had thereby become a son of God. The inherent absolutist potentialities which this rapidly developing theocratic kingship harboured, were proportionately neutralized by the simultaneous elaboration of the checks just mentioned, notably his subjection to a basic law enunciated as it was by the very same ecclesiastics who were powerfully instrumental in detaching the king from the people itself (above p. 54) and in drawing him, so to speak, into their own orbit. By making him a *persona ecclesiastica* (above, p. 88) they could control him all the more easily: the scope of his governmental actions became considerably restricted. True enough, he appeared and was the superior of the people entrusted to him, yet he was in numerous and essential respects constrained in his government and legislation by the very premises which had made him adopt the theocratic kind of kingship – the religious and biblical view of the divine grace to which alone he owed his position as king. What must be pointed out is that rulership permeated by this religious connotation exercised profound influence far beyond the Middle Ages. Yet it was this kind of rulership which within European civilization first brought about the thesis that the Ruler was subjected to law. The conferment of divine grace on the king through the medium of unction and the simultaneous solemn undertaking by the king to observe the law and fulfil the role of a tutor, were the two central features of the coronation

APPENDIX C

service: it comprised all the essential ideological and constitutional elements which were made accessible to understanding by means of a carefully structured concrete symbolism and a concise doxology, the whole culminating in the rebirth of the king.

INDEX

INDEX